39.95

THE QUEST FOR VOICE
IN CONTEMPORARY
PSYCHOANALYSIS

THE QUEST FOR VOICE IN CONTEMPORARY PSYCHOANALYSIS

CARLO STRENGER, PH.D.

INTERNATIONAL UNIVERSITIES PRESS, INC.
MADISON   CONNECTICUT

INTERNATIONAL UNIVERSITIES PRESS ® and IUP (& design) ®
are registered trademarks of International Universities Press, Inc.

Library of Congress Cataloging-in-Publication Data

Strenger, Carlo.
    The quest for voice in contemporary psychoanalysis / Carlo
Strenger.
        p. cm.
    Includes bibliographical references and index.
    ISBN 0-8236-5762-0
    1. Psychoanalysis. 2. Psychoanalysis and philosophy. I. Title.

RC506.S773 2002
616.89'17—dc21

                                                2002027377

Manufactured in the United States of America

CONTENTS

INTRODUCTION: WE'VE MADE IT THROUGH THE CENTURY, ALIVE AND KICKING

WE'VE MADE IT THROUGH THE CENTURY

It is no matter of course at all for an intellectual and cultural movement to be able to say that it has made it through the eventful twentieth century. As opposed to Marxism, existentialism, structuralism, pragmatism, neothomism, and many other movements that have claimed attention at some point, psychoanalysis is still alive, and doesn't seem to have any intention of quitting the scene. It exists as an identifiable movement with a wide institutional network distributed throughout the Western World (and gradually outside of it as well). Daily millions of hours of psychotherapy are conducted in ways that are to some extent shaped by psychoanalytic ideas. The educated middle classes understand their lives in terms of psychoanalytic provenance, even if these terms are more often than not diluted and distorted in use and meaning.

1

At several crucial junctures it looked as if psychoanalysis was going to suffocate as a result of overinstitutionalization and overadherence to its traditions, but somehow it has succeeded in renewing and reinventing itself for a century in ways that have kept it alive. In the last decade or so, psychoanalysis has undergone another change of a crucial nature. Psychoanalysis is now entering a *postmythological stage*. What I mean by this is that current avant-garde psychoanalysis, as exemplified in the New York relational perspective and the work of individual authors like Christopher Bollas and Adam Phillips, has become keenly aware of the fact that psychoanalytic theories are metaphors and narratives that are used to construct viable versions of human experience. Myth that becomes conscious of its own nature is no longer myth; it becomes the existential–hermeneutic endeavor of generating meaning.

This book revolves around one central question. Now that the avant-garde of psychoanalysis does not believe in psychoanalysis as a science anymore, what kind of practice and discourse can it legitimately claim to be? If the psychoanalyst cannot and should not conceptualize her authority as grounded in a theory of human development and mental functioning, what is her authority? What uses can be made of psychoanalytic theories that can only be taken to be narratives and metaphors about what it is like to live a human life?

Throughout the chapters of this book I argue that this state of affairs should not be deplored. As Adam Phillips (1995, p. xiii) has pointed out, contemporary citizens of the West tend to anxiously look for experts for every detail of their lives, from how to make love to how to raise their children. In such an age, the psychoanalyst's most useful function might be to refuse the role of the expert, and to instead give people a chance to take some more freedom to ask how they want to live, rather than what the "healthy" way of life is.

What I will present here is a late modern psychoanalytic perspective. I take the term *late modern* from the sociologist Anthony Giddens (1991, 1992) who in a series of books has presented an interesting analysis of the late modern condition of the Western world. I prefer this term to *postmodern,* because the latter carries a whole bag of implications that I do not necessarily subscribe to. In particular I have little sympathy for a certain opaque and hermetic style that often permeates writings that are self-professedly postmodern.

My ideal in many ways is the somewhat more sober, and yet distinctly humanist voice of the philosopher Isaiah Berlin, who passed away in 1997. One of Berlin's most famous works, *The Hedgehog and the Fox* (1951), was central to the writing of chapter 2 which is meant as a homage to this man whose work has been with me for the last twenty years. Berlin distinguishes between two forms of intellectual temperament: Hedgehogs look for one, integrative picture, foxes resist the temptation of big pictures because they think that the complexity of reality is recalcitrant to grand theory (cf. chapter 2 for an elaboration of the theme).

I have always been fascinated by the grand visions of hedgehogs. I love the beauty of their constructions and the coherence of their vision. This is one of the reasons why I fell under Freud's spell ever since I began reading him at age 16. It is precisely because I find these grand theories so enticing that I am aware of their intrinsic dangers. And these dangers are most apparent in a discipline which, like psychoanalysis, is supposed to help people be less afraid of being themselves. Grand conceptions instill fear because they purport to know what the good life is, how mature people should look.

Psychoanalytic discourse of the last decade has become acutely aware of this danger. I think that the "foxish" element has been strengthened. Psychoanalytic writing has become more musing, tentative, playful, and open-ended. Hence another way of looking at the current situation of psychoanalysis is to ask what psychoanalysis could be when it turns from a hedgehogish into a foxish mood.

It is possible to give a preliminary and schematic characterization of late modern psychoanalysis by juxtaposing it with basic tenets of classical psychoanalysis. The latter was characterized by six basic assumptions:

1. Psychoanalysis is capable of producing an integrated theory of human nature by combining the theory of personality, developmental psychology, psychopathology and etiology, and the theory of therapeutic technique and cure.
2. Psychoanalysis is the only theory and technique that touches upon the roots of psychopathology; all other treatments are superficial methods of symptom removal. Psychoanalytic clinical material can verify these claims.
3. Psychoanalytic theory reflects the deep structure of the human mind, and no other theory does.
4. Psychoanalytic developmental theory reflects natural standards of maturation that allow both for a hierarchical ordering of psychopathologies and for a definition of the one state of mental health.
5. Psychoanalytic institutions, ranging from institutes to training programs to the four or five times a week treatment format are somehow a reflection of some natural necessity.
6. There is a fundamental epistemic asymmetry between the patient and the analyst: the analyst knows the patient's mind better than the patient herself, and the treatment consists in the patient's gradual acceptance of these truths against his or her own resistances.

Contemporary avant-garde versions of psychoanalysis have completely changed these assumptions.

1. The ambition of psychoanalysis to create an integrated scientific theory of human behavior is rejected. Instead there is a tacit consensus that understands psychoanalysis in constructivist terms as an existential–hermeneutic discipline.

2. Most avant-garde analysts continue to think that psychoanalysis has distinct advantages in terms of depth and
   breadth of conceptualization and treatment. But they
   would not claim that psychoanalysis uncovers the one
   truth that all other forms of treatment somehow miss.
3. Contemporary psychoanalysis has become deeply suspicious of notions of deep structure, and sees them as a
   potential reflection of an authoritarian system of normalization. Instead psychoanalytic theory and practice
   are mostly understood in constructivist terms.
4. Developmental hierarchies are being dropped and instead a plurality of possible life-styles is assumed.
5. Many of the most creative current writers have been
   educated in psychoanalytic institutions that were outside the International Psychoanalytic Association, and
   the latter has begun a rapprochement with institutions
   that are not affiliated with it. There is a growing process
   of reflection on what constitutes good psychoanalytic
   education.
6. The hierarchical understanding of the clinical situation
   is replaced by dialectical conceptions of intersubjectivity and mutuality. The analyst is not understood as a
   neutral observer, but as a participant whose subjectivity
   is involved in the therapeutic process.

Reading the contemporary literature gives the impression that psychoanalysis has settled for being a clinical
discipline that has common borders with literary, sociological, political, philosophical, and at times theological concerns. Current discussions focus on the importance of the
analyst's subjectivity, and the implications of this on the
ethical and clinical essence of the psychoanalytic endeavor. There is a growing consensus that psychoanalysis
is an inherently dialectical discipline that works in an intersubjective field that cannot be fully objectified. The growing impact of feminist theory and cultural criticism has
made constructivism into something like a tacit orthodoxy.
In this introduction I intend to provide a bird's eye
perspective on the developments that have led to the late

modern version of psychoanalysis, and I will briefly place the various chapters of this book within this larger perspective.

FROM GRAND THEORY TO DIALECTICAL CONSTRUCTIVISM

For most of its history psychoanalysis had assumed that it was a scientific discipline, and that its theories could adequately be tested on the couch. This has turned out not to be true. Critics from outside psychoanalysis like the philosopher of science Adolf Grünbaum (1984), and practitioners of psychoanalysis like Donald Spence (1981) and Roy Schafer (1976, 1983) came to the conclusion that psychoanalysis had to reconceptualize its own foundations.

There were three positions, roughly: Grünbaum argued that psychoanalysis was essentially a scientific theory, but that none of its basic tenets were confirmed, and that it had to be tested extraclinically. Donald Spence wavered between detailed analyses of the hermeneutic structure of psychoanalysis and the belief that indeed psychoanalysis should and could be tested with extraclinical, systematic tools. Schafer went all the way: he reconceptualized psychoanalysis as the art of retelling lives, and therefore came to see it as a literary undertaking only to be measured by standards of narrative coherence.

In my own *Between Hermeneutics and Science* (1991) I tried to take an intermediary position. On the one hand I agreed with the hermeneuticist position with respect to the logic of psychoanalytic clinical work. I tried to show that nondogmatic psychoanalytic work could be seen as an extension of commonsense psychology, and that its methodology was similar to that of other disciplines in the humanities, like literary criticism and history. On the other hand I agreed with some of the misgivings Grünbaum (1984) had voiced about the hermeneuticist construal of psychoanalysis: it could not differentiate between acceptable and nonacceptable narratives of how patients had become what they had become. Therefore, I argued, psychoanalysis had to be in constant contact with neighboring disciplines in order to maintain external coherence with established bodies of knowledge.

By and large I still stand behind most of the theses of *Between Hermeneutics and Science,* except for one. I still saw a chance at the time for psychoanalysis to become the center of an ongoing research program, that in due time might generate some indirect corroboration of psychoanalytic theory. I no longer believe this to be the case, and I would like to explain why, and what the implications of this change of mind are.

About a century ago psychoanalysis began its evolution toward a program of vaulting ambition. By 1930 the program of psychoanalytic theory was to offer an integrative theory of the human mind and behavior. It was to unify developmental psychology, psychopathology, the theory of personality, and the theory of treatment.

Psychopathology was supposed to be ordered along the lines of psychoanalytic developmental psychology. The depth of pathology was correlated with the developmental phase in which it originated. Schizophrenia was correlated with the early oral phase; depressive illnesses with a later oral stage; obsessive neurosis with the anal stage; and hysteria with the phallic stage. Of course the details of both psychoanalytic developmental theory and the interpretation of psychopathology was to change through the years. Kleinian and Winnicottian ideas changed the terms of the developmental framework. Margaret Mahler's developmental axis of separation-individuation introduced another central theme, but the basic idea remained the same. Psychoanalytic theory was to order the universe of mental phenomena in a developmental hierarchy. This became the foundation of a research program on a grand scale. Anything from developmental psychology to the theory of treatment was to be integrated into one theoretical edifice (e.g., Rapaport, 1960).

Now, at the end of the twentieth century, this grand program has met the fate of most grand theory in the social sciences. The postmodern distrust of grand meta-narratives (Lyotard, 1979) has changed psychoanaly-sis—and for good reasons. Psychoanalysis has not kept its promise to come up with a testable, powerful, theory that would gradually generate hypotheses that could be empiri-cally verified.

This development implies a drastic loss of ambition. Psychoanalysis no longer even strives to provide empiri-cally testable theory of *any* sort. When Christopher Bollas, to take an example of one of the most articulate contem-porary psychoanalysts, writes about his "theory of the true self" (1989, chapter 1), the term *theory* must be under-stood in the rather minimal sense as currently used in *literary theory*. No systematization is implied, and I would be surprised if Bollas ever thought of his ideas as the foun-dation of something that can be researched with the tools of statistical hypothesis testing. Instead he creates an evoc-ative set of metaphors that provides a rich, consistent framework for the narrativization of the clinical process. He is willing to use metaphors from all psychoanalytic schools in an associative manner, and thus continues the ecumenical tone of current, pluralistic psychoanalysis (even though he disassociates himself from New York rela-tional psychoanalysis).

There are certainly authors and currents that try to build bridges with empirical disciplines like infant re-search, but there is less and less of the patient, almost dogged persistence an earlier generation of authors like Hartmann, Rapaport, Holt, and Rubinstein exhibited in its attempts to find out what the precise theoretical context of psychoanalysis was supposed to be, and how it could be tested. The new paradigm of psychoanalysis is that of an existential endeavor that is more concerned with subjec-tive experience, social meaning, and personal growth than with systematic theory building.

The yearning for grand theory fails at any rate, be-cause it is now highly unclear *what* could be the object of testing psychoanalytic theory. Widely used positions range from models that put almost exclusive emphasis on unconscious processes (Klein, Lacan), to models that hardly make use of the notion of the unconscious at all (self psychology in some of its variations). There are models that claim that psychopathology is a function of defensive operations against unacceptable impulses (Kleinian, Freudian), others think in terms of interpersonal patterns (interpersonalists). Some put crucial emphasis on affect states (self psychology, Kleinians), others consider them to be almost irrelevant to psychoanalysis (Lacanian). Some approaches believe that transference interpretations are the centerpiece of analytic work (modern Freudians, Kleinians), others believe that they should primarily be used to reestablish a workable selfobject bond (intersubjectivism). At the risk of slight exaggeration I should say that I doubt that there is a single nontrivial theorem to which all current psychoanalytic schools would subscribe.

FROM PSYCHIATRIC ESTABLISHMENT TO CULTURE OF SELFHOOD

The internal changes in psychoanalysis were driven by several major changes on a large social scale. Psychoanalysis, particularly in the United States, is undergoing a change of crucial importance in terms of its status (for much of the following, cf. Hale [1995]). In the decades after the Second World War, psychoanalysis conquered American psychiatry. Many of the central university chairs in psychiatry were taken over by psychoanalysts, and the language of psychoanalysis became the lingua franca of psychiatric discourse. The concomitant result was that psychoanalysis became deeply enmeshed in the power–knowledge web of society: anything from expert witness status to the question of whether to institutionalize patients became a central topic of psychoanalysis.

In the last three decades psychoanalysis largely lost its public status in the medical world. Psychiatry has come to see itself almost completely as a natural science discipline based on neurobiology. The biological paradigm seems to have won the battle for the domination of psychiatry almost completely, and many psychiatrists are happy that psychoanalysis has lost its hold on the field (Shorter, 1997).

The second development that contributed to the change of status of psychoanalysis was the opening up of the psychotherapy market to competing approaches in the 1960s. Whereas psychoanalysis seemed to be the only serious therapeutic approach in the forties and fifties, there arose a serious competitor in the form of behavior therapy. Then came the boom of the psychotherapeutic culture of the 1970s: catalogs of therapeutic approaches listed up to four hundred therapeutic approaches. There seemed to be no end to what could be called therapy, and it became progressively less clear why psychoanalysis should be unique in any way.

The third social factor was the drastic change in insurance policy. It all began with the psychotherapy outcome studies that purportedly showed two things: first, that there were no significant differences in the therapeutic results of different therapeutic approaches. Second, it was claimed that long-term therapy did not demonstrably show better results than short-term therapy (Garfield and Bergin, 1978).

Insurance companies loved this: they now argued that they would only cover therapeutic methods that had been scientifically proven to be effective, and that they would no longer cover more than about fifteen sessions a year, i.e., the length of a short-term therapy. The reform of the health care system and the rise of managed health care only strengthened this tendency: by and large long-term therapy, psychoanalytic or other, is no longer covered by medical insurance in most countries.

These three factors led to a drastic change in the status of psychoanalysis: it lost what was once a near monopoly; it ceased to have a strong standing in the medical world; it lost the funding privileges associated with this standing; and it became largely excluded from the power positions that society confers on the medical establishment.

So far this sounds like a story of decline. But I think that the depsychiatrization of psychoanalysis also opened a space of freedom that had progressively been closed down by the institutionalization of psychoanalysis. While psychoanalysis had held power positions, it was necessary to keep the profession tightly organized, the language theoretical, and to create the semblance of a scientific discipline. The medical language also required that psychoanalysis formulated itself as a procedure that cured people of illnesses.

Thus psychoanalysis for many decades became an instrument of normalization. Ego psychology, as has been argued many times (Lacan, 1953; Drews and Brecht, 1971), became a psychology of adaptation. The efforts to create a psychoanalytic–psychiatric nosology with learned discussions about the differences between, say, borderline personality disorder and narcissistic behavior disorder, reflected the social need for order and predictability.

Currently the practice of psychoanalysis largely moves back to where it started from: the private interaction between a client and a practitioner. By losing the more strictly psychiatric patient to medicine, and the social cases to clinical social work, the psychoanalytic practitioner gradually gets to see primarily the middle-class patients whose suffering is often vaguely defined, and who primarily need a language and a practice that will allow them to make sense of their lives.

My main point is that psychoanalysis at this point is no longer an identifiable body of thought. It is rather becoming a form of life in Wittgenstein's (1953) sense. It is a cultural movement that makes sense of the plight of the late modern individual. It creates narratives for understanding the complexities of life and for dealing with existential dead-ends. It is also an institutionally entrenched practice of shaping and disciplining the self according to

an ethics and an aesthetics centered on the values of authenticity, autonomy, interpersonal relatedness, and tolerance (cf. chapter 3 below). The various schools differ from
each other in the styles of life and values according to
which the individual is supposed to live.

I don't think that this state of affairs is deplorable.
The spirit of the age favors plurality over singularity, paradox over systematic elaboration. Many authors have
pointed out that the neat ordering of mental phenomena
and personality styles on a developmental scale by classical
theories has a strong judgmental streak. The language of
moral judgment has been replaced with a language of maturity, that nevertheless continues to maintain an implicit
dimension of what might be called developmental moralism. Borderlines are somehow less valuable as human
beings than neurotics, and this judgment is rationalized
by arguing that borderlines have a less integrated identity
and rely on developmentally earlier defense mechanisms.

In an age of pluralism, psychoanalysis has become far
more open to the possibility that a wide variety of personality styles, sexual choices, and life goals are legitimate. It is
interesting to note that the historical place of psychoanalysis has changed greatly, though. During the first half of
this century psychoanalysis was the iconoclastic spearhead
of social developments toward openness. It introduced
controversial notions like infantile sexuality, the congeni-
tal bisexuality of all human beings, and through the idea
of the unconscious decentered the human subject. As opposed to that the recent changes in psychoanalysis were,
often belated, reactions to large-scale cultural and social
developments ranging from feminism and cultural criticism to experimentation with new forms of raising children, and the rise of multiculturalism as an ideal.

THE NARRATIVE TURN

I now want to trace two crucial steps that led to the current
climate of open, multifaceted, approaches to psychoanalysis. The first step could be called the *narrative turn in*

psychoanalysis. This turn can be closely associated with two landmark works.

The first was Donald Spence's *Narrative Truth and Historical Truth* (1981). In this densely argued, precise, rich, and well-documented book Spence challenged the most basic tenet of classical psychoanalysis. He showed in detail that clinical work could not possibly provide the objective data that could ground a scientific theory, and that psychoanalytic interpretation was based on assumptions that it could not possibly verify in itself. The idea that transference contents reflect central conflicts, that the unconscious directs the flow of association, that interpretation of unconscious content generates further therapeutic flow, are theses that need independent verification. In this respect Spence's position is quite similar to that of the philosopher of science Adolf Grünbaum (1984), who argued that psychoanalysis cannot rely on clinical testing of its major hypotheses.

Instead he showed in detail how psychoanalysis is a hermeneutic activity guided by a variety of interpretive conventions. The real tour de force of the book shows in detail how analogous psychoanalytic clinical work is to literary criticism. Ultimately, Spence argues, the psychoanalyst is engaged in what he called the *normalization* of the analysand's discourse. There are a set of interpretive conventions that guide this process: the ideas of defense, resistance, transference, and the major developmental narratives are the blueprints into which the analysand's discourse is to be fitted in order to make it psychoanalytically intelligible.

This is standard procedure in textual interpretations in the humanities. The major work of philosophical hermeneutics, Gadamer's *Truth and Method* (1960), had shown that the interpreter of necessity lives within horizons of intelligibility that provide the basis for any interpretive activity. Gadamer's main thesis had been that there could be no interpretation without such preunderstanding of what is meaningful and what is meaningless. Therefore it is conceptually impossible ever to start from scratch, and to question such preunderstanding radically. In other words, if psychoanalysis is a humanistic discipline, the fact that it lives within the hermeneutic circle is not to be deplored because it is unavoidable (Strenger, 1991, chapter 2).

Spence's *Narrative Truth and Historical Truth* ended on a note that was rather confusing to many readers. After ten chapters of precise demonstration of the hermeneutic structure of psychoanalysis, Spence suddenly made a 180-degree turn, and argued that psychoanalysis needed to revert to careful empirical research that would corroborate its central causal hypotheses. At the end of the book it suddenly turned out that Spence was deeply uncomfortable with the constructivist–hermeneuticist picture of psychoanalysis. He seemed to see his book as a prolegomenon for the claim that psychoanalysis needed something else if it was to be a respectable discipline. Judging from his later publications, Spence has never come to terms with the tension between a more scientistic conception that has guided his empirical research and his insight into the hermeneutic nature of clinical activity.

The second major work in the narrative turn was Roy Schafer's *The Analytic Attitude* (1983), and in this book no misgivings were to be found about a hermeneutic interpretation of psychoanalysis. This book was the culmination of one of the most spectacular changes of mind in recent psychoanalytic history. In 1968 Schafer had published *Aspects of Internalization,* an erudite and brilliant exercise in ego psychology which took a very realistic stance toward accepted theory. Schafer asked questions that took the structural model completely seriously; e.g., which of the mental agencies of the structural model contained introjects. He still spoke in terms of psychic energies and their transformations, and seemed to be happy in participating in the construction of the edifice of ego psychology.

In 1970 his publications began to change tone completely. He began to question the very possibility of natural science as an adequate model for psychoanalysis. Until 1976 Schafer tried to develop a systematic alternative to the language of metapsychology which he called action language. He then gradually moved away from the more specific proposals of action language, and instead began to develop his picture of psychoanalytic clinical work as the art of retelling lives.

The Analytic Attitude is a sustained exploration of many aspects of psychoanalytic work from the point of view of narrative action. The picture is essentially that the patient, like every human being, constructs his experiential work by the way he narrates it. Schafer's basic idea is that the patient's suffering is a function of the reductive nature of his life narratives. The goal of psychoanalytic work is therefore an increase in flexibility of the patient's narrative repertoire. The result of good work is not the construction of the one, final biography, but the construction of multiple histories.

Schafer had moved to the language of modern literary criticism as the central frame of reference for psychoanalytic metatheory. He renounced the notions of one objective truth that was to be uncovered, and instead moved toward a dialectic epistemology in which the subject of knowledge and its object mutually constitute each other. Schafer's work became one of the most sustained expositions of psychoanalysis as a humanistic discipline that is about stories and their coherence rather than about causal hypotheses and developmental psychology.

THE RELATIONAL TURN

The narrative turn was a first, crucial step toward the current, playful, pluralistic universe of psychoanalysis, but it took a further development to transform pluralism from a necessity to a virtue. In the late nineteen eighties, New York psychoanalysis began to evolve a new center of creative thinking. Most of its major analysts had several characteristics in common: first, most of them had been born after the Second World War. Their adolescence and early

adulthood had taken place in the sixties. The sexual liberation of that decade was an integral part of their mental
landscape and identity. The student unrest of 1968, which
had irretrievably changed the notions of academic and
professional authority, was part of the social reality into
which they grew. Feminism had already become an established movement.

It is probably not a coincidence either that most of
them are not M.D.s but Ph.Ds. The obvious concomitant
was that their thinking was less influenced by natural science models, and more by the humanities. Their rhetorical mode was closer to the language of literary and cultural
criticism than to more authoritarian styles of discourse
that had dominated psychoanalytic thought and writing
up to then.

The fact that they are Ph.Ds also has a further implication: the American Psychoanalytic Association since its inception had only accepted M.Ds for training (Hale, 1995).
This association in turn was the official partner of the International Psychoanalytic Association. The place where
Ph.D.s could train in New York was therefore primarily the
interpersonally oriented William Alanson White Institute,
which had been founded by renegades like Clara Thom-
son and Erich Fromm. The second place where they could
train was the New York University Postdoctoral Program
in Psychoanalysis, which very soon became one of the epi-
centers of creative thinking (Aron, 1996). Both these institutions were not inhibited by the fear of not being
recognized by the International Psychoanalytic Association, since they did not seek recognition to begin with.

By what looks to me to be a typical quirk of intellectual history, this movement was originally associated with
the introduction of object relational thinking to American
psychoanalysis. The text which may well be considered the
founding document of the relational movement was
Greenberg and Mitchell's *Object Relations and Psychoanalytic Theory* (1983). This book stood out for two reasons:
first, it was a superb piece of scholarship and integration
which came to be useful to a generation of students. This

is what made the book unproblematic in the eyes of many. Its second feature was subversive, though. The main argument and narrative line of the book organizes psychoanalytic history on the dimension from drive to object relations.

The old paradigm of drive psychology was, of course, the language of classical American ego psychology, and therefore the language of the establishment (Hale, 1995). This paradigm, in Greenberg and Mitchell's formulation, was a one-person psychology. This meant that it was inherently undialectical, made a strict distinction between the observer and the observed, and therefore created the illusion that the psychoanalyst could be an observer of a psychic reality not influenced by who she was and how she worked. In addition the Freudo-Kleinian idea that the mind is a closed system governed by intrapsychically generated fantasies had come under attack from several quarters—most of all from empirical research on infant development.

Daniel Stern's *The Interpersonal World of the Infant* (1985) was another landmark work in the development of the relational turn, even though Stern has never been part of the relational group, to the best of my knowledge. Stern is both a psychoanalyst and a systematic, empirical researcher in the field of infant development. His book had many outstanding qualities. First of all it was beautifully written, lucid, and convincing in its argument and outlook; second, most of it was based on detailed, empirical research of two decades, and was therefore scientifically respectable; third, it was irreverent and iconoclastic.

Stern used Kohutian self psychology as the dominant framework of interpretation for his findings. But his main argument could be stated without relying on any particular theory. The baby, Stern showed, was by no means a closed system regulated by drives and intrapsychically generated fantasies. Instead he showed the exquisite detail of the dance by which mother and child mutually regulate each other. Gone was the stimulus barrier of Freudian metapsychology, gone was the Kleinian idea that some internal drama of life and death instinct irrevocably determined the adult's fate. Instead there was a much more friendly, commonsensical image of an infant who gradually built a sense of self and other based on her evolving experience of the interchange with her caretakers. Stern provided the relational emphasis on interpersonal interaction and attunement with the scientific respectability of controlled research.

Retroactively this marriage between object relations theory in its various forms and dialectical, constructivist, nonauthoritarian, and postmodernist metatheory was (as most marriages are) the product of historical and geographical coincidence. It happened to be the case that the dominant paradigm of most psychoanalytic societies in New York was ego psychological Freudianism. It also happened to be the case that British object relations thinking had not been considered respectable in the established psychoanalytic institutes in New York, particularly in the orthodox New York Psychoanalytic Society. Hence the new dialectical, constructivist relational approach initially created an amalgam of object relations theory and postmodern epistemology.

In recent years many authors in this movement have recognized that this amalgam was a historical accident rather than a necessity (Aron, 1996; Mitchell, 1997). Relational metatheory, the more relaxed and interactive clinical style of the new generation, could be combined with any theoretical predilection. The relational reconceptualization of psychoanalytic theory as a set of narratives and metaphors provides the clinician with a space of freedom. The analyst who is enthralled with Kleinian metaphors is entitled to use them, provided that they are not taken too literally. Ogden's (1986) reinterpretations of Kleinian concepts like the paranoid–schizoid and the depressive position constitutes a paradigm for how to use metaphors while detaching them from their original theoretical context.

It even became possible again to use beloved Freudian concepts. Even the clinician who does not believe in the literal truth of Freudian developmental theory can use concepts like *oedipal, phallic, primal scene*, and *castration anxiety* as long as they are not taken literally and not used in an authoritarian manner and with sexist implications. These concepts are, after all, metaphors that have hypnotized generations of analysts and nonanalysts alike, and have therefore proved to be powerful organizers of human experience.

INTERSUBJECTIVITY, MUTUALITY, AND PLURALISM

Contemporary avant-garde psychoanalysis is not committed to any particular theory. Intersubjectivism (e.g., Stolorow, Brandchaft, and Atwood, 1987) is inspired by Kohutian self psychology. Christopher Bollas (1989, 1992) writes within the tradition of the British independent group in London. Jessica Benjamin (1989, 1995) of the New York University relational track moves freely between Freudian, Lacanian, and Mahlerian metaphors, and is steeped in feminist literature, and has lately (1998) made extensive use of Frankfurt critical theory. Stephen Mitchell (1993, 1997) is primarily influenced by the interpersonal school of the William Alanson White Institute, but makes use of Freudian and Kleinian concepts.

What characterizes these writers is not a set of theoretical assumptions, but a climate of opinion, a set of values, and a common metatheoretical stance. More than anything, late modern psychoanalysis has reflected consistently on the fact that the conceptual armamentarium of psychoanalysis, all of which is derived from writings from the first half of this century, cannot be relied on as established theory. In doing so, two crucial achievements were combined. On the one hand, the danger of indoctrinating patients was drastically lowered. Once an analyst is aware that his or her theoretical framework is ultimately just a preferred perspective on life and the clinical process, it becomes almost impossible to stretch patients on a procrustean bed. Resistance becomes a relativized notion, and it is supplanted for many by the idea of the intrinsic difficulty of building a shared language.

The main merit of relational psychoanalysis is that it has created a form of psychoanalytic discourse which takes full account of the intellectual and social situation of psychoanalysis. It has made theoretical pluralism an integral part of its metatheoretical position. The common denominators of the current avant-garde of writers and clinicians is characterized by a clinical style that is exemplified by two of the catchwords of the new generation: intersubjectivity and mutuality. Intersubjectivity has become central both in the understanding of developmental and social processes and of the clinical situation. Human beings are not taken to have a timeless, biologically fixed essence. Personal identity is understood to evolve within the context of socially defined categories that are in turn mediated by interpersonal processes of mutual recognition. Emphasis is put on the ways in which the child, adolescent, and adult recognizes herself in the eyes of significant others. Hegel's idea that self consciousness arises through recognition by others has become a central tenet of contemporary psychoanalysis.

This has profound implications for understanding the clinical process. No longer is the analyst taken to be an objective observer external to the patient's mind. Instead it is taken as an axiom that the analyst's actual subjectivity (as opposed to the patient's transferentially tainted perceptions) is a crucial ingredient of the therapeutic interchange. Every intervention of the analyst reflects a subjectivity formed by cultural forces, theoretical predilections, and personal experience and character. The patient is changed by the impact of an, albeit professionally formed, actual subjectivity. Recognition by the analyst becomes a core experience for the analysand.

Recognition is not a one-way process, though. The New York relational version of late modern psychoanalysis has been crucially formed by the publication of Ferenczi's *Clinical Diary* (1987), and its description of Ferenczi's experiments in mutual analysis. Even though Ferenczi's temporary change of place and role with the analysand is deemed somewhat extreme, even by today's avant-garde analysts, the idea of mutuality as a crucial ingredient of every analytic encounter has become one of the centerpieces of today's more egalitarian conceptions of analytic work.

The deconstruction of the hierarchical understanding of the clinical situation was aided by the influence of feminist thought and cultural criticism. The feminist influence reaches far deeper than the deconstruction of paternalistic conceptions of femininity. Late modern psychoanalysis has come to question notions of hierarchical authority conferred by professional status that have informed classical visions of analytic work. The emphasis on mutuality and recognition reflects the feminist view that subjects mutually constitute each other through recognition, and that there cannot be a position of authority that is outside the context of human interaction, from an Archimedean vantage point of complete neutrality and objectivity. Analytic authority has not been abolished, but it has received a human face. Authority is no longer the abolition of the analyst's subjectivity, but the ability to put it to disciplined use.

Current psychoanalytic themes reflect a change in the cultural climate. Even in philosophy there has been a move away from the patient, careful conceptual analysis. Moral, aesthetic, and social concerns have moved to the center of attention, and epistemology, metaphysics, and classical philosophy of science are less *en vogue* nowadays. The philosophical climate of the day is characterized by acquiescence with the fact that we seem not to be capable of making our own thought transparent to ourselves.

This tendency has left its mark on psychoanalytic discourse. It is as if the psychoanalytic clinician and the theorist who tries to make sense of clinical experience do not have the time to ask the type of questions leading toward

scientific systematization. Social developments push psychoanalytic thinking and practice into new and exciting
areas that need to be dealt with: feminism, gender construction, the changing needs of patients, and a deeper
understanding of the place of psychoanalysis in current
cultural fields.

OVERVIEW OF THE CHAPTERS

This book reflects my preoccupation with the philosophical foundations of psychoanalysis, and I hope forms a coherent contribution to the current late modern
reconceptualization of psychoanalysis as a discipline that
tries to assist human beings in their endeavor to become
fully developed individuals.

Part I develops my own version of psychoanalytic constructivism. Chapter 1, "Psychoanalysis as Art and Discipline of the Self," takes constructivism one step further
than is generally done. Even though a number of late modern analysts have pointed out systematically to what extent
psychoanalytic interventions are expressions of the analyst's subjectivity, not enough attention has been paid to
a further point. Every therapeutic style is based on an
ideal of developed individuality. In previous years such
ideals were called conceptions of maturity, because it was
assumed that nature pretty much prescribes what it means
to be healthy. Nowadays such a view is deemed obsolete,
because we have become more tolerant of a range of lifestyles.

Correspondingly the clinician must be aware that she
proposes a particular ideal of what it is like to live a good
life. I make use of the work of authors like Hadot (1995)
and Foucault (1983) on Hellenistic philosophy as a practice intended to shape the self, and I propose to look at
various psychoanalytic (and nonpsychoanalytic) therapeutic styles as disciplines of the self. They are practices designed to give the self ethical and aesthetic coherence,

and thus to allow the individual to feel at one with herself. In other words, I try to push constructivism one step further by arguing that every clinician has a culturally entrenched view of the ideal self ("capable of intimacy"; "geared toward self-realization"; "authenticity"; "genitality," are some examples), and that a fully democratic conception of psychotherapy would demand that the therapist be conscious of her particular ideal, and present it to the patient, if necessary.

Chapter 2, "Critical Pluralism: How to Live with Our Yearning for Unified Conceptions," deals with what I consider to be one of the crucial weaknesses of psychoanalytic thought and practice in almost all of its versions. Psychoanalysis has always sought unified conceptions that integrate a view of human nature and a pure technique. This purism was codified in Eissler's 1953 paper on the effect of technique on the analysand's ego, that argued that there is such a thing as pure psychoanalytic technique, and that divergence from such technique must always be justified.

It is fascinating to note that every psychoanalytic school has tried to present its own version of pure psychoanalytic technique. I use Bion (1961) as an example of the purist conception of psychoanalysis, but he stands for the whole tradition that takes seriously Freud's metaphor of the "pure gold of psychoanalysis." Freudians believe that ideally you should do nothing but interpret resistances and unconscious contents; Kleinians tend to focus on unconscious phantasy. Self psychologists believe that empathic resonance to the experience of selfobject failure is at the center of psychoanalytic work, whereas Lacanians believe in punctuating the analysand's discourse to loosen alienating identifications. The list could be continued.

It is interesting that the late modern deconstruction of earlier psychoanalytic certainties has not fully tackled the belief in a unified technique. I think that there are neither good a priori reasons nor any empirical evidence to support this idea of a unified technique. I use the work of the existentialist psychotherapist Irvin Yalom (1975,

1980, 1989) as an exemplification of therapeutic pragmatism, because at this point in history no major psychoanalytic author can be found who is truly pragmatic in the
choice of therapeutic technique.

Chapter 2 eschews a purely eclectic position by showing that the pragmatic clinician can make use of the great
purist conceptions of psychoanalytic work. Each of these
conceptions embodies an ideal of developed individuality
(cf. chapter 1), and each of them has its own attractions.
The position I advocate, critical pluralism, allows the clinician to be fascinated by each of these purist conceptions
without subscribing to any of them, and instead move between them on pragmatic grounds.

Part II exemplifies one of the central theses of this
book, namely that it is impossible to do psychotherapy of
any sort without being guided by some Weltanschauung.
I believe that many of the central disputes in psychoanalysis are based on diverging views of what human life is
about. It gives concrete exemplifications of one of the
main theses of chapter 2, that the practicing clinician
needs to navigate her way between conflicting ideals that
pull in different directions.

Chapter 3, "The Classic and the Romantic Vision in
Psychoanalysis," shows how psychoanalytic work, theoretical and clinical, is invariably shaped by general philosophical views. I try to identify what I believe to be one of the
central tensions in psychoanalysis both in theory and in
practice. As clinicians we keep being faced with the dilemma between two perspectives. We can look at the patient from the outside, and judge the adequacy of his
representation of and adaptation to external reality. This
perspective gives clinical interventions a somewhat critical
angle, since they show the patient where she fails to make
full use of her ability to think, perceive, and act rationally.

We can also try to understand the patient's experience from within and see our task in helping the patient
to crystallize and express her subjective experience, no
matter whether this experience is reasonable or not. This
latter activity is often denoted by the term *empathy*. I try

to show that these two perspectives are historically allied with the classicist view of human nature originating in the Enlightenment, and with the romantic reaction to the Enlightenment as paradigmatically expressed by Rousseau.

I avoid an identification with either the classicist or the romantic vision both theoretically and technically. I show how each of the perspectives contains highly important ingredients for a balanced clinical approach. In chapter 4 I go one step further: I argue that even though it is humanly impossible to work without a guiding framework of values, one should avoid the dilemma of looking for one, inclusive framework uniting philosophical vision and technique. Pragmatic considerations may lead the clinician to adapt a romantic approach clinically even though she does not accept the romantic view of human life. In other words, I may not believe that psychopathology is primarily due to environmental failure, and yet think that it is clinically fruitful to focus on the patient's subjective experience of such failure. On the other hand, I may believe that environmental failure is the crucial determinant of psychopathology, and nevertheless feel that certain patients need classicist interventions, at least at times.

Part III contains two exemplifications of the late modern, pluralist way of seeing individual styles. Chapter 5 reflects on the process I underwent writing my recent book, *Individuality, the Impossible Project: Psychoanalysis and Self Creation* (1998), which exemplifies many of the theoretical theses in this book through clinical examples and analyses. It juxtaposes two extraordinary individuals, one of whom I had worked with. "Tamara," who is the subject of the first chapter of *Individuality, the Impossible Project*, lived a life on the edge, and constructed an intricate neosexuality. The second is the French philosopher Michel Foucault, who judging by James Miller's biography (1993), was haunted by the demons of his past, and spent his life trying to liberate himself from them.

Both Tamara and Foucault were deeply involved in the world of S&M, and they therefore fall under the category of what has traditionally been called *perversion*. The question I ask in this chapter is whether indeed people like Tamara and Foucault must be taken to deny important aspects of reality, and are therefore not fully developed, as classical psychoanalytic theory has claimed (e.g., Chasseguet-Smirgel, 1984). My work with Tamara gradually led me to accept that her life choices, her sexuality, and her intricate gender construction had been a conscious project of self creation. She had made every effort to shape her self and her life as a work of art.

This is what Michel Foucault had tried to do for a lifetime. His *oeuvre* was, as he said explicitly, an attempt to deal with the dramatic anxieties of his life: madness, medicine, incarceration, and sexuality. Miller's (1993) biography shows that Foucault's life was a direct extension of his work, in this respect. Foucault lived a truly philosophical life, and his notion of the discipline of the self was one of the foundations of chapter 1, "Psychoanalysis as Art and Discipline of the Self."

In writing *Individuality, the Impossible Project,* I often reflected on what seems to be a paradox: psychoanalysts are nowadays, supposedly, more open and pluralistic than ever. And yet the normalizing gaze is not easy to tame. The field of mental health is preoccupied with what is healthy and normal, and with classifying the sick and abnormal in numbered schemes. Society often expects mental health professionals to be experts on what the right way to live is. The very idea that an individual makes conscious choices to create the self in a different way arouses suspicion. I therefore wanted to present Tamara and Foucault as authentic examples of what was once called the philosophical life; the attempt to shape one's self according to one's beliefs, values, and aesthetic preferences.

The final chapter of this book explores varieties of individual styles in psychoanalysis. The psychoanalytic avant-garde is no longer preoccupied with hiding subjectivity and individuality behind impersonal formulations. This chapter is first and foremost a celebration of the achievement of psychoanalysts who have developed distinct, rich, and interesting voices. Furthermore it tries to show how these voices exemplify options of psychoanalytic individuality both in writing and in the clinical dialogue.

If contemporary psychoanalysis has become open to a variety of ways of being human and humane, it is necessary for us to part with the idea that there is one right way of doing psychotherapy and psychoanalysis. Difference in clinical style should be celebrated rather than deplored. As I show in chapters 1 and 2, and as I hope to have demonstrated in *Between Hermeneutics and Science* (1991), pluralism need not slide into sloppy relativism. We should therefore pride ourselves on the fact that psychoanalytic discourse and clinical practice are evolving into an art form that helps people to find their voices and individual styles of life.

PART I

CRITICAL PLURALISM
AND PSYCHOANALYSIS
AS ART

1 PSYCHOANALYSIS AS ART AND DISCIPLINE OF THE SELF

INTRODUCTION

There have been three basic ways in which psychoanalysis has understood its practice: for the first two-thirds of its history the self-understanding of psychoanalysis as a science was almost unquestioned. The growing number of competing psychotherapeutic approaches, as well as increasing methodological and philosophical criticism, gave birth to the hermeneuticist understanding of psychoanalysis which gained a considerable following. Self psychology and intersubjectivism have developed the view of psychoanalysis as an essentially phenomenological undertaking.

During the last decade or so, more constructivist approaches have evolved. The relational approach in the United States has begun to conceptualize the analytic process as a construction and creation of meaning rather than seeing it as the uncovering of a preexisting reality. This approach can in many ways be seen as a continuation of the hermeneuticist approach.

The goal of the present work is a radicalization of the constructivist approach along Nietzschean and Foucaultian lines. The main claim will be as follows: cultural developments of the last decades have undermined the very idea that there is such a thing as a biologically predetermined mature personality. Instead, modern liberal societies have evolved in the direction of pluralistic frameworks which contain various subcultures. Each of these subcultures is centered around ideals of accomplished individuality (the successful businessman/woman, the expressive artist, the cool street kid, the sensitive new-age man/woman, etc.).

The plurality of therapeutic approaches has presented a problem for those who continued to see psychotherapy and psychoanalysis as sciences which describe the biopsychological nature of human beings. Instead I propose to understand psychotherapeutic schools as cultural traditions centered around particular ideals of individuality (the Freudian ideal of stoic self-control, the Winnicottian ideal of spontaneity, the Bionian ideal of the capacity to bear lack of knowledge, etc.). From these traditions cultural practices have evolved which help individuals to shape the self along the lines of their ideal of accomplished individuality. Therefore I use Foucault's term of the *discipline of the self* to characterize these psychotherapeutic schools—some of which have become major cultural forces in themselves.

SOME FEATURES OF LATE MODERNITY

Changes in Existential Problems

Psychoanalysis has been conscious of the fact that something has changed in the types of problems generally seen in the consulting room. Given the combination of the medical model and developmental thinking, psychoanalysis has tended to conceptualize these changes in developmental and diagnostic terms: patients, it was argued, were less differentiated, there was a preponderance of preoedipal disturbances (and hence the patients were "more disturbed").

From the position of radical narrativization it seems that this explanation is not tenable. Given the profound changes from the beginning of this century to late modernity, it is very likely that the changes in patients are due to the fact that the tasks of individuality have changed greatly since the beginnings of this century. Freud's patients lived in a relatively well-defined cultural and moral universe, as Freud himself did. For most of them the goal of staying within the social class they belonged to and the ability to adhere to its behavioral and moral standards was not questioned. The dynamics of repression was, as has been pointed out, a reflection of the social structures of the time: the unacceptable was relegated to the lower classes, to red-light districts, and images of depravity. Psychoanalysis was certainly responsible for opening the discursive boundaries between the domains of excommunicated content and the respectable, but it did not question the assumption that normality was the ultimate goal.

Late modernity has changed this set of basic assumptions (Giddens, 1991). Probably the most salient change is to be seen in the domain of sexuality: heterosexuality has gradually lost its claim to be the only acceptable and legitimate form of sexual behavior. Similarly, reproduction and the founding of a family are no longer considered to be the only way in which an individual can live a life deemed to be acceptable. The various sexual subcultures have created a space in which what was once considered transgression is now a cultural alternative in lifestyle.

Life trajectories are no longer clearly defined, and the psychoanalytic conception of developmental stages which one must traverse toward maturity has ceased to be a reflection of the cultural space within which we live. The ideal of personality seems to change: Freud saw the healthy personality as a personality in which the boundaries between the id and the ego are strongly established. The new ideal which is emerging is that of the individual who is open to a wide variety of experiences, who is willing to explore various constructions of gender and sexuality, and is not bound by a single, traditional model of gender roles and personal identity.

Of course the form of life which is and will probably remain the predominant one is that of the family. Nevertheless, the self-consciousness of the family is changing dramatically as the possibility of wider options is accepted. The traditional definitions of motherhood and fatherhood are being called into question. Structures like male dominance, which have been claimed to be essential aspects of the human mind even by deconstructivist authors like Lacan, are being criticized by cultural critics of various persuasions. Late modernity has introduced the democratization of politics into the sphere of personal life, and opens the vista of a different conception of the family (Giddens, 1991, chapter 7).

Late Modern Personal Identity

In traditional societies personal identity is primarily defined by the individual's membership in a particular group. Primary identity is defined by family, the place where one has grown up and lives, and the individual's ethnic group and religious affiliation. The individual has the possibility of living a life in which he grows into a more or less preassigned place in society which defines who he is.

The modern Western world has changed this greatly. The globalization of postindustrial society makes it possible for many individuals to envisage living their lives almost anywhere. A large number of people have grown up without ever having belonged to a community: children of managers become used to moving from one place to the next within one or two years. Attachment to people and places cannot form the frame of orientation through which the individual can define personal identity.

Freud's patients lived in a relatively tightly knit community. Chances were that one would begin and end one's life in the same environment. The late modern individual's frame of reference is his or her career rather than a community, and this career quite often takes precedence to attachments to places, people, and cultures. Hence the individual must find the psychic resources with which to maintain a direction in life primarily within himself, since support systems often change rapidly through the various parts of a career and a lifetime.

The safety of the constraints that existed in earlier periods, the knowledge that there were standards that had to be taken for granted if one wanted to belong to the social class into which one was born, is not available today. The individual is expected to cherish the choices of styles, values, and identities at his or her disposal. The middle and upper middle classes, who constitute the primary clientele of individual psychotherapy, live with the often anxiety-laden consciousness that they must make a career of their lives, that they must go out into the world and conquer it.

With increased freedom of choice and the growing awareness of the plurality of possible lifestyles and value orientations, the complexity of the task of living a life has increased greatly. The contemporary individual who tries to live a life is inundated with images, ideals, and possible identities. It often seems that a late adolescent or young adult can sit in front of a TV and choose between the various images as one chooses between the various goods on the shelves of a supermarket. The point is, of course, that identities are not put together from various elements in a do-it-yourself manner. The image of a desired identity must be merged with a personal history, with memories, attachments, talents, interests, fears, and hopes into a lived reality (Gergen, 1991).

More than ever the Renaissance idea that individuality is a creation has become a lived reality for a sizable part of the middle-class population. The notions of the true self which must evolve, of personal development as the fruition of a preexisting self, are giving way to the idea that a person's individuality is the central creation of a life (Strenger, 1998).

The project of individuality has always been about forming oneself. The Renaissance ideals of *virtù* had already emphasized that the individual could form himself according to an image he had himself formed. Late modernity has given this project of self-formation a different slant: self-creation now seems a matter of choosing the image according to which the individual wants to create himself, and then shape himself along the lines of this image in next to no time: some career success combined with some body building could do the job in just a few years!

The nineteen eighties have strengthened the sense that personal identity can be shaped at will. Provenance or social class seemed to be no constraints whatsoever on who the individual could be. Twenty-five-year-old brokers found themselves millionaires just because they had the talent for buying and selling money in split-second decisions. Twenty-year-old rock musicians became international celebrities overnight because they had been catapulted into the limelight by MTV charts.

The epitome of the difficulty in orienting oneself in a surreal reality is shown in the motion picture *Blue Steel,* in which another successful commodities broker turns into a serial killer. There is a scene in which he has a dialogue with God while he works out on his body-building machine. He is tortured by his loneliness, he begs God not to leave him alone. Suddenly something snaps and he understands that he *is* God. The combination of seemingly unlimited possibilities with the lack of significant attachments can create a combination of omnipotence and complete despair which psychoanalytic clinical descriptions have pointed out as a typical phenomenon of narcissistic and borderline psychopathology. It might well be, though, that this emotional configuration reflects the social realities of modern cities rather than developmental fixations.

Changing Personality Patterns

The emphasis of classical psychoanalysis on repression and on the unconscious reflected the normalizing pressures on the individual around the fin de siècle. Morality, decency, uprightness, and adherence to a strict code of propriety were crucial elements of education, and continued to be exerted by society later on. Impulses, wishes, and thoughts which were incompatible with the predominant social mores were experienced as a threat to one's standing as a moral and healthy human being. Some of this remained true through midcentury, when, for example, many women were still brought up with the image of sweetness described and attacked by Betty Friedan in *The Feminine Mystique* (1965).

At present the normalizing pressures are of a different sort: the middle-class individual is supposed to "make it," she has to fight the fear of failing, the fear of losing her footing on the rung of the social ladder associated with self-respect, safety, and a life worth living.

Psychoanalysts have noted that narcissistic and schizoid personality dynamics are more frequent than they used to be. The linear, biologically inspired developmental thinking characteristic of the first generations of analytic thought led to the tendency to think that present-day patients suffer from preoedipal rather than oedipal pathologies. It seems to me that the different problems presented by patients today are a function of the changing difficulties in the project of individuality. The pressures on the individual are far less those of having to disavow unacceptable impulses than those of having to negotiate a hypercomplex social reality. Most human relations are not characterized by the moral weight associated with traditional forms of life but by the necessity of getting along with those who have an impact on one's career and social standing.

The danger situations of the late modern individual seem to be less those of being crushed by guilt than being inundated by the shame of not living up to the images of

being a success (Giddens, 1991, chapter 2). The humiliation of seeing one's desire to be somebody thwarted is one
of the most central fears I encounter in young adults who
seek therapy. They live with the dreadful consciousness
that they must be well into a career track by their early
thirties, since otherwise they will be left out.

Kohut (1971) and Kernberg (1975) agree on one feature of the narcissistic personality: the tension between
the depleted, humiliated, worthless self and that of the
grandiose, omnipotent self. My own clinical impression is
that this constellation is particularly salient in early adulthood. Young people turn to therapy because they are in
a state of panic. They live with a kaleidoscope of images
of the successful life, and they are incapable of linking
any of these images to a lived experience. They vaccillate
between the hope of turning themselves into embodiments of those images and the fear that they will be left
on the side, without a positive identity which will give them
a sense that life is worth living.

The gradual process in which children and adoles-
cents can grow by internalizing stable images of their parents, who provide the foundation for the idealized
imagoes defining values and a positive identity, has ceased
to be a good description of present development. The
media present the child and adolescent with an inunda-
tion of ideal images which mostly outshine his parents,
who are experienced as being out of touch with what is
"in," "hip," and with current lifestyles. Many parents indeed do not feel that they have the resources to deal with
the complexity of developmental demands made on
their children.

The reverse side of the freedom for self-creation is
that inner experience and external identity often do not
cohere with each other. The disintegration products of
identities glued together from media images are documented by the motion pictures mentioned above and the
novels of Bret Easton Ellis (1991, 1994). The anxiety of
having to "make it" and the middle-class fear of failing

(Bellah, Madison, Sullivan, Swidler, and Tipton, 1985), often do not leave enough internal space for the individual to find out what his or her desires really are. As a result the haven of the therapeutic relationship may be one of the few places for people to sort out who they are and who they want to be.

Liberal Democracy and Ideals of Individuality

The loss of the sense of community, shared values, and a clear-cut view of maturity which characterize late modernity is deplored by some and celebrated by others. Nostalgic attempts à la Heidegger to restore some primordial experience of rootedness are less than convincing, and the conservative belief that religion and family values are the cure for all ills are often a danger to the achievements of liberal democracy. At any rate the globalization of the lifeworld, the changes in the experience of lived space-time are probably irrevokable.

The vista which is opening up is both frightening and fascinating. The number of individuals who have a wide spectrum of life choice is growing enormously. The ideals of liberal democracy are in certain respects coming to fruition. With the loosening of ties of kinship and community, and the price it entails, the contemporary individual has more possibility for forming his or her self according to a chosen image than most people in history ever had.

The growing number of subcultures and lifestyles constituting late modern civilization allows more individuals than ever to find a lifestyle which suits their temperamental leanings and desires. Traditional societies demanded the acceptance of one more or less rigid moral and behavioral set of standards. As opposed to this, the late modern individual has the possibility of asking himself what type of life is most likely to give him a sense of self-actualization. Until midcentury those who wanted to find ways of living which did not suit the accepted mores had to pay the price of marginality. Only those with artistic temperaments had the option of a more or less acceptable identity as bohemians which gave them some leeway.

The price paid by the individual is that it takes much more mental strength to shape one's individuality and to live one's life. Late modern society provides less structure than any previous high civilization. Few can build their identities without a conscious effort, few feel that they have an established identity in early adulthood, and many continue deep into midlife to feel that they are not living the life they want to lead.

The Protest Against Social Categorization

Late modernity is characterized by the rejection of social norms as necessary or "natural." Many movements flourish, such as feminism, gay liberation, and the various ethnic groups, who fight for legitimacy of their rights, desires, sexual preferences, and cultures. Western society is approaching the realization that nature has not left us any clues; that ethics is a human creation rather than a copying of the hidden order of nature.

Feminism had to fight against the age-old idea that nature provides an order which is ethically compelling, and that this order relegates women to a second-rate place in society. For a while some feminist theorists made the mistake of arguing that there were no relevant differences between the sexes, and thus feminism inevitably weakened its own position. It acquired its full force by taking the position that whatever the natural differences between men and women were, these could not justify the maintenance of a social order which deprived women of equal rights and opportunities (Chodorow, 1994).

Gay liberation had to tackle the issue head on from the very beginning: obviously "nature" defines masculinity and femininity by their sexual function in procreation. Hence gays had to fight the idea that nature could prescribe the rightness of sexual behavior and preferences, if they were ever to escape their status as an ostracized minority.

Gay liberation began with legal and political issues, fighting discrimination, persecution, ostracism, prejudice, and the darkness of stupidity. There were preliminary successes ranging from the abolition of criminal prosecution of homosexuality in Britain, to its legalization in other countries. Then the gay community won the fight against the definition of homosexuality as an illness. Its success is documented by the exclusion of homosexuality as a psychiatric illness from the DSM-III onwards (APA, 1980).

Once gay communities could flourish more openly, they created a cultural search for new forms of community (Browning, 1993). New forms of family life, new conceptions of belonging, new forms of solidarity emerged; some arose for obvious reasons—gay long-term relations are mostly not centered around child rearing. Some were rooted in a community of fate: the emergence of AIDS in the eighties forced gays to make sense of the tragedy they were undergoing. They learned to live under most difficult circumstances with the ubiquity of death.

The gay movement became an expression of cultural creativity per se. It was forced to search for new ways of experiencing and forming the self, for new understandings of the relationship between self and society, for a reexperiencing of what it meant to be male or female, a new understanding of the relationship between gender and sex. All this is not meant to idealize the gay liberation movement, which has its inherent paradoxes and complexities (Foucault, 1987). Its importance for our context is that its brief history is the most tangible instantiation of the attempt of human beings to transcend the order of nature and to create forms of life in full consciousness of the fact that they were creating them, rather than imitating a presumed order of nature.

Truth and Creation

Gay liberation, feminism, and other late modern developments have helped to bring to the fore an issue of crucial

importance. Classical psychoanalysis assumed that the subject's coming to know the truth about himself will by itself
engender a process of maturation. This assumption was
based on developmental moralism: the subject's coming
to know about his fixations will lead him inevitably to fulfill
the epigenetically predetermined goal of development.

Postmodernism has come to cast doubt on this very
idea. History since the sixties has allowed us to watch new
cultural forms come into being at a higher speed than
ever before. Many of them were related to sexual preference and sexual identity, a topic psychoanalysis originally
thought to be predetermined by nature itself. The politics
of sex in the last decades has raised doubts about this
certainty. It has opened the possibility that human beings
have the freedom to create their style of life with respect
to sexual identity as well.

Joyce McDougall (1983) has come close to recogniz-
ing this fact by exchanging the term *perversion* for her
interesting term *neosexualities*. This term emphasizes that
neosexualities are indeed creations. They are new forms
of life which are meant to meet the needs and satisfy the
desires of those who cannot fit into the dominant mores
of society without feeling stripped of their individuality.
As Chodorow (1994, p. 63) has pointed out, though,
McDougall continues to see perversions as being of necessity pathological, arguing that they are of an addictive
character, that perverts are of necessity less free, and
hence ill.

I am not taking issue with the question of whether
neosexualities are indeed correlated with a sense of com-
pulsion to act on them, because I do not have enough
empirical evidence either way to take a stance. Yet Chodorow (1994, p. 63) has a point in saying that McDougall
seems to have a somewhat sterile conception of "normal"
sexuality. Aren't we heterosexuals "compelled" to act out
our sexuality as well, and is not sexuality that is devoid of
demonic force somewhat pale?

Let us now return to the relationship of truth and
creation: I tend to think that indeed neosexualities are

often attempts to deal with early trauma. In particular I find Stoller's argument convincing that masochism is an attempt to deal with unbearable humiliations and impingements that occurred in early childhood, and I have found this idea empirically useful in understanding individual patients.

I have been faced with the following problem, though: at least one patient I worked with gained considerable insight into the origins of her neosexuality (Strenger, 1998, chapter 1). Nevertheless she felt that her neosexuality had become an essential constituent of her identity. She could not envisage giving it up without obliterating who she was. Masochism for her had become the embodiment of her relentless fight for individuality in a family and society that pushed her toward "normality" at the price of losing herself.

Michel Foucault, this highly gifted and creative woman, and others have made me question the idea that development toward normality is the only conceivable goal. These people found rich ways of living their lives, to contribute to knowledge and art, and I have come to doubt seriously the wisdom of adopting the position of enlightened psychoanalytic superiority and stating that they have not reached some predetermined goal of development. Their lives (*pace* McDougall's insistence) seem to me as deep, rich, and vibrant as that of any heterosexual "well-adapted" person I know.

Psychoanalysis: From Purported Science to Discipline of Self

Psychoanalysis, in many ways the richest tradition of psychotherapy, has generated a body of precise phenomenological description and of imaginative construction of mental states. It has also developed the tradition of a craft and a discipline designed to help individuals to gain more inner freedom.

The problem is that psychoanalysis has for most of its history labored under an illusory notion of theory. Freud's writings elaborate an intricate system of thought in which the transformations of psychic energy were to be described in analogy to such description in physics. Further elements of the theory were to be a developmental psychology and a theory about the genesis of psychic structure. None of these concepts has stood the scrutiny of philosophers of science and academic psychologists. Either they have turned out to be too vague to allow for scientific testing, or, to the extent that they have been tested, they have not received scientific confirmation (Grünbaum, 1984).

Yet psychoanalytic theoretical writing, as well as that of other schools of depth psychology, is sometimes fascinating, sometimes inspirational, and often illuminating to the individual searching for self-understanding. It is certainly of prime importance to the clinician who needs narratives which make sense of his patients' plights.

If these writings are not scientific theory, what are they? My claim is that the best way to understand psychoanalytic theory is as a set of metanarratives governing possible disciplines of the self, and as such continuous with religious practices, the Greco-Roman schools of philosophy, and other disciplines of the self (Ellenberger, 1970, p. 501).

On the Very Idea of a Discipline of the Self

Every civilization has a multitude of ideals of what it means to be an individual. These ideals have fulfilled vital roles; they have provided educational guidelines for cultural institutions, and narratives which inspired individuals in the formation of their personalities. Such ideals included the sage, the warrior, the man of justice, the craftsman, the just ruler, the honest citizen, the artist, the romantic lover, the healer, and many more. Every civilization has a set of virtues which are put forward as goals for self-formation. Examples include courage, justice, temperance, compassion, determination, foresight, and wisdom.

The paradigms of fully developed individuality and the conceptions of virtue were justified by some metaphysical picture like the Platonic theory of the fight of the mind not to be tainted by the body; the Jewish view of the fight between the *yetzer ha'tov* and the *yetzer hara* (the good and the bad instinct), the Christian conception of the fight between the spirit and the flesh; the Chinese doctrine of yin and yang; or the Buddhist view of the struggle toward enlightenment. These metaphysical pictures provided the underpinnings of the disciplines of the self devised by each culture to provide tools for the formation of the individual.

Conceptions of ideal selfhood and virtue cannot remain purely theoretical, if they are to guide individuals in the development of their personalities. They must receive concrete embodiment in cultural institutions which create practices of disciplining the self (Foucault, 1983). Well-known examples for such institutions are schools of meditation which are geared toward training individuals to achieve control over their state of mind and autonomous bodily functions. Military academies, besides the theoretical knowledge and skills they teach, are supposed to develop personality characteristics desirable for a military officer. Monastic orders which teach theological knowledge and pastoral skills, also train novices to develop personality traits such as humility, temperance, love of God, and the like.

The practices of these institutions depend on the ideal type of personalities they want to develop: Zen masters want to develop emptiness, the ability to attain immediate experience, calmness, and effortlessness of concentration in order to reach enlightenment. Hence meditative practices are geared toward dissipation of thought, training the imagination toward certain images and metaphors, and the ability to focus on immediate bodily experience (Buswell, 1992). Military academies work toward subordination through drill, leadership through exercise of judgment in maneuvers, stamina through prolonged physical exercise and standing up to hardship, reliability through development of relevant skills and the like. Monastic orders try to instill belief by prayer, temperance through abstinence and fasting, humility through subordination to one's superiors, love of God through meditation, study, and the like.

Psychotherapeutic Schools as Traditions of Disciplines of Self

I propose to view psychotherapeutic schools as cultural institutions which embody traditions of practices of disciplining the self. Psychoanalysis is the foremost example of such a tradition. It has been in existence for nearly a century, and has developed well-entrenched practices and a clearly delineated mode of training. For the time being I will skip the complexity introduced by the wide variety of theoretical and clinical approaches to be found in psychoanalysis today, and sketch a modern Freudian picture.

Like every institution designed to impart a discipline of the self, psychoanalysis is based on theoretical underpinnings: psychoanalytic theory as it has developed since Freud. This theory is taught in theoretical seminars. The clinical skills of interviewing, diagnosing, the creation and maintenance of a therapeutic setting, understanding unconscious content, the formulation of interpretations, are taught in clinical seminars and developed further through supervision of cases by training analysts.

Psychoanalytic training is based on the assumption that a psychoanalyst must achieve a certain level of personal maturity in order to be capable of exercising this profession. This implies access to one's own unconscious motivations and fantasies, a lack of rigid defense mechanisms which would prevent rational self-understanding, and what psychoanalysis calls a genital character structure—meaning roughly an orientation toward generativity in work and love (Greenson, 1967, chapter 4). In brief, the analyst should embody the ideal of the rational, fully analyzed human being. This goal is to be achieved primarily by undergoing one's own personal training analysis by a recognized training analyst, who presumably has already achieved the personality characteristics and degree of maturity demanded by the psychoanalytic ideal.

Psychoanalysis is much more than a theory or a therapeutic technique. It is an organization, a language, an ethos, a "climate of opinion" (Auden, 1939). For the practicing clinician it is a way of life, a worldview. Psychoanalytic institutes often constitute the center of the lives of those involved in them. These institutes are private organizations, and this is not just due to the historical contingency that psychoanalysis was not accepted into universities at the beginning of its history. The explicit goal of psychoanalytic institutes is to shape the candidates' personalities, and the structure of these institutes is in many ways modeled on that of an extended family rather than an academic institution.

Psychoanalysis provides an (albeit extreme) exemplification of the idea that psychotherapeutic schools are disciplines of the self which aspire to transmit a whole way of life. I do not think that the authoritarianism which has been criticized by authors both internal (Kernberg, 1987) and external (Gellner, 1985) to psychoanalysis is a necessary concomitant of this goal. The rigid structure, the constant tendency of psychoanalysis to keep itself "pure" are indeed problematic, and it has undermined the goal psychoanalysis has always been identified with: that of increasing the autonomy of both its practitioners and patients.

The Basic Dilemma of Secular Psychotherapy: How to Help without Infringing on the Patient's Autonomy

The above description must strike the modern reader as highly problematic. Modern psychotherapy is supposed to provide professional guidance toward change and not to propose what the Eastern religions and disciplines of the self call "a way" (of life). A therapeutic procedure that is based on a value-guided process of development smacks of indoctrination, even brainwashing. Is not psychotherapy expected to safeguard and even enhance the patient's autonomy?

Psychoanalysis has been centered around an extremely interesting conception which was supposed to bypass the problem of the impact a secular psychotherapist's authority could have on the patient's autonomy. The one and only tool of psychoanalysis was supposed to be self-understanding of the patient. Insight into the genetic and dynamic roots of his affliction was supposed to cure the patient in and of itself. Jürgen Habermas, the most important representative of the classical ideas of the Enlightenment alive today, has argued that psychoanalysis is *the* paradigm of the emancipatory function of knowledge (Habermas, 1968). He defines this empancipatory function as the process in which the very acquisition of knowledge of the causal roots of an individual's behavior liberates the individual from these causes, and is hence exclusively geared toward the emancipation of the individual, i.e., the enhancement of autonomy.

Habermas's model is extremely attractive: it raises the possibility of a modern discipline that fulfills the Socratic dream of personal development through self-knowledge, and it argues that a completely nonauthoritarian mode of psychotherapy is possible. If Habermas's model were indeed a good description of the psychoanalytic process, one could rightly argue that there is a secular form of psychotherapy which truly safeguards the patient's autonomy, and is therefore essentially different from older, nonsecular forms of healing and confession.

The Problems of the Emancipatory Model of Psychoanalysis

There is no doubt that the intention behind the psychoanalytic model of healing through self-knowledge is highly laudable. I was committed to it, and I still feel in deep sympathy with it, since its program of work, which is purely in the service of the enhancement of an individual's autonomy, appeals deeply to my liberal intuitions. The problem, alas, is that this model rests on some crucial simplifications which, once exposed, can be shown to be, at times, dangerous distortions of what really happens. To put it simply: a close look at actual therapeutic practice combined with philosophical analysis of the notion of interpretation shows that there is no such thing as neutral guidance toward self-knowledge.

As many authors have argued (e.g., Spence, 1981), and as I showed in detail in *Between Hermeneutics and Science* (1991, pp. 115–123), the analyst's interpretation of the patient's mental content is always guided by a theoretical understanding of what these contents are supposed to be and by a normative conception of what process the patient is supposed to undergo in order to come closer to some—again value-laden—conception of maturity or mental health. The danger of the psychoanalytic conception of therapy is that even with the best intentions it can undermine the patient's autonomy quite deeply. The analyst who hides behind the notion of total neutrality while by necessity applying a heavily value-laden conception of mental functioning, development of personality, and individual maturity ends up being deeply manipulative precisely because he does not put his normative conception up front (Gellner, 1985, chapter 2).

Psychoanalysis and the Ideal of Autonomy

It is important not to throw out the baby with the bathwater: the fact that the emancipatory model of psychoanalytic practice is flawed does not mean that the ideal of safeguarding the patient's autonomy is not valuable and important. But, as Kant (1787, pp. 670–732) argued, it is important to distinguish between concepts that have empirical reality ("constitutive concepts") and ideals which we can strive for, but never implement fully ("regulative ideals"). The idea of an emancipatory psychotherapy which does not indoctrinate the patient is a regulative ideal in Kant's sense. However, as with every regulative ideal, the misidentification of this ideal as constitutive, i.e., as capable of literal realization, is dangerous: its result can be indoctrination rather than emancipation.

This becomes painfully obvious through the history of psychoanalysis: for decades this history looks more like a war between competing religious factions than a dialogue between enlightened disciplines (Grosskurth, 1986, 1991). Dogmatic assertions have abounded, about the centrality of the Oedipus complex in neuroses (Freud); the necessity to work through the depressive position (Melanie Klein); individuation as the integration of the collective unconscious into the personality (Jung); or the crucial importance of empathy and the provision of selfobject needs (Kohut). Denunciations of competing factions as "not really analytic," "superficial," "just providing support but not analysis," and the like recall accusations between religious factions that the "heretics" have abandoned the path of true faith.

How can the very idea of secular psychotherapy, which safeguards patients' autonomy, be saved? To me the only way seems to admit that every psychotherapeutic process involves the transmission of an ideal of individuality, that no psychotherapist can be neutral. Once we are aware of this fact we must grant every potential patient the possibility of understanding what the guiding assumptions of this ideal of individuality are. Since there is no such thing as the one true method, it is impermissible to interpret the patient's difficulty in entering the therapeutic language of his therapist first and foremost as resistance. If, as I believe, psychotherapy cannot be done without such ideals, the only way of safeguarding the patient's autonomy is to train practitioners to have a pluralist self-consciousness.

PSYCHOTHERAPY AS ART

The Idea of a Liberal Society

I propose to use the art world instead of science as a paradigm for the organization of psychotherapy and psychoanalysis. Psychotherapy should be a domain in which styles of individuality can be created and where they can compete with each other. This space, the location of *culture*, like the art world, should be governed by a combination of plurality and quality.

Postmodernism takes art rather than science as the paradigm for an ideal organization of society. The sociological dynamics of science is characterized by the desire for consensus. Since Thomas Kuhn's *The Structure of Scientific Revolutions* (1961), historians of science have made us increasingly aware of the normalizing mechanisms, and the inherently conservative tendencies of the organization of science.

The history of Western epistemology has been governed by the fear of chaos. Since Plato, it was a matter of course that if there is no *one* truth to be found, total relativism would result. Modern theory of science from Descartes to logical positivism had an unquestioned starting point: there must be *one* method of evaluating theoretical claims, since otherwise rationality would succumb to total anarchy (Putnam, 1981).

Art is interesting in its combination of two tendencies which seem prima facie mutually exclusive: an inherent drive toward plurality and an attempt to judge standards of quality. Since the romantic period art has been governed by the ideal of new creation: a work of art is considered to be great if it does not continue an existing tradition but initiates a new style. The history of art is the history of competing styles which coexist within a common cultural space. The art world is the paradigm of a cultural institution which *thrives* on plurality.

Yet art is not possible without judgments of quality. The history of art is characterized by the constant competition between artists and artistic styles. Such competition is impossible without the idea of quality. Yet a set of rules by which art is judged does not exist. What then are the standards of judgment?

The art world generates these standards by creating a canon, a historical account of the works and styles which constitutes the history of art. A canon defines standards of judgment by including certain artists and works and excluding others (Bloom, 1994). Standards of judgment evolve along with this canon, which in turn is constantly rewritten and expanded. Just as there are various ways to write the canon, there are of necessity various ways of judging art, which compete among themselves.

In other words, the standards of judgment do not logically and historically precede the creation of art, but rather evolve as an intrinsic part of the history of art. New styles challenge existing standards which are modified to integrate novel valuable art—even if the art world must violate and redefine existing standards in order to sustain judgment that a new style is indeed valuable.

THE ART WORLD AS MODEL FOR PSYCHOTHERAPY

The model of the art world has interesting consequences when applied to psychotherapy. The plurality of coexisting approaches becomes a virtue rather than a problem. Psychotherapy should thrive on the tension generated by plurality and not be bogged down by it. Every school should feel forced to constantly rethink and develop its approach and feel challenged by other approaches without losing its identity.

I do not think that psychotherapy without coherent styles is possible. Every single therapy is a journey in a metaphorical space which is constituted by the narrative of the journey. This metaphorical space is constituted by the conceptualization of the journey by both the patient and the therapist. The patient mostly lives in a closed narrative space; he has lost a sense of direction in life, or he feels that the direction he wants to travel in is blocked by a wall. The therapist's task is therefore to reconceptualize the narrative space of the patient's life in a way that opens new vistas.

The creation of a therapeutic process demands that there be a sense of continuity between the sessions, between the various parts of the therapeutic dialogue. This continuity is engendered by two major factors: one is the stability of an evolving relationship between patient and therapist, the second is the presence of guiding themes which connect the various parts of the therapeutic journey. A therapeutic relationship is created through the reliability of the therapist's personality, his way of interacting with the patient, the constancy of his attitude, in brief, the coherence of his therapeutic style. This style is embodied in many, more subtle ways as well: the therapist adopts a stance, an attitude toward the patient, toward the hardships and pitfalls of life, toward romantic strivings, and feelings of failure, as well as an interpersonal attitude.

The patient, by entering a therapy, learns the language and the conventions of a discipline of the self: he acquires new ways of narrating his life, techniques of shaping his personality, and normative conceptions of what life could look like. Otherwise he would be faced with a mass of conflicting and possibly contradictory messages which do not allow him to enter a process.

Every practitioner feels the necessity of developing a coherent style of work, but he should be conscious of the fact that his style is one of many possible ways of working. Every clinician must be conscious of the fact that in adopting a particular style of work he makes a choice not based on the truth about human nature, but on stylistic preference and affinity to the ideal of individuality guiding his preferred school. If the therapist is informed by pluralist, liberal self-consciousness he does not enforce this attitude and hence indoctrinate the patient, but offers it as a possible way to experience and lead one's life.

The fact that the schools do not die, but continue to exist, the fact that psychotherapy does not become an eclectic discipline organized around techniques rather than styles, is not to be deplored: it is the best safeguard for the maintenance of pluralist self-consciousness without which psychotherapy can become an instrument of domination rather than guidance toward freedom.

The Difficult Art of Living a Life

Ideals of accomplished individuality are not descriptions of a state of biologically prescribed maturity. They are expressions of culturally created images of the characteristics an individual must have in order to successfully live a life of a certain type. In that respect they are more similar to the prescription of an academic discipline or an art academy regarding the skills and training a member of the field or craft must have in order to be able to succeed.

Taking the perspective of the individual ideal rather than that of social morality does not mean that judgments of quality do not enter our thinking. Looking at life histories we can still ask to what extent an individual has succeeded in living the life she wanted, how much coherence, flow, and satisfaction this life contains, whether it contains rich and meaningful personal relationships. This judgment should be an internal one: a life should be understood according to the implicit or explicit criteria the individual herself applies in the experience and assessment of her life. In this respect an understanding of lives from the point of view of individual ideal is more similar to art criticism than it is to moral and legal judgment.

The situation of each individual who tries to live her life bears a similarity to the situation of the artist. The development of the analogy may help us to highlight some of the structures of existence which are relevant to a therapeutic understanding of individuals.

The painter stands in front of an empty canvas. He knows a great deal about how his predecessors have filled such canvases. In fact, his very choice of standing in front of a canvas puts him into this tradition. This position has been depicted countless times. His associations while painting can range from Velasquez's *Las Meninas* to Van Gogh's self-portraits.

No painter works in a vacuum. The history of art and the present art world create a field of force which influences his hands in every stroke. His historical position, his teachers, other painters who have gripped his imagination, and the styles which have defined his art crowd his studio. A painter is never alone, even though in a sense he is free to do as he pleases. He knows that there is no right way to fill the canvas, but his empty canvas is structured by the standards and expectations which are the background of his identity as a painter.

To be an artist is also to live in a world of critics. The art world is constituted by those who write about and judge art, who organize exhibitions, and sell art, no less than by those who produce it. The canon of art history is defined by what is integrated in major surveys of periods and schools. Personal influence by teachers, colleagues, and friends is superimposed on the influence generated by museums, books, and the amalgam of factors called culture.

The art world is structured by aesthetic judgment, and could not exist without the discourse of art criticism which judges quality (Danto, 1978). The creation of art is inextricably intertwined with the institutions that try to evolve criteria of what is good art and what is not. Good art criticism tries to make explicit what the artist has tried to achieve in a particular work. The artist's project is judged internally, not from the perspective of some general theory of art. A novel, for example, is criticized in terms of its inner flow and coherence, the extent to which its characters are developed and convincing, and the interest its plot commands. The novel's genre is taken into account, and the criteria of success are a function of that genre. A good critic always takes into account the possibility that a writer may have found ways of mixing genres, or even developing a category sui generis. Only bad and unimaginative criticism begins from some preconceived theory of the novel, its purported moral and aesthetic purpose, and then judges it from that point of view.

Understanding lives entails a similar process, in which lives and characters are assessed according to the individual's own standards. Of course lives evolve within a context no less than works of art do. Images of the good life are always generated against a background of cultural para-digms of accomplished individuality. Images of a life worth living are mostly of a certain genre: the pursuit of financial success and social status; the desire to build a family; the wish to be creative; the search for close personal relation-ships; the yearning for spiritual meaning are some exam-ples of the culturally entrenched ideals which individuals can adopt. In the terms of classical psychoanalytic theory, there is a constant interaction between self representation and ideal self. The existential pain which often leads pa-tients to seek help can be a function of their experience of the distance between the ideal self and their experience of their actual selves. This makes them feel that they do not live a life they experience as worth living.

Again, as in art criticism, the therapist's understand-ing is not based on complete identification with the pa-tient's perspective. The individual's goals and their interrelationship are assessed according to criteria of rea-sonableness, feasibility, and coherence between different goals. The question then, of course, arises where these criteria come from. The ideal of completely neutral, purely empathic understanding is a regulative ideal which guides us, but cannot be achieved. The therapist's own understanding of the good life and accomplished individu-ality will play an ineradicable role in his understanding of every patient.

Psychotherapeutic Schools and Disciplines of the Self

In the last years of his life Michel Foucault began to de-velop the idea that persons turn themselves into subjects by submitting (subjecting) themselves to disciplines which form them. The double meaning of the idea that subjects (qua agents) must subject (qua patients) themselves to a discipline was engrained in his notion of *modes d'assujetisse-ment,* modes of turning oneself into a subject. Foucault began to explore the idea that we are always guided by an aesthetics of existence, by an aesthetic ideal of the subject.

In my own terminology, the need for individuality is the attempt to realize in oneself an aesthetics of existence (Foucault, 1983).

The analytic therapist who sees his own authority in this way, by necessity takes a different stance. He sees himself not as an extension of power systems, but as an expert in forming the self according to certain ideals. Many such ideals can be drawn from the tradition of depth psychology: Freud's ideas of dignity and truthfulness; Jung's ideal of spiritual directedness; Winnicott's ideal of the spontaneous gesture; Bion's idea of bearing uncertainty and pain in order to find new modes of thinking; these and many others can be used again in the search for new aesthetics of existence.

Psychotherapy is the twentieth-century equivalent of disciplines of the self which have existed in every culture. I define a discipline of the self as a cultural form of life which offers a traditionally entrenched model of the virtuous individual and teaches the practices by which such virtue can be achieved.

Modern psychotherapy is continuous with such disciplines of the self as the Greco-Roman philosophical schools, the monastic orders of various religions, schools of martial arts, and military academies, in that it fosters the development of virtues. Yet it also constitutes a true innovation: modern, secular psychotherapies at their best respect the right of the individual to have a mind of his own and to choose between various ideals of the good life. The condition for maintaining this commitment to liberal individualism, and this is my central point, is contingent on maintaining a pluralist self-consciousness. This in turn is, I think, made easier by the perspective on psychoanalysis as art.

The Irreducibility of the Personal Element in Psychotherapy

Every psychotherapeutic school develops ways to shape the therapist's personality. The clinician must be a practical master of the discipline of selfhood he wants to impart to his patients. This formation of the therapeutic self is linked to one of the most consistent findings of psycho-therapy research: something in the therapeutic relation-ship seems to be essential to the success of therapeutic work (Garfield and Bergin, 1978, chapters 7, 8). Mostly the elements investigated concern the extent to which the patient trusts the therapist, the therapist's acceptance of the patient, and the quality of the relationship between patient and therapist.

Hence it seems that an essential part of the therapeu-tic craft is the ability to form the type of relationship with the patient which will be helpful. The psychoanalytic tradi-tion has tried to identify this ingredient in the relationship from early on as neutrality: the ability to abstain from judgment, to subdue one's personality, and to maintain a consistently analytic attitude. In other words, the psycho-analytic tradition has assumed that there is something like a technique of forming a therapeutic relationship.

Published case material (and even more conversation with colleagues) creates a different impression: the thera-pist's personality has a tremendous impact on the thera-peutic relationship. The original tendency of the psychoanalytic tradition to attribute whatever perception the patient has of his analyst to transferential distortions has turned out to be unrealistic, and the number of ana-lysts who maintain this view is rapidly shrinking.

It is certainly true that there is a great amount of discipline involved in acquiring the capacity to form thera-peutic relationships. But this discipline is not about neu-tralizing one's personality, but about making constructive use of it. Let me return to the analogy with art, and this time I want to use the example of the performing musi-cian. The musician must obviously acquire a sound techni-cal basis if he is to play well. The question is *what* he will be able to play well; this is a function of his personal musi-cal *idiom* (to appropriate Christopher Bollas's term). There are natural jazz players, natural rock players, natural classical musicians. As a matter of sheer empirical fact there are very few musicians who are good at more than one musical idiom: examples like Friedrich Gulda who is both a classical pianist and plays jazz are a small minority (and many will argue that he does not belong to the first class of either category). Technique must merge with personality elements like personal idiom, temperamental qualities, and preponderant perceptual Gestalts into a seamless whole if the artist's performance is to be more than a medley of competently applied techniques.

Looking at psychoanalysis from the point of view just developed, we can begin to see why the development of the practicing clinician is inextricably mixed with his personal development.

1. The ability to form consistent therapeutic relationships depends on the therapist's capacity to make use of her personal idiom in ways which integrate this idiom naturally with what is useful for the patient.

2. The clinician's perspective on the patient's personality and life cannot possibly be detached from her own life experience as the matters dealt with in therapeutic processes are highly personal. Any attempt of the therapist to go consistently against her own grain in understanding and intervening in the therapeutic process will inevitably lead to a stilted relationship, and the therapist will be highly unconvincing.

3. Yet, it is illusory to think that the therapist can simply spontaneously "be herself." No human being (at least no human being I know of) is naturally built in ways which are suited to the highly differentiated and subtle modes of relating, understanding, and intervening which are needed in psychotherapy. Hence the personal idiom needs to be formed and trained in the same way as a musician's, if the individual is to be a good therapist.

4. Most of all, the clinician is supposed to guide metaphorical journeys through mental space. If he does not actually experience life, in particular his own life in terms of this journey, if these metaphors do not inform his perception of life, he will not be capable of providing his patients with a convincing view of what this journey is like.

Psychoanalysis as a Stylistic Category

It might rightfully be argued that the description above does not differentiate between psychoanalytic clinicians and other approaches. I agree. In order to provide such characterization we must look at each clinician and ask what his stylistic preferences are, and what tradition he identifies with most. This criterion is, of course, not one which seeks for the essence of psychoanalysis; if anything it seeks family resemblances between various approaches. Psychoanalysis is, in this sense, a loosely knit family, with members of varying degrees of centrality. Not unlike the Hapsburg family with their protruding chins and their fleshy lips which seem both sensual and pouting, the family of psychoanalysis has a variety of features which make its members easy to identify.

The first sign of psychoanalysis is its search for hidden unities. The individual is not taken at face value, the varieties of life manifestations are not taken as a set of behavioral data which carry their meanings on their sleeves. The assumption is always that there is hidden unity, a small number of common themes which are the locus of the individual's intelligibility. Inevitably this leads to thinking in terms of depth and surface. Psychoanalysts always seek motifs which underlie the patient's overt functioning. No symptom, no behavior is taken in isolation. It is always assumed that the basic hidden themes will turn out to shed light on the bewildering variety of behavioral manifestations.

In musical terms one could say that the psychoanalytic clinician always assumes that an individual's life must be understood as a symphonic structure. He looks for a small number of basic themes and motifs, and takes the composition of a life to be a development of these themes. It would never be enough for a depth psychologist to see a life as a series of compositions which have some resemblance to each other.

The second sign of psychoanalysis in thinking in terms of coexisting levels of functioning. The theme of various levels of experience is played out over and over again: primary process and secondary process, unconscious phantasy and symbolic thought, the archetypal and the discursive, the infantile and the mature—these levels are the basic bread of psychoanalysis. The ideas of hidden unities and levels of functioning are tightly linked in the thinking of most psychoanalysts. The hidden unities of life are mostly sought at the more basic (generally unconscious) level, and the more conscious levels are taken to be elaboration of these themes.

The third sign of psychoanalysis is its emphasis on listening rather than instructing. The psychoanalyst does not look for strategies, does not seek to actively change the patient. The assumption is always that when the therapeutic process is stalling, this is an indication of a theme at the basic level that has not yet come to the fore. This emphasis on change from within is due to a common denominator of all depth psychologies: psychoanalysis is committed to the Western tradition of internality. Its ethics is to believe that subjects are determined from within; it conceives of the individual from the inside outwards, so to speak, and not from the outside inwards. It assumes that individuality as such has depth; individuals are never just reactive to an environment. Hence it is distasteful to a psychoanalyst to think that a behavioral change can in itself make an important difference. And even if there is a behavioral change which obviously has some impact, the depth psychologist always assumes that this impact is a function of some deeper meaning the symptom and its disappearance have had for the individual.

The fourth major sign of psychoanalysis is that it dislikes looking at minor themes. It always assumes that the drama of the individual is connected to some major, existential theme: life and death, sexuality, and sexual identity, control versus loss of control, love and hate, dependence versus independence, time and eternity.

This last sign goes along with a certain distaste psychoanalysts generally have for the comic vision of the world: this comic vision assumes that small, inessential things can make a big difference; that big entanglements can be a function in themselves of unimportant details. The literary forms which suit the psychoanalysts are those of the tragic drama, the romantic epos, not the comic miniature.

Psychoanalysis as Literature

Of the various ways psychoanalysis has evolved to seek unity of understanding of human lives some are richer, more compelling, possibly therapeutically more efficient than others. The problem is that there seems to be no way to establish such a ranking. Within the confines of the International Psychoanalytic Association there are roughly a dozen styles which can be identified as distinct. The fact is that none of them has managed to convince the others of its superiority.

My contention is that the—ultimately aesthetic—preferences of each school cannot be backed by a theory of human nature. It seems more honest to simply say that one's mind just works that way; that this is the way one prefers to understand human beings; that other, more pragmatic, less encompassing modes of thinking simply do not strike a chord in one's soul.

It is possible, though, to argue for one's style: one can try to show that one's view of life is richer, more compelling, than alternative modes. Such arguments of necessity are of an aesthetic, almost literary character. One could try to show that competing approaches do not have the same amount of differentiation; that they simplify too much; that the life narratives generated by them turn out to be more stereotypical, more schematic than one's own accounts.

Psychoanalysis has been good at doing two things: describing complexities of human experience and providing narratives which make sense of such experience. The other professional class of people which has been good at this is writers of fiction and poetry. Proust, to take one of the best examples, has developed one of the most fascinating ways of showing the recurrence of basic childhood themes throughout life in his *À la recherche du temps perdu* (1913–1927). In fact this work might well serve as a basic textbook for psychoanalysts. But no one in his right mind would argue that the *Recherche* contains a scientific theory. It develops a certain mode of narration. And the right approach to the *Recherche* is to analyze its mode of narration—something Nabokov does quite masterfully in his *Lectures on Literature* (1980).

I think that exactly the same thing can be said about Freud, Jung, Klein, Winnicott, Kohut, and the other heroes of psychoanalysis. Each of them developed a particular mode of telling human lives. Psychoanalysis is best understood as a discipline which tries to provide interesting ways of telling and living human lives through the pitfalls and difficulties provided by life. Because it was not conscious of this fact, psychoanalysis has been essentially mythological for most of its history. What happens to myth when it becomes conscious of its own nature is that it becomes literature. The hermeneuticist interpretation of psychoanalysis has made it possible for us to become conscious of the fact that we have been speaking prose all along.

2 CRITICAL PLURALISM: HOW TO LIVE WITH OUR YEARNING FOR UNIFIED CONCEPTIONS

THE NEED FOR VOICE

Every clinician needs a voice, a presence in the consulting room that is both authentic and therapeutic. Voice is an amalgam of style, guiding values, modes of relating, and content of message. Therapeutic voice necessitates a more or less coherent presence in the consulting room, an identity and a style which provide the analyst with the stamina to conduct his work, and the patient with the safety of facing an individual he can gradually come to trust. In other words, psychotherapy isn't just about techniques. No technique has been found yet which in its own right constitutes either a necessary or a sufficient condition for therapeutic success.

In the previous chapter I have argued that the art world can serve as a useful model for psychoanalytic culture, because it allows us to make better sense of the plurality of styles. The present chapter will put an important caveat on this thesis. Art is about aesthetic coherence. Psychotherapy is about helping people. Even though every practitioner needs a coherent style, we must not forget that the therapeutic encounter is never art for art's sake.

One of the important tensions in the search for a clinical voice is defined by the opposition of purism versus pragmatism. This tension can be felt in the daily dilemmas of clinical practice: should I provide a clear, unambiguous, aesthetically and existentially coherent presence and narrative line? Or should I do what might be helpful at the present moment? Should I give the patient the opportunity to find his own way through the maze of life, his thoughts, and feelings, or should I employ some technique which might shorten the process considerably and provide important relief?

The tension between purism and pragmatism is the tension between the yearning for a single voice that unifies all of a therapist's modes of relating, interventions, and messages, and the insight that no such single voice is likely to be useful for all patients, or even for any single patient in all situations. The main question I would like to deal with is how we can live with this tension.

The psychoanalytic clinician needs to find a relationship to the canonic voices and texts of the past, if he is to see himself as part of the psychoanalytic tradition. The second question I want to address is, therefore, how can the clinician who is skeptical with regard to the truth value of the great theories of the past make constructive use of them?

The goal of this chapter is to delineate a position, which I will call *critical pluralism,* that allows the clinician to make use of the great purist conceptions of the past without either dogmatically asserting their truth value, or sacrificing the patient's needs on the altar of the purity of approach. I will begin by using Isaiah Berlin's description of two types of intellectual temperament, and I will try to show that critical pluralism is capable of integrating between the need for purity, beauty, and coherence and the pragmatist's skeptical insistence that the map is not the territory, and that being helpful is often opposed to purist practice.

Hedgehogs and Foxes

Isaiah Berlin, the intellectual historian and political philosopher, has delineated this tension between the one,
overarching vision and the careful attention to the empirical details and pragmatic demands of a situation, in his
book *The Hedgehog and the Fox* (1951), which takes its title
from a fragment of the Greek poet Archilochus which says:
"The fox knows many things, but the hedgehog knows one
big thing." Berlin characterizes the difference between
hedgehogs and foxes as follows:

> For there exists a great chasm between those, on one side,
> who relate everything to a single central vision, one system
> less or more coherent or articulate, in terms of which they
> understand, think and feel—a single, universal organizing
> principle in terms of which alone all that they are and say
> has significance—and, on the other side, those who pursue
> many ends, often unrelated and even contradictory, con-
> nected, if at all, only in some *de facto* way, for some psycho-
> logical or physiological cause, related by no moral or
> aesthetic principle; these last lead lives, perform acts, and
> entertain ideas that are centrifugal rather than centripetal,
> their thought is scattered or diffused, moving on many
> levels, seizing upon the essence of a vast variety of experi-
> ences and objects for what they are in themselves, without,
> consciously or unconsciously, seeking to fit them into, or
> exclude them from, any one unchanging, all-embracing,
> sometimes self-contradictory and incomplete, at times fa-
> natical, unitary vision. The first kind of intellectual and
> artistic personality belongs to the hedgehogs, the second
> to the foxes: and without insisting on a rigid classification,
> we may, without too much fear of cons tradition, say that,
> in this sense, Dante belongs to the first category, Shake-
> speare to the second; Plato, Lucretius, Pascal, Hegel, Dos-
> toevsky, Nietzsche, Ibsen, Proust are, in varying degrees
> hedgehogs; Herodotus, Aristotle, Montaigne, Erasmus,
> Molière, Goethe, Pushkin, Balzac, Joyce are foxes [Berlin,
> 1951, p. 22].

The psychoanalytic tradition is characterized by the
predominance of hedgehogs: Freud's metaphor of the

"pure gold of analysis" has had a tremendous impact on the whole history of the field. Psychoanalysis is laboring under the weight of the idea that for it to maintain its identity, it must have an integrated, pure conception of itself. It must define its field by a particular epistemology, and its clinical practice must be centered around a central line.

Something in the cultural tradition of psychoanalysis seems to make it difficult to accept that we may not be capable of producing purist conceptions of psychoanalytic practice. And yet the plurality of approaches seems to be there to stay. The hope for the grand integration, the new system that will provide unitary theory and a foundation for purist clinical practice seems less realistic than ever.

Freud was the hedgehog par excellence, Melanie Klein, Wilfred Bion, and Heinz Kohut followed close by. Each of them had a unitary vision which guided their interpretation of every phenomenon they met. Freud's vision was centered around the belief that life is a permanent fight between pleasure principle and reality principle, animal nature and civilization, irrationality and rationality. His theory and practice formed a seamless web guided by a stoic ethics that assumed that only the introduction of civilization and truthfulness into the furthest recesses of the mind could guide the patient to full mental health.

On the other, romantic, end of the spectrum of hedgehogs we have Heinz Kohut whose theoretical, ethical, and clinical vision is centered around the belief that a life worth living is centered around the two poles of a sense of worth and vitality on the one hand, and established ideals and values on the other hand. His romantic ethics assumed that it was up to the parental environment to provide the child with the resources which allowed for cohesive selfhood to evolve.

Ferenczi, Balint, Lacan, Erikson, and Greenson are good examples of foxes. Even though each of them had a distinct voice, they were guided by encountered complexity rather than by unity of vision. Ferenczi's lifelong search for ways of being therapeutically useful made him change positions on many issues. He was never sure that a final position could or should be achieved, and his *oeuvre* is more a set of important contributions to various questions than it is an integrated body of thought. Greenson is a vibrant presence in the history of psychoanalysis, and he has an unmistakable voice. Yet his concerns are always clinical, theory is subservient to the pragmatic needs of helping the individual patient, and of resolving particular problems encountered in daily practice.

THE CHARMS OF PURISM: WILFRED BION

Without hedgehogs the profession would lack the major magnets which shape the field of possible voices. Their attraction is partially a function of the power of integrated visions which give unequivocal significance to every phenomenon that is to be encountered. By creating such unitary perspectives they provide Gestalts which are paradigms for the interpretation of human lives. None of them withstands detailed criticism, but they are valuable precisely because they show us the implications of certain ideas by pushing them to their logical extremes.

The ideal of the "pure gold of analysis," much belittled and ridiculed, has a certain grandeur, the beauty characteristic of forms of life geared toward perfection of discipline. The extreme of the purist approach is to be found in Bion's notion of faith: Bion believed that pure psychoanalysis should work without memory and desire, that it should put its faith into an absolute reality which would at some point shine through if only the psychoanalyst would refrain from interfering with this process. Bion transcendentalized psychoanalysis to the point of thinking that it was a unique setting in which the patient could actualize his or her personhood buried under the masses of symptoms. He provides us with the quintessential example of purist thought and practice, which in certain ways brings to mind the great meditational practices of the East. The set of rules regulating analytic interaction is tightly woven in order to avoid any type of effect which might spoil the goals of pure analytic work.

One of the most salient characteristics of Bion's vision is his uncompromising yearning for true meaning, and his relentless attempt to decipher the human tendency to avoid thought, suffering, and individuation. Psychoanalysis for him became a transcendental undertaking: the search for something like a true personality inside human beings who are so pitifully weak and infantile.

> Somewhere in the analytic situation, buried in masses of neuroses, psychoses and so on, there is a person struggling to be born. It seems to me that the analyst's function is not to demonstrate all these neurotic and psychotic mechanisms, excepting as an incidental in the course of freeing the patient. It doesn't seem to be fanciful to say that just as Michelangelo, Leonardo, Picasso, Shakespeare and others have been able to liberate this mass of material, actual forms which remind us of real life, so the analyst is engaged in an analogous occupation—an attempt to help the child to find the grown up who is latent there, and also to show that the grown person is still a child [Bion, 1987, p. 41].

The transcendental element in Bion's thinking derived from his unwillingness to say much about what this person was. The real person became a limited concept, not unlike the God of negative theology, around whom everything revolves and nothing can be said.

His yearning for truth and his disdain for what he saw as the tendency of psychoanalysts to interpret automatically without sufficient evidence, led him to his most famous dictum: the analyst, he said, must enter the analytic session without memory and desire (Bion, 1970, chapter 4). He should try not to remember that he has known this person from many sessions. He should have no desire to achieve anything in the session; no vision of health; no vision of who this person could or should be.

The analyst's state of mind should be that of an act of *faith*. Faith in the existence of an ultimate reality (symbolized by capital "O"), which cannot be known, but can only *be*. This psychic reality is not sensuous in nature; hence the analyst cannot rely on his senses in knowing it. He cannot know the patient's psychic ultimate reality in any other way either; all he can do is to *be* what he can be in this room with this patient at this time. His faith is that at some point this will lead to a transformation in which meaning will emerge out of chaos, a person out of the "masses of neuroses and psychoses."

Bion is talking about a mystical state of mind; a state of emptiness which allows true knowledge to emerge; a knowledge which is existential and experiential rather than another concoction of verbiage automatically produced. Bion was perfectly aware of his affinity to mystical experience and practice and on several occasions (Bion, 1970, chapter 6) spoke about the relation between the mystic and the society around him, quite obviously referring to himself when speaking about mystics and the inability of society to accept them.

Bion's perspective is an interesting amalgam of a central Freudian idea and Kantian philosophical epistemology. The Freudian idea to which he returns endlessly is that the capacity to *think* evolves out of the baby's encounter with *frustration*. Freud's belief that the pleasure principle is replaced by the reality principle only because the baby experiences that there are some experiences of the breast which are followed by satiation, whereas others leave the baby hungry. Hence the baby is forced to accept that some experiences are veridical perceptions and others hallucinations. If there were no frustration, the reality principle, the acceptance of reality, would never be established (Bion, 1961).

Bion's development of this idea is as follows: the infant's inborn preconception of the breast (roughly something like a Piagetian primary schema of finding and sucking the breast) sometimes meets with sensory fulfillment, and sometimes with frustration. It is the meeting of preconception and frustration which decides the fate of the infant's, and the future adult's, mind. If frustration tolerance is sufficient, the infant can form the thought of the absent breast. *Thought is about the desired object when it is absent.* If frustration tolerance is low, the experience of absence cannot be maintained, and instead the experience of rage, lack, and frustration is reified and turned into a positive presence: a new experiential object is created, the *bad* breast. This hallucinatory object is painful, and the infant tries to rid itself of it by fantasizing it outside itself. Thus begins the reign of omnipotent fantasy: if the personality contains pain, the pain is not experienced but evacuated in fantasy. The result is a psychotic universe full of bad experiences projected onto it, and both inner and outer reality are distorted, since the subject becomes incapable of really experiencing ("suffering" as Bion says) its own pain, and since external reality becomes the container of disowned experiences.

Authenticity of human experience for Bion is a function of but one question. How willing are you to suffer? If your willingness is sufficiently strong, you will be capable of true thought. You will perceive and conceive of yourself and the world in a relatively realistic manner and you will be a fully human person. To the extent you try to evade pain, you will twist and turn yourself into a neurotically and psychotically distorted animal who only *seems* to think. In reality you will be busy fantasizing away whatever you do not like, and you will neither truly experience yourself nor the world.

The second element of Bion's thought is a piece of Kantian epistemology. An important part of Kant's theory of knowledge centers around the relationship of conceptual thought and intuitive sensation. His view is that these two are ontologically and logically distinct. Concepts are the organizers of experience, but they are in themselves empty. Sensations are the material of experience, but they are in themselves blind. The theory of knowledge is to show the logical relationship between the two.

Bion's use of Kant revolves around Kant's dictum: "Concepts without intuitions are empty, intuitions without concepts are blind" (1787). Bion's term for Kant's "empty" is *unsaturated.* The mind's tendency is not to accept lack of saturation. To the same extent as the mind wants to evade frustration of bodily needs, it wants to evade the frustration of not knowing, the state of having a thought without knowing its truth value. Hence the mind evades nonknowledge and doubt by lulling itself into certainties where none are to be had.

I consider Bion's sharp distinction between true theory and myth to be one of the most important aspects of his thought. Theory is a formalized structure of concepts and propositions combined with more or less clear statements of the conditions that would count as evidence for these propositions. Myth is a narrative construction which may allow for the elucidation of experience and the generation of meaning, but not of truth and falsity, and certainly does not have clear conditions for epistemic acceptability.

One of Bion's most important realizations was that most of psychoanalytic theory has the logical structure of myth and not of theory. He was highly impatient with all kinds of pseudocertainties in the psychoanalytic world, exasperated by theoretical talk which is pseudoknowledgeable, where analysts lull themselves into a sense of safety by endlessly repeating the same formulae, feeling that they have explained where they have just reiterated the same mythical structure again and again. In Bion's terms, they are unwilling to accept a state of nonsaturation.

His demand for entering analytic sessions without memory and desire was precisely the demand to be able to bear nonsaturation, uncertainty, and lack of knowledge. Hence he turned psychoanalysis into a strict, ascetic discipline tolerating pain without distortion: the pain of frustration, of uncertainty, and of the existential isolation of the individual.

Bion's ideal is that of the skeptic, the relentless, uncompromising seeker of purity, the ascetic who demands the utmost in terms of being able to bear uncertainty, isolation, and the pain of nonfulfillment. Bion is a mystic who seeks modes of expression which are unconventional in order to break through the molds of what has become too familiar and automatic to still count as thought. He seeks emptiness, for translucency, the peace engendered by pure being without desire, the monastic silence beyond the endless chatter in which most of our lives are immersed.

Bion's disdain is geared toward those who seek saturation and cannot bear emptiness. The virtue of the mystic is not to shy away from pain, but to transform pain into thought. And this was what Bion tried to do in his analytic work and in his writing. Hence his attempt to create new symbols which would force analysts to go back to sheer experience and to shun their own desire for the sense of certainty engendered by entrenched phrases and pseudo-technical language.

It is instructive to note where Bion failed to quite stand up to his own ideal, most particularly in his uncritical acceptance of Freud's ideas of the pleasure principle and the reality principle, and his adherence to the Kleinian conception of mind, and sometimes to their clinical practice. Whenever he gives clinical examples (which is rare), it is interesting to see the extent to which he uses essentially Kleinian interpretive lines, even though his stated goal is to work without memory and desire. Bion exempts important aspects of Kleinian theory from his insight that psychoanalytic theory largely has the structure of myth and not of theory. He keeps using the terms "The Kleinian *theory* of projective identification" and the "Kleinian *theory* of the paranoid–schizoid and depressive positions."

This is a fascinating case of selective blindness. These Kleinian formulations in no way stand up to Bion's own criteria for what constitutes a theory. They are metaphoricomythical creations like any other psychoanalytic formulation. In other words, there was a point at which Bion himself was not capable of maintaining the state of nonsaturation.

These criticisms are meant to point out the extent to which the total openness, the mystical waiting for truth is not a realistic model of anything that truly can be done. We all apply Gestalts to what we hear and see, and these Gestalts are by necessity historically informed. The old mystical idea that we can clean our minds completely has the unfortunate tendency to overlook that experience is *always* informed by structures of meaning. Hence emptiness if often primarily a rhetorical concept geared toward opening oneself to the metaphors preferred by some particular theorist.

The second point of selective blindness concerned Bion's belief in the special status of psychoanalytic practice. He believed in it with the fervent intensity of a mystic who has seen the light. For him psychoanalysis as he conceived of it was the path to truth. Bion violently disliked anything which did not approach his ascetic ideal of bearing uncertainty and being capable of emptying one's mind. He interpreted much of what patients said as evidence of destructive evacuation of pain and attempts to destroy the analyst's analytic ability. This must have turned him into a fairly difficult analyst. In his seminars he time and again says that it is surprising if patients come to analysis, since they do not truly want it, since they do not want pain, and they do not want truth (Bion, 1987).

He was not particularly concerned with the fact that most people who turn to psychotherapeutic help do so neither to seek a spiritual search for purity of thought, nor to cleanse themselves through the experience of pain. He seemed to be oblivious to the fact that there might be something legitimate in patients' bewilderment at entering a strange kind of ritual instead of a more cooperative, commonsensically intuitive enterprise.

Bion more than any other writer on psychoanalysis shows the greatness and misery of purism in the field. On the one hand he upholds a lofty ideal of self-discipline which evokes respect and has guided many clinicians to greater openness toward experience. On the other hand his writings and clinical practice show the extent to which transcendentalization of a ritual can land a man as imaginative as Bion in unwitting dogmatisms and risk disregarding the patient's subjective experiences in the name of a transcendental notion of full personhood.

THE VOICE OF PRAGMATIC SANITY

The problem with purism is that no therapeutic encounter as I experience it can be described within the confines of purist constraints. Irvin Yalom has been more willing than any other author I know of to describe his learning post facto, the sheer groping for sense, the ways in which fate plays tricks on you, and the ironies which defeat your therapeutic wisdom. By and large the therapeutic encounter is of a messiness, of a sheer humanity and contingent lawlessness which cannot be captured by any of the purist approaches. It might be argued that Bion is no less willing to accept lack of knowledge and understanding. But Bion is highly purist in his belief that meaning will emerge if he sticks to a strictly defined setting, and the types of meaning he finds are, as I argued, always of a particular sort.

The cost of the belief in a particular setting and type of interpretation is great: there is the risk that patients come to feel that they have been tied onto a Procrustean bed and cut or stretched to fit its size. Pragmatism's belief is that we do not deal with art for art's sake or theory for theory's sake, but ultimately with a craft committed to helping people. Hence it is not willing to sacrifice common sense, flexibility, and sheer humaneness on the altar of purity of approach.

The pragmatist voice safeguards the patient's interest in being helped in his own terms and according to his own understanding as quickly as possible against the paternalism often implicit in purism. At its best pragmatism is the voice of enlightened skeptical empiricism with its long heritage from the seventeenth century onwards. It distrusts big ideologies and single-mindedness in the pursuit

of the One Truth. It is keenly aware of our epistemic fallibility, and demands that we never forget our propensity
to err. Pragmatism puts the serving of human needs above
beauty, coherence, and nobility, and it thinks that this
demands that we sometimes grope for what works rather
than striving for purity of procedure.

The most defining aspect of pragmatism is its insistence that the map must never be confused with the territory. It sees theory as a tool rather than as a mirror of
reality, and hence judges its validity by its usefulness. Purity of approach and unity of theoretical outlook are valued by pragmatism to the extent that they are subservient
to the practical goal at hand, and in psychotherapy this
means being helpful to the patient.

The pragmatic voice in psychotherapy is well exemplified by Irvin Yalom. He begins his book on existential
psychotherapy (1980) by telling the story of the Armenian
cooking course he once participated in. The Armenian
matron who taught the course gave them explicit recipes,
but on the way to the oven she would walk by a table with
an assortment of spices. She would add them *en passant,*
without giving much of an account of how and why she
determined the precise quantities.

The participants would replicate the recipes, and, not
surprisingly, would always be disappointed by the difference between their own product and the matron's dishes.
They soon came to the conclusion that the difference in
quality was accounted for by the little asides that were not
stated in the recipes.

Yalom's point is that he doubts that the success of
therapeutic work is due to adherence to the official guidelines codified in theories and canonical papers. He assumes that the difference between good and not so good
therapeutic work is to be sought in the little asides which
we often disregard precisely because theory tells us to disregard them.

Yalom has an integrative ethical vision which pulls
together many elements of existentialist thought into a

therapeutic philosophy, but he is thoroughly open-minded about the techniques that are helpful. He has done extensive research into the therapeutic factors in group therapy (1975), and is willing to work along the ways indicated as fruitful by empirical evidence. Because Yalom believes that technical purism can never match the complexity and opaqueness of either life or therapeutic processes, he consciously uses a wide variety of techniques in the service of the philosophy of freedom and lucidity which he advocates. Pragmatism can combine an ethical vision with practical flexibility, and its distrust toward theoretical ambition need not prevent it from thinking which captures depth and complexity.

Yalom's later writings are the most extreme example available nowadays of the renunciation of theoretical ambition for the sake of precision of experiential description. His collection of case histories, *Love's Executioner* (1989), is a masterpiece of literary transformation of therapeutic experience. Yalom has the courage to put himself on the line. He does not bother to put distance between himself and the reader by writing about his "countertransference." Instead he makes his experience much more transparent to the reader, and shows in detail how his personality and his convictions enter the therapeutic process.

He opens himself completely to criticism because he does not disguise his personality behind the fiction that all his reactions are the result of interaction with the patient, one of the favorite fictions entertained by the constant use of terms like *projective identification* in psychoanalytic writing. He is willing to fully acknowledge the complexity of the fact that the therapist always sits there as a human being, and he does not disguise the sheer groping for understanding behind verbose theoretical statements.

He makes it much easier for the reader to say, "I would have done this differently." There are junctures at which I disagree with his therapeutic tactics, but when I ask myself why, I become more fully aware of the extent to which my own way of working is a function of convictions which I cannot fully defend and of personality traits which I cannot rationalize by theory. One of many things I have gained from reading Yalom is that today I have no problem in telling patients at certain junctures that this is the way I do things because I don't know how to do them otherwise. I am happy to be told about what they experience as useful and what they experience as impediments to their growth and an intrusion into their individual freedom.

It is not surprising that Yalom is rarely, if ever, quoted in the strictly psychoanalytic literature. Psychoanalysis often discards what he does as superficial, as insufficiently geared toward the subtleties of unconscious life. It is important to acknowledge that he is pointing to a basic feature of psychodynamic discourse: that it touches upon the sheer contingency of human existence. Our search for understanding must often settle for literary presentation of what happened. If we are honest with ourselves, our yearning for hidden continuities, deep meanings, and processes buttressed by established theory often remains unsatisfied.

Yalom forces us to acknowledge that what maintains our therapeutic backbone is professional ethics, our commitment to trying to do our best to be helpful, rather than theoretical axioms about the natural necessity of this or that form of the therapeutic setting and process. The opacity of our patients' lives and the processes they undergo defies our need for total understanding. Finally Yalom's courage in putting his personality on the line goes beyond the willingness of many current psychoanalytic writers who acknowledge openly (Stolorow, Atwood, and Brandchaft, 1987; Bollas, 1989, chapter 3) that the therapist's subjectivity is never abolished.

The danger of pragmatism is that it can verge on a technocratic conception of psychotherapy. If finding the right way to help the patient change becomes a matter of finding the right technique, the price paid can be that the therapist can lose the perspective of the patient's being a subject who may be expressing something that does not immediately meet the eye. I do, for example, have problems with single-minded technical approaches like that of Habib Davanloo (1980). His therapeutic ambition produces a degree of intrusiveness which I experience as disrespectful to the patient's individuality and subjectivity. I also sometimes wonder whether the impressive therapeutic results he claims to have are not sometimes gained at the price of silencing the patient's search for a truer voice of his own.

This extreme is even more developed in the work of Milton Erickson (Rosen, 1982) and some of his followers like Jay Haley (1973). Their resourcefulness and technical creativity in finding ways out of therapeutic deadlocks is often admirable. Yet I am often shocked by the fact that this school sometimes comes to the point where the patient seems to become an object to be fixed rather than a human being with a subjectivity of his own. Erickson's famous case of the "February man" raises this question: Is the hypnotic implantation of fake memories a legitimate technique? Is there not a limit to what can and should be done to provide symptomatic relief?

I think that such excesses can only be prevented if psychotherapy does not see itself as a technology of change. Pragmatism must be prevented from turning into a manipulative discipline by guiding philosophical assumptions, by discourse about normative conceptions of individuality and subjectivity. This is well exemplified by Yalom: while being far removed from purism, Yalom maintains a constant dialogue with philosophical traditions which emphasize the importance of preserving freedom and autonomy. His existentialist ethics provide the touchstone for what he will and won't do.

Pragmatism must therefore be tempered by a dialogue with ideals which are not of a pragmatic nature. We saw the limitations of purism in the context of Bion. Yet Bion's transcendental notion of personhood may well be used as a corrective to the tendency of changing the patient by all means, and prevent manipulative excess. By the same token the ideal of helping the patient as efficiently as possible is useful in tempering the purist tendency to put a single-minded purist conception above the patient's desire to be helped as quickly as possible. I will therefore turn to the development of a position which makes such dialogue between ideals an explicit theme.

CRITICAL PLURALISM AS A DISTINCT VOICE

Critical pluralism is singularly suited to mediate the tension between purism and pragmatism. For me this voice has a distinct flavor, and it has been a strong presence in the political discourse of Western culture since the nineteenth century, even though it is less strongly heard lately. I briefly want to define this position and exemplify it in the context of political philosophy and I will then apply it to psychotherapy.

The term *pluralism* has become a catchword in so many contexts that I would gladly refrain from using it, if I knew of a decent alternative. In the last two decades the (justified) fight of ethnic cultures for recognition has taken a turn which obscures important issues. It is one thing to argue that the imperialism of Western culture has been lacking in respect for other cultures. It is quite another thing to buttress this claim with the idea that there is no way to judge the quality of theories, art, and forms of political organization.

Unfortunately pluralism has acquired a strident quality in fights for equal recognition of all possible perspectives, and it is often taken to mean that there are no differences of quality between competing positions. Critical pluralism does accord ontological validity for perspectives per se, and accords respect to the subjectivity of individuals, groups, and cultures. But it wants to preserve the right to argue that Bach wrote music qualitatively superior in deep ways to most of what has been written in the West and in other cultures, or that Western astrophysics

is a better account of the universe than the Greek cosmog-
onies of the fifth century B.C., the account of the Bible, or
African myths.

In particular it argues that liberal democracy is superior to any other form of political organization. One of its
deepest advantages is that it is the only political ideology
which makes dialogue and the possibility of dissent an
intrinsic part of its point of view. I will therefore call it
critical pluralism to indicate its unrelenting opposition to
facile relativism (Strenger, 1991, chapter 6).

The basic assumption of critical pluralism is that human understanding is intrinsically limited; that no conceptual framework can capture all possible perspectives on
reality, human or otherwise, and that the coexistence of
competing conceptual frameworks is in itself of enormous
value. The argument for the necessity of plurality has, to
my mind, never been stated better than by John Stuart Mill
in his treatise *On Liberty* (1859). Human societies cannot
afford to deny any voice the right to speak up. Our understanding is deeply fallible, and shutting up the opposition
will make it impossible for us to hear criticism.

Mill and his followers never intended this to mean,
though, that all positions are of equal validity. The price
of liberal democracy is that it must give room to positions
a liberal loathes. Critical pluralism will find itself in deep
accord with Voltaire's immortal saying to one of his cleri-
cal opponents: "I disapprove of what you say, but I will
defend to the death your right to say it."

In what sense then, is pluralism a distinct voice? Why
is it not a metaposition rather than a voice? A political
analogy might help: in a democratic parliament all parties
are supposed to accept the basic tenets of democracy and
to abide by its rules. Yet most Western parliaments contain
a liberal faction which has as its main goal the maintenance of the democratic goals themselves. Within the political discourse of democracy liberalism is in itself a
distinct voice.

The voice of critical pluralism as I hear it is a voice
of sanity. It tries to avoid the strident qualities of both

fanaticism and relativism and tries to make the effort to maintain the capability of listening and to appreciate the inner logic of alternative positions.

Isaiah Berlin exemplifies the voice of critical pluralism by dealing with the theme of a basic tension in human understanding which has run through the history of Western thought. Let me quote Berlin in full:

> One belief, more than any other, is responsible for the slaughter of individuals on the altars of the great historical ideals—justice or progress or the happiness of future generations, or the sacred mission or emancipation of a nation or race or class, or even liberty itself, which demands the sacrifice of individuals for the freedom of society. This is the belief that somewhere, in the past or in the future, in divine revelation or in the mind of an individual thinker, in the pronouncements of history or science, or in the simple heart of an uncorrupted good man, there is a final solution. This ancient faith rests on the conviction that all the positive values in which men have believed must, in the end, be compatible, and perhaps even entail one another. "Nature binds truth, happiness and virtue together as by an indissoluble chain" [Berlin, 1958, p. 167].

Berlin does not denounce this belief in the convergence of all ideals into a coherent whole as idiocy, metaphysical gibberish, or infantile fixation. He sees it as a deep longing engrained in the structure of the human mind, the hope and desire that all our values ultimately cohere. His treatment of intellectual history is permeated by a warmth of understanding, a capacity for empathic elucidation rare in any field.

In many ways his undertaking can be compared to Kant's dialectic of reason. Kant showed that the mind finds itself in contradictions when speculating about the structure of the totality of the universe. He argued that these contradictions were due to the fact that organizing categories of experience were stretched beyond what they could contain. Notions of substance or cause are valid when applied within the context of empirical experience but lose their validity when stretched beyond that. Kant argued that the very nature of reason is such that it formulates questions which it cannot answer. He does not see the great metaphysical questions about the nature of the universe and its first cause, and the nature of the human soul as expressions of stupidity. He shows how these questions and the desire to answer them are intrinsic to reason, and that the human predicament is to ask questions forever which cannot be answered.

Isaiah Berlin is the Kant of political reason: his analysis of the human striving for total, final solutions is not devoid of sympathy and understanding for the yearning for an overarching answer. His analyses of the vagaries of political reason and cultural sentiment are never reductive and are always geared toward sympathetic understanding of the human roots of the illusions behind them, but intransigent in the emphasis on the dangers of totalitarianism, intellectual, political, and otherwise.

> It may be that the ideal of freedom to choose ends without claiming eternal validity for them, and the pluralism of values connected with this, is only the late fruit of our declining capitalist civilization: an ideal which remote ages and primitive societies have not recognized, and one which posterity will regard with curiosity, even sympathy, but little comprehension. This may be so: but no skeptical conclusions seem to me to follow. Principles are not less sacred because their duration cannot be guaranteed. Indeed, the very desire for guarantees that our values are eternal and secure in some objective heaven is perhaps only a craving for the certainties of childhood or the absolute values of our primitive past. "To realize the relative validity of one's convictions," said an admirable writer of our time, "and yet stand for them unflinchingly is what distinguishes a civilized man from a barbarian." To demand more than this is perhaps a deep and incurable metaphysical need; but to allow it to determine one's practice is a symptom of an equally deep, and more dangerous, moral and political immaturity [Berlin, 1958, p. 172].

I have quoted Berlin extensively to provide a taste of his voice. It is a voice not necessarily *en vogue:* Berlin lacks the self-reflexive virtuosity and search for sophistication *à tout prix* typical of much current intellectual debate. His search for a rich perspective is colored by a humanist leaning (and learning) which has become somewhat unfashionable in our poststructuralist age, in which use of the notions of authors, subjects, selves, and intentions have become indications of a writer's lack of sophistication. The humanist underpinnings of Berlin's voice are reflected in his willingness to look for the human core of every cultural manifestation, to think through the motivations pushing us beyond what we can achieve. Berlin shows the possibility of accepting the historical contingency of one's own position without falling into cynicism. His ability to stick to his beliefs without being dogmatic about them may indeed be one of the marks of "civilized [wo]man," and the ultimate test of character for the individual.

CRITICAL PLURALISM AND THE CLINICIAN'S PREDICAMENT

Given the plurality of coexisting approaches in psychoanalysis and psychotherapy, it is hardly possible to deny the basic validity of the pragmatist insistence that no purist approach can contain the therapeutic wisdom necessary for all cases and situations. Does this mean that the purist voices must simply be discarded as obsolete, as remainders of a rationalist age that believed in the basic intelligibility of reality and the possibility of finding final truths?

Personally I would find discarding the purist voices saddening. They have the beauty, the ability to fascinate that can only be achieved through the singlemindedness of purpose and the unity of design of unified visions. In addition I think that they command an interest that goes far beyond the historical. The purist positions offer the clinician paradigms of therapeutic voice which show him what it is like to do clinical work based exclusively on one ideal.

Critical pluralism is, among other things, meant to present the possibility of using purist positions in clinical work without demanding commitment to any of them. Critical pluralism is different from eclecticism in one central respect. Eclecticism assumes that psychotherapy is, or should be, a collection of techniques which should be adapted to patients and symptomatic pictures. It assumes that the professionalism of a therapist is a function of his or her command of some of the existing techniques and the ability to use them appropriately. In some respects eclecticism takes psychotherapy to be a discipline that should be similar to medicine: in the same way as the medical practitioner uses tools, medications, and procedures, the psychotherapist uses techniques.

Critical pluralism assumes that techniques are somewhat incidental in psychotherapy. It assumes that no therapy can be done without having some ideals of accomplished individuality. These ideals, often cast as conceptions of mature personality, guide the therapist's understanding of the patient's problems and the nature of the process the therapist must undergo in order to come closer to the ideal of accomplished individuality. Critical pluralism assumes that the plurality of approaches reflects a plurality of ideals and values which lay claims on individuals living in today's society. The psychoanalytic clinician's predicament of living in a discipline with a plurality of approaches is a function of experiencing the pull of a variety of ideals. Critical pluralism makes the multiplicity of competing approaches and styles an explicit theme. It emphasizes the possibility of standards of quality while denying that these allow narrowing down of the alternatives to one course of action only.

Critical pluralism is singularly suited to address the predicament of psychotherapy. The practicing clinician constantly deals with human fallibility, because, by its very nature, human frailty is at the center of psychotherapy. He must be capable of doing so without falling prey to nihilism. Illusion, fantasy, misguided hopes for total happiness, and self-defeating strategies to achieve safety and self-esteem are the stuff of psychotherapy.

The demand on the psychotherapist is to combine lucidity with sympathy; absolute acceptance of the individual's subjectivity with an unflinching eye for the irrational and self-defeating; adaptation to the patient's needs with an ability to maintain sanity and hope throughout the periods of confusion and despair. The present-day psychotherapist must be able to combine all these features without the assurance of having the one right theory. In fact, if the therapist is honest with herself, she knows that anything she does is done differently by other people whom she respects.

The task of the analytic psychotherapist is therefore akin to the predicament of the political theorist and activist as described by Berlin, namely, to combine respect for a subjective point of view with the possibility of criticism. Without respect for subjectivity and individuality the analytic therapist loses the foundations of his profession. Critical pluralism recognizes that the human capacity to have a point of view is of indelible importance. To have a point of view means first and foremost to have subjectivity: thought, feeling, and desire. It is an inalienable right to be the person one is.

In the context of psychotherapy critical pluralism is the type of voice which is first and foremost concerned with the importance of a plurality of voices. It recognizes that it is itself in a paradoxical situation: for it to exist there must be nonliberal voices. As critical pluralism is concerned with the fruitfulness of dialogue and dissent, it is aware of the fact that it must not be allowed ever to be the only position, as otherwise there is no one left to argue with. At the same time the critical element of this pluralism entails that not all positions are equally valid. Besides the human, ontological validity it accords to subjectivity per se, it recognizes a second type of validity which is intersubjective. This type of validity must be demonstrable, and it allows for degrees of quality.

USING PURIST POSITIONS AS IDEALS

The starting point of this chapter is that one of the clinician's crucial needs is to develop a voice as a crucial aspect of one's professional and personal identity. In analogy to other aspects of identity, clinical voice evolves largely in interaction and dialogue with ideal-type models—for example, supervisors and one's personal analyst. We pick up a type of presence from one clinician, an interpretive line from another, a certain way of relating to one's countertransference from a third.

The clinician lives in a cultural field of force which is defined by paradigmatic voices. Each of the salient, well-defined, forceful voices of the history of psychoanalysis provides a possible existential and clinical option. The major voices of the tradition, particularly the purist's, generally present more than just a clinical approach. A purist's clinical view is based on a general vision of the human condition. A purist has a view of what it means to live a human life, what a worthwhile life is, what a fully developed individual is, and the major pitfalls of the journey from childhood to maturity.

The identity of the psychoanalyst in the purist's view embodies all the features of what it means to be a fully developed individual. The purist assumes that it is necessary for the clinician to be aware of the major difficulties of what it means to live a life, that he has largely resolved those difficulties, or at least knows how to tackle them when they appear in clinical situations.

Let me exemplify this point schematically with three major figures. For Freud human life is a constant struggle to maintain lucidity as to one's true motivations. He sees the individual as involved in a battle between the tendency to seek immediate satisfactions irrespective of the long-term price paid. He believes that we are all under the spell of the gravitational pull of archaic wishes which we cannot acknowledge to ourselves, and that hence we all tend to fool ourselves as to what we really feel and why we really do what we do.

Freud's ethic is stoic: he believes that the clash between inner nature and external reality is essential to the human condition. There is no preestablished harmony between the structure of the world and the nature of our desires. Like all stoics from Zenon through Seneca to Spinoza he points out the extent to which our ability to influence fate is extremely limited. Hence he believes that the one way we have to live a more or less decent life is to curtail our own desires. Freud does not believe that happiness is a goal we can reasonably strive for. The reward for lucidity, truthfulness, and self-control is not necessarily happiness, since we are all at the mercy of fate. What we can reasonably aim for is dignity, the sense of standing up to the hardships and complexities of life without losing our integrity and lucidity (Strenger, 1989).

Correspondingly the demand Freud puts on the psychoanalyst is first and foremost that of lucidity. The analyst who is prone to illusions about the true nature of human nature in general and his own personality in particular, is not capable of being truly helpful. He will collude with the patient's regressive yearnings, he will fall prey to his own desires of being a savior, a genius, omniscient, gratifying, larger than life. In his "Observations on Transference-Love" (1915), Freud gives a grim yet moving description of the multiple battles the analyst must fight against the internal and external forces that attempt to divert him from his analytic task. Only a deeply entrenched professional ethics and a deep understanding of the workings of the mind and the nature of the analytic process can prevent the analyst from succumbing to the temptations of the flesh and the seductions of illusion.

The skeptical clinician need not accept the details or even the broad outlines of Freud's vision of human nature in order to see the attractions of his view of the ideal

clinician. Whether Freudian or not, every practicing clinician knows the junctures at which he is being seduced into
the space of illusion, in which he is being offered a role
that is larger than life, in which he is seen as the ideal
man. The power of these offers is often overwhelming,
since they promise the possibility of transcending the limitations of life and of one's therapeutic power.

Even though I am far from being Freudian in my
approach, my personal experience is that at the crucial
junctures of therapeutic work in which the transferential
pressures and offers of the patient pull me in a direction
which would be detrimental to the therapeutic process,
Freud's ideal of the stoic healer is helpful to me. It functions like a magnetic pole which pulls me back into the
line of duty. Being part of a tradition and community
of those who are willing to and capable of renouncing
immediate satisfaction for a higher goal, who can maintain
lucidity and dignity in the face of seduction and adversity,
can give the strength to navigate successfully through the
dire straits of intricate transference–countertransference
entanglements.

The Freudian ideal of stoic lucidity for me is counter-
acted by the Winnicottian ideal of going out of one's way
to meet the patient's needs. Winnicott's vision is organized around the image of the child who must negotiate
the complex process of coming to accept the externality
of the world without losing touch with his inner nature. If
Freud's focus is on the manifold ways in which individuals
refuse to accept things as they are and to fall into the traps
of self-deception, Winnicott's emphasis is on the many
ways in which the caretakers can fail to provide the child
with the type of environment which allows him or her
to succeed in the negotiation between inner nature and
outer reality.

Winnicott's metaphor of the spontaneous gesture denotes the individual's ability to be truly alive, to retain a
sense of creativity under the pressures of having to adapt
to the pressures of external reality. His narrative of the
true and the false self points to the ways in which we cease

to relate to the world because its impingements become unbearable. His story line of the regression to dependence is about the ways in which the analyst creates an environment sufficiently attuned to the patient's needs and sufficiently reliable to allow the patient to renounce the defense of nonrelatedness by which he has protected himself. For Winnicott it is the analyst's task to muster the patience and the endurance which allows the patient to come out of his withdrawal and to bring his true self in touch with external reality, and Winnicott himself was willing to go very far to provide the patient with the needed environment.

I have experienced the pull of Winnicott's ideal of the good-enough therapist at crucial junctures. When I thought that patients needed the chance to experience that the external world could meet their deepest needs, the image of Winnicott enabled me to endure significant intrusions into my life and great strain to see these patients through those crucial periods I conceptualized as regressions to dependence (Strenger, 1998, chapters 3 and 7).

Quite obviously, the Freudian and Winnicottian ideals are in certain aspects diametrically opposed to each other. The Freudian ideal demands that the therapist stick to the limitations of the setting by all means and thus represent the inexorable demands of the reality principle. The Winnicottian ideal demands a reality be created which allows the patient to recreate the space of illusion that allows him to return to the point at which he had to disrupt contact with the external world. It is possible to say that Winnicott demands that the analyst embody the patient's fantasy, to accept the offer Freud sees as destructive seduction away from the analytic task.

The critical pluralist does not try to find a synthesis between these two ideals. He believes, with Isaiah Berlin, that there are equally valid values and ideals which put demands on us and that contradict each other. Critical pluralism assumes that it is illusory to believe that all valid ideals cohere with each other, and that conflict between ideals can be avoided.

Finally I want to mention briefly where Bion's idea of the act of faith has helped me in several therapies. With some patients I have been faced with the predicament of losing track completely. I did not have a clear understanding of what was going on in the therapy, none of my interventions were really helpful in generating therapeutic movement. All I knew was that these patients continued to come to therapy despite their skepticism, cynicism, and despair.

The presence of Bion's voice helped me through these protracted periods of stalemate. Even though my style was probably not Bionian, I accepted that it was my task to maintain the hope for the emergence of meaning and for the possibility that the patient's potential for a full life would be realized at some point. In one case this meant going through a period of months of silence in the sessions. In another it meant that I took it upon myself to generate dialogue just in order to maintain some psychological contact with the patient, whose despair led her to disconnect from the therapeutic relationship if I did not make the effort.

The purists (or *hedgehogs*, to use Berlin's term) of the profession provide us with visions that are unitary, and with images of what it is like to live and to do therapy according to one ideal only. Their importance, I believe, does not reside in presenting the one right, or best, or even good way of doing therapy. The insight of the fox, who sees many little things, reminds us that there is no one map, theory, or approach that can encompass the complexities of life and clinical experience. Hence each of the purist ideals is by its very nature deficient. Instead these ideals confront us with existential and clinical options which can give us the kind of stamina needed at moments when our more standard practices fail.

I would find a clinical culture without hedgehogs drab. Given that the golden middle way that would always work is no less of an illusion than the one purist ideal that provides all the answers, the existence of mutually incompatible ideals reflects the conflicts we encounter in clinical practice. The individual clinician's negotiation between the variety of these ideals is conflictual, complicated, and sometimes painful. But it also provides the unique taste of a profession which can never rely on algorithms to decide about the right way of doing our job.

PLURALIST VOICES IN PRESENT PSYCHOANALYTIC WRITING

I briefly wanted to mention three authors who embody the voice of critical pluralism: Christopher Bollas, Stephen Mitchell, and Andrew Samuels.

Bollas's voice has emerged as a dominant force in the last seven years. He has published four books in quick succession which are widely read and discussed (1987, 1989, 1992, 1995). I will focus only on the aspects of his work which make him a good example of critical pluralism. Bollas's associative range is impressive: Winnicottian metaphors are his homeground, but he resonates strongly with Bionian thought. He is well versed in postmodernist writing, which he brings to bear through the use of Lacan and Derrida's work. He reappropriates Freud in his own terms; for example, in his brilliant meditation on the theme "Why Oedipus" (1992, chapter 10). For him the psychoanalytic tradition is a field of objects which are there for him to use in the elaboration of his own personal *idiom* (to use Bollas's term).

Bollas's voice plays variations on the major theme of his work: his narrative of the development of personal idiom by use of objects. This narrative guides his finely honed clinical perception. He paints clinical pictures which are highly original (e.g., his concepts of the "ghostline personality," the "antinarcissist," and others [1987, 1989]) and never simplifies richness of texture in the analytic encounter. He is able to maintain consciousness of the fact that at any moment a multiplicity of perspectives can be brought to bear on this encounter, without losing the central thread of his particular vantage point.

A second example is Stephen Mitchell, whose voice has most fully emerged in his *Hope and Dread in Psychoanalysis* (1993). Mitchell exemplifies critical pluralism in two ways. First, he has a keen sense of the interplay between the metatheoretical and the theoretical. He is capable of seeing through the enmeshment of the empiricoclinical and the metaphorical levels of psychoanalytic thought and practice, and combines these perspectives effortlessly in his writing. Second, one of the greatest virtues of the critical pluralist is to be able to combine passion with pluralism, distance, and involvement. Mitchell strikes a delicate balance between ironic distance from techniques, theories, and concepts on the one hand, and a passionate stance for the values of psychoanalysis on the other hand.

My third example is that of Andrew Samuels, a British Jungian who has made pluralism one of his main themes. One of the most impressive features of Samuels's work is the way he has been able to combine Jungian thought with a postmodern perspective (1989, 1993). Prima facie this seems an almost impossible undertaking; most of the history of Jungian thought is formed by a slightly archaizing style typical of the tradition of modern Protestant theology which Jung was deeply involved in.

Samuels has been able to develop Jungian themes without succumbing to the tone of spiritual mentorship quite often to be found in Jungian writing, His ability to fuse the political thinking of movements like feminism, gay liberation, and environmentalism with Jungian analytic psychology into a distinct voice has created one of the more interesting perspectives to be found in the field of depth psychology today. Incidentally, he has also continued the dialogue of the British Jungians with British object-relations theory, and he seems to make very fruitful clinical use of this amalgam.

CONTAINING A MULTIPLICITY OF VOICES
WITHOUT LOSING ONE'S VOICE

A characteristic common to Bollas, Mitchell, and Samuels is their ability to create a distinct voice out of the wide range of materials they incorporate into their thinking and writing. In doing so they exemplify one of the prime virtues of critical pluralism, the ability to maintain one's voice while containing within oneself a multiplicity of voices. I am using the metaphor of containment, possibly Wilfred Bion's most suggestive idea, because it is pregnant with possibilities. My own development of this metaphor need not be what Bion precisely had in mind. Containment is first and foremost containment of complexity. There is an almost invincible tendency in human minds to reduce complexity, to refuse the multifacetedness of experience. We want monovalence. Clarity for us mostly means to have only one thing to take into account.

Critical pluralism is not meant to dilute voice; it is meant to create an amalgam which in itself has power. Containment is meant not to create a hodgepodge, but a space in which the various voices can relate to each other. Listening to the *Kyrie* of Bach's Mass in B-minor, one is struck with Bach's awesome ability to create a space in which the various voices are relating to each other. He succeeds in maintaining the distinctiveness of the various individual voices while creating an overall voice. This is a paradigm of the containment of complexity. The precondition is to have sufficient inner space to let each of the voices have its say, and yet maintain an overall voice which is created by the inner richness.

Critical pluralism is meant to do exactly that. It is not supposed to be a compendium of alternatives, or an arid type of learned intellectualism. Isaiah Berlin's exemplifies critical pluralism at its best; he maintains his own philosophical view in the way he presents over voices. Whether he deals with Tolstoy, Vico, Herder, or John Stuart Mill, he succeeds in amplifying their perspective while letting his own voice shine through clearly.

This is what I take psychoanalytic therapy at its best to be about: the therapist's task is to amplify the patient's subjectivity and to develop her voice. This cannot be done by sheer neutrality or absence. Just being there for someone to develop her voice turns out to be a highly active and personal matter. Great therapists (Greenson, for example) have a distinct presence in their writings and clinical work. Their voice is strongly present, but it is a voice which fosters the presence of others instead of drowning it.

Psychoanalysis tries to provide a space within which the analysand can find himself. The terminology of potential space, and the unfortunate term *object* which often denotes individuals, have obscured the fact that the analytic space is intensely personal. The patient's need is for dialogue, not for a sounding box. Such dialogue as she needs must be carefully attuned to the patient's needs in order to prevent her losing her own voice again, as she has many times before in her life. The art of letting the patient's voice reverberate is inevitably one of having a voice of one's own which is offered to the patient for consideration, and not imposed as fact or dogma.

INDIVIDUAL VOICE AND TRADITION

The therapist's ability to let other voices develop while maintaining his own in the therapeutic situation is closely paralleled by his ability to find his own way in the cultural space of therapeutic presences in the literature. Psychotherapists, whether psychoanalytic or other, are part of a tradition. This tradition provides a cultural force field, the poles of which are delineated by the major voices of the field. The task of psychotherapists is to find voices of their own while containing within themselves the complexity of perspectives this field is of necessity condemned to.

The anti-intellectualism of many psychotherapists is

often the reflection of a sense of helplessness in the face of overwhelming intellectual and experiential complexity. It is as if they feel that since the One Theory is not to be had anyway, gut feeling and intuition are to be their only guides. The problem is that intuition is the integrative reaction of a whole personality on the basis of its whole past, knowledge, and experience. Those who fool themselves into thinking that their intuition can be used without schooling simply deny themselves and their patients an intuition which is truly informed. Theirs will be an impoverished intuition lacking the achievement of generations of writers who have created metaphors and visions to describe human experience.

At the other end of the spectrum there are the believers in a single theory who simply deny that there is anything worth learning outside their own tradition. They blindfold themselves to what may threaten their safety, and they are those who are most likely to sacrifice the patient on the altar of the purity of their approach.

The demand critical pluralism places on psychotherapists is great indeed: it is to maintain an inner space which can at any time contain a multiplicity of perspectives. Psychotherapists must keep a constantly shifting equilibrium between unity of style and consciousness of alternatives. This demand is imperative, because if psychoanalytic psychotherapy is a craft, then metaphors, narratives, points of view, pictures of human nature, and visions of human lives are its tools. We expect a medical doctor to be up to date with the current state of the art, we expect lawyers to know the relevant precedence cases of their field, and architects to know the available materials, techniques, and styles of their craft.

The situation of the psychotherapist is more complicated since this discipline does not have anything like a definable state of the art; it has a multiplicity of styles instead. This is, as I have argued repeatedly (Strenger, 1991), desirable. Unsurprisingly, the state of psychotherapy reflects something about life: there are no algorithms about how to live. As individuals we can just try to do our best at every moment, and to be as truthful to ourselves as we can in assessing our choices and course of action. As psychotherapists we can, and should, use the accumulated experience of millions of hours of psychotherapy done by others. But we must be aware of the fact that what counts as theory is always just an attempt by other therapists to make sense of their attempts to do the best they can, and their failures to achieve it. As in life, theory cannot replace the development of human powers of judgment, it can only help to form it (Murdoch, 1992, p. 206).

Lest I be misunderstood: I am not arguing for intelligent diletantism, but for responsible professionalism. Yet, maybe in a profound sense, being a psychotherapist you always remain (possibly should remain) an *amateur* in the original sense of the word: a lover of what you do. Respect for the soul demands that *high professionalism* be combined with some degree of awareness of the strangeness of the very idea of being a professional in a discipline which, after all, is about living lives.

PART II

PSYCHOANALYSIS AND WELTANSCHAUUNG

3 THE CLASSIC AND THE ROMANTIC VISION IN PSYCHOANALYSIS: FREUD AND KOHUT

INTRODUCTION

If psychoanalysis is a discipline of the self, a form of life that is meant to help individuals to deal with the difficult art of living a life, it is, of necessity, governed by intuitions of what human lives are all about. Freud's categorical denials that psychoanalysis is a Weltanschauung are belied by the simple fact that his own *oeuvre* is one of the most compelling twentieth-century interpretations of human life as a totality.

In the postmodern era we have become suspicious of grand metanarratives. We know that there is no good reason why there should be total interpretations of life. This does not mean, though, that such grand interpretations do not have a hold on our imagination. Critical pluralism is the attempt not to deny the charm of great images of life, but to put this charm into perspective, and to live with the paradox that conflicting ideals can have a hold on us.

101

There is a tension which has been characteristic of psychoanalytic thought since the nineteen twenties, and which has increased in the last decades. This tension is not often discussed explicitly, and yet it is unmistakably there. It is manifested in the tone of papers and the narrative structure of case histories. It colors disputes about developmental theory, metapsychology, and analytic technique, and it is, I believe, one of the strongest determinants in the heated emotional overtones in many of these disputes. I will call it the tension between the classic and the romantic vision of human reality.

I will here grapple with the twilight zone of the psychoanalytic vision of human reality. It is a twilight zone because it is rarely addressed explicitly. The typical paper or book deals with clinical or theoretical problems. The overarching view of human reality which is an amalgam of metaphysics, values, and an attitude, a stance which is not purely cognitive, is not often deemed to be a worthy topic for discussion. And yet, like the basic mood of a human being which colors all his experiences, this attitude toward human reality colors all manifestations of psychoanalysis, whether in the consulting room, in conferences, or in academic journals.

The presentation of the classic and the romantic visions in psychoanalysis will have to proceed by creating ideal types in order to demonstrate the salient features of each of the visions. As we will see later on there are reasons to think that these visions are generally amalgamated in varying proportions. The dimensions as I want to use them are summarized by T. E. Hulme in his classic paper "Romanticism and Classicism" as follows:

> Put shortly, these are the two views, then. One, that man is intrinsically good spoilt by circumstance; and the other than he is intrinsically limited, but disciplined by order and tradition to something fairly decent. To the one party man's nature is like a well, to the other like a bucket. The view which regards man as a well, a reservoir full of possibilities I call the romantic; the one which regards him

as a very finite and fixed creature, I call the classical [1924, p. 117].

I will first present this tension by showing how it expresses itself in the body of thought of psychoanalytic theory. Freud will serve as the embodiment of the classic attitude, Heinz Kohut as the most typical representative of the romantic stance.

This choice is easily motivated in the case of Freud, as his exposition of the tenets of the classic vision is eloquent, profound, and relatively uncontaminated. Later developments of the classic vision can be found in psychoanalytic currents which are opposed to each other in many respects. Examples are American ego psychology as it developed around the work of Hartmann, Kris, and Loewenstein; the work of Melanie Klein and her school; and the French school of psychoanalysis, particularly as exemplified by Janine Chasseguet-Smirgel (1984).

The romantic vision began to evolve in psychoanalysis with the ideas of Sandor Ferenczi. It was taken up by Michael Balint, who was also the first to see a tension between a classic and a romantic vision of cure in psychoanalysis (1935). It developed further in the British object-relations school, and particularly in the work of Donald Winnicott. Heinz Kohut's work is particularly suited to show the central features of the romantic approach because, at least since *The Restoration of the Self* (1977), he saw his theoretical and therapeutic approach as explicitly trying to change the central outlook of psychoanalysis.

After this exposition I will try to show that the tension between these attitudes is not primarily one between different theoretical positions. It is essential to the psychoanalytic endeavor as a whole, and indeed of the human condition in general. We will see that the patient and the analyst must at every moment find their way between the classic and the romantic attitude, and that ultimately one of the goals of analysis must be to find the right balance between the two.

The notion of a vision as it is used here is not quite easy to explain. Since the days of Gestalt psychology we know that sense perception is not the connection of sensory atoms by association. The whole of a Gestalt is more than the sum of its parts. A Gestalt constitutes an overarching structure which has many properties which are not determined by its parts. In particular we know that the same visual stimulus can be perceived under different Gestalts depending on the background, the motivational state, and knowledge of the perceiver and a host of other factors.

One of the central emphases of the Gestalt psychologists (cf. especially Koehler [1938]) was that perception is value laden. We do not first perceive an object and then associate aesthetic qualities with it. Instead the value element of the perception is intrinsic to the percept itself. The laws of Gestalt are such that we try to organize percepts into good Gestalts. The aesthetic properties are therefore as essential to the content of a percept as color, size, and form.

It is not easy to formulate the analogue to Gestalt in the intellectual and emotional domain. I will introduce the idea by an old joke: the optimist says this is the best of all possible worlds. The pessimist says: yes indeed. The point of this joke is that the cognitive content of the statements of the optimist and the pessimist is identical. Both think that the actual world is the best world conceivable. The optimist sees that the world could not be better, because it is the richest possible world, the one which includes most variety and ultimately most moral value. The pessimist thinks that the world could not be better and he adds with a sigh: this is the best possible world; look at how terrible, absurd, and ridiculous it is. But if you think things could be better, you're profoundly wrong. At best they could be worse.

Part of the difference between the optimist and the pessimist is the way they structure their thought about the world into figure and ground. The optimist sees a rich tapestry of phenomena, he focuses on the beauty of what he sees. For him the suffering, the inexplicabilities of the world are nothing but byproducts of how the world *must* be if it is to be rich and beautiful. They are the ground on which the figure of the richness of the universe can be perceived. The pessimist structures his idea of consciousness differently. For him the universe is a set of absurdities, moral outrages, and needless suffering. He does not see how it could be different, but a rich tapestry of absurdities for him is still an absurdity.

We know the very same phenomenon of interpretation of reality under a particular vision from our patients. The depressed patient is not able to see any value in what he does and has. The narcissistically unstable patient sees the bad, the meaningless, and the ugly in himself wherever he looks; when he sees something good, it evokes pain in him because of the tremendous envy it arouses. Patients with phallic–narcissistic traits often cannot help but see every interpersonal situation in terms of sexual seduction and competition. Other patients interpret every interpersonal encounter as a struggle between two persons, one of whom will end up being humiliated and the other one victorious. All of them stick rigidly to a certain type of interpretive categories and story lines in their understanding of themselves and others. That is, all of them tend to interpret the facts under one particular vision; they impose the same story line over and over again.

We know this phenomenon from our daily life and the changes of mood we undergo. In a joyful mood everything looks bright, what we encounter is interesting, and difficulties are just minor obstacles to be overcome. When our mood is depressed everything looks meaningless, bothersome, and like a burden; obstacles look like mountains which it takes terrible effort to climb only to find more obstacles afterwards.

In the intellectual domain we generally talk about Weltanschauung when we want to refer to the value-laden traits of a manner of experiencing and interpreting reality. The great philosophical systems are the paradigmatic embodiments of such visions. This is one of the main reasons why we deem philosophers such as Plato, Aristotle, Spinoza, Leibniz, and Kant to be worth studying even though we do not agree with their factual assumptions. Beyond their claims about what the world consists of, they show us a way to look at and to experience our lives and the world. In what is to follow I will use the terms *vision, mood, attitude,* and *stance* more or less interchangeably to denote the value-laden cognitive–affective mode of looking at human reality.

One of the few authors who has noticed the great importance of visions of reality in psychoanalysis is Roy Schafer. His "The Psychoanalytic Vision of Reality" (1970) characterizes psychoanalysis along the dimensions of the tragic, the comic, the romantic, and the ironic. He shows how psychoanalysis is characterized primarily by an emphasis on the tragic and the ironic aspects of human reality. Drawing on Schafer (1970), Messer and Winokur (1980) have argued that there are limits on the integration of psychoanalysis and behavior therapy, since their visions of human reality are profoundly different. They have shown that the vision of human reality of a form of psychotherapy is no less essential to it than the particular techniques it uses. The categorization of two visions in psychoanalysis I want to propose can be related to Schafer's taxonomy, but it is not identical with it. What I call the classic attitude roughly corresponds to a combination of the tragic and the ironic in his presentation; what I call the romantic is not quite the same as what he means by the same term.

The classic and romantic visions as I understand them can be placed historically. In the eighteenth century they are embodied in the conflict between the more rationalist streak of the Enlightenment and the romantic reaction against it. The classic view is to be found most clearly in Kant's thought: man must strive toward autonomy and true autonomy is identical with the reign of reason. Reason is the ability to know the general, the lawful in reality. The fully rational man is able to submit his more idiosyncratic, subjective side to the voice of reason. If he succeeds in doing so, rather than being driven by his animal nature he will turn into a fully autonomous person.

Kant is profoundly suspicious of human nature to the extent that it is not governed by reason. Hence his ethics is purely rationalistic. To the extent that an act is purely rationally motivated, it is good. If it is not, it may happen to conform to the good, but this would be a pure coincidence. Man's emotions cannot be relied on: they are egotistic, antisocial, and not much is to be expected from them. Hence human nature needs constraints which are to be imposed by reason.

The value of human life is to be found in the specifically human ability to transcend the drivenness of our animal nature. Kant's ethos is one of freedom. Our ability to be self-directed turns us from insignificant specks in a vast universe into those beings who are truly valuable. The human activities which express this are science in the cognitive domain, the reign of the categorical imperative in morals, and in the aesthetic domain, the order playfully imposed on nature. The value of the individual does not reside in his uniqueness, but in the way he embodies the ability to transcend the individual and idiosyncratic by applying reason.

The romantic view was developed by Rousseau (particularly in *The Social Contract*, 1762) and flourished most fully in Goethe's work. The supreme value is the development of the individual. Each person is a unique self, with a unique perspective on the world. The fully developed individual is characterized by true spontaneity, by the richness of his subjective experience. He has ideals which provide the motive force of his life, and these ideals are fueled by his awareness that they express his own personality in its concrete, unique individuality.

Rousseau saw the foundations of ethics not in reason but in an emotion which he believed to be intrinsic to human nature: compassion. Identifying with the other and feeling his suffering and sorrow is as natural to man as sexual desire and hunger. Not only did Rousseau therefore not see the need for constraints on human nature; he thought that human nature unadulterated was intrinsically good. Whatever has gone wrong with man is a function of distortions on human nature which have been imposed artificially by society. The incarnation of Rousseau's view of human nature is epitomized in his idea of the *noble savage.*

The romantic and the classic vision in the eighteenth and nineteenth centuries have one value in common: that of autonomy. But their understanding of what autonomy consists of is profoundly different, as can be seen in later works as well. Hegel, the great representative of the classic vision in the nineteenth century, sees autonomy in the individual's recognition that he is but an aspect of the general structure of reality and submission to the laws of the whole (Taylor, 1975). As opposed to that, Kierkegaard, one of the great figures of the romantic view, considers autonomy in the individual's ability to attain his own subjective truth. When we now turn to psychoanalysis we will see how these varying ways of understanding human beings and freedom are expressed in theory and practice.

THE CLASSIC VISION IN FREUD

There is a theme which runs through Freud's writings, starting with the "Project for a Scientific Psychology" (1895) and ending with the posthumously published "An Outline of Psycho-Analysis" (1940). It is the dichotomy between the pleasure principle and the reality principle. It would be possible to organize much of Freud's thought, metapsychological and clinical, around this central dichotomy. It is reflected in many other conceptual polarities in his writings: primary vs. secondary process, id and ego, symptom formation vs. sublimation, fixation vs. renunciation, and ultimately neurosis vs. mental health.

The neurotic, for Freud, is governed by the pleasure principle, and has therefore not really grown up. He has not been able to renounce infantile wishes, and where he cannot satisfy them in reality, he seeks substitutions in fantasy, neurotic symptoms, and character traits. The motives for defense are rooted in the pleasure principle as well. Instead of facing unpleasurable aspects of inner and outer reality without distortion, the neurotic activates defenses which prevent him from experiencing anxiety, guilt, shame, and other unpleasurable affects.

The essence of personal maturation in Freud's vision consists in the gradual transition from the domination of the pleasure principle to a state in which the reality principle has a firm hold on the adult's mental functioning. The newborn infant is a pure pleasure ego, or, in Freud's later terminology, pure id. The infant wants nothing but pleasure and avoidance of unpleasure. The metaphor which describes this state is that of the infant hallucinating the breast to immediately relieve a state of hunger (Freud, 1895). Human beings are always drawn back to the state in which they can disregard the nature of reality as it is, and hence the battle against the pleasure principle is never won for good.

Both in his attitude to the individual patient and to whole cultural phenomena, Freud takes the side of reason as opposed to the instinctual and infantile. In analysis the patient wants to enact his wishes, but Freud demands of him that he must understand and verbalize instead. Where the patient wants to make insight into an intellectual, one-time event, Freud patiently forces him to work through the manifold manifestations of his infantile wishes and fantasies. Where whole cultures want to perpetuate illusions, Freud exhorts them to achieve maturity and renounce the comforting distortions of reality (Freud, 1927).

Ultimately the whole setting of classical psychoanalysis is an expression of this attitude. The patient lies down and hence cannot discharge tension through motility. He must say everything which comes to his mind, but no wish—except for that of being understood—should be gratified by the analyst. Nothing but the truth can cure, since the essence of neurosis is the avoidance of reality. Freud tried to show to both his patients and his disbelieving contemporaries that this reality was more complex and less reassuring than they wanted to believe.

Freud is a cultural pessimist. The clash between man's instinctual nature and the demands of reality is unavoidable. Culture is and will always be founded on renunciation of instinctual aims, and hence man must learn how to master his inner nature. Whatever the degree of mastery of external nature, conflict and the demand for renunciation will remain essential to the human condition (Freud, 1930).

This cultural pessimism is combined with a passionate belief in the possibility of human autonomy and maturity. Freud denies his patients everything except insight by which they will come to know the truth about themselves. Even though Freud is a determinist he believes that persons can truly take responsibility for themselves. He refuses to accept the excuse, "that's just the way I am, this is my character," which human beings often use to disclaim responsibility for what they do and are. Freud always relates to the person as responsible for his character traits and symptoms. This is why he believes that change can only come from within. The person must acknowledge his wishes and fantasies, take responsibility for them, and thus acquire the freedom to change.

Freud's view of happiness is akin to the notion of *eudaimonia* in Greek, particularly Stoic, philosophy (cf. Copleston, 1946, p. 139). For the Stoics the end of life is virtue which in turn is defined as life according to nature. For the Stoic, man's inner nature is reason. Virtue ultimately consists in the capacity of man to master his passions, and to lead his life according to his understanding of both internal and external nature. Both aspects of reality are considered to have a relatively immutable essence and hence happiness can only consist of the acknowledgment and acceptance of the inescapable complexities of life.

It may sound as if Freud's vision of what human life can be like at its best is rather grim, and there is some truth to that. Freud ends the *Studies on Hysteria* (Breuer and Freud, 1893–1895, p. 305) by relating that he sometimes told his patients: "much will be gained if we succeed in transforming your hysterical misery into common un-happiness. With a mental life that has been restored to health you will be better armed against that unhappiness."

What, then, do we have to live for? Freud never ques-tioned that sexual satisfaction and love are among the peaks of human experience. Nor did he deny that "power, success and wealth" are what keeps men going even though he does not think that these are the true values in life (1930, p. 64). He views these latter goals with the warm irony given to him through the wisdom that human nature is frail, and that theories should not create illusions about man's sublimeness. Freud had no sympathy for utopia, and he did not believe in the perfectibility of man, as shown in his assessment of Marxism as based on illusions about human nature (1933, pp. 180). Freud's real respect is re-served for those moments in which man overcomes his immediate, biologically based strivings and acts out of his deeper understanding of the nature of reality.

This ethos of truthfulness and striving for maturity is expressed most strikingly in the concluding paragraphs of Freud's paper "Observations on Transference-Love" (1915). The main problem Freud discusses in this paper is how the sometimes passionate love of female patients for male analysts should be handled. He mentions all the subtle ways in which the analyst might defuse the complex-ity of the situation by denying the reality, intensity, or genuineness of the feelings the woman patient experi-ences. He rejects all of them, and demands that the analyst face the situation as it is: "the patient's love is genuine, and the doctor might be strongly moved by the way in which a woman of high principles . . . confesses her pas-sion" (1915, p. 170). Freud's final statement is worth quot-ing in full:

> And yet it is quite out of the question for the analyst to give way. However highly he may prize love he must prize even more highly the opportunity for helping his patient over a decisive stage in her life. She has to learn from him to overcome the pleasure principle, to give up a satisfac-tion which lies to hand but is socially not acceptable, in

favour of a more distant one, which is perhaps altogether uncertain, but which is both psychologically and socially unimpeachable. The analytic psychotherapist thus has a threefold battle to wage in his own mind against the forces which seek to drag him down from the analytic level; outside the analysis, against opponents who dispute the importance he attaches to the sexual instinctual forces and hinder him from making use of them in his scientific technique, and inside the analysis, against his patients, who at first behave like opponents but later on reveal the overvaluation of sexual life which dominates them, and who try to make him captive to their socially untamed passion [1915, p. 170].

In these paragraphs, Freud shows what he considers to be true human maturity. The seductions and pressures of reality are manifold. Society presses the analyst to stop talking about the threatening realities which undermine its soothing and yet repressive official picture of what things are like. The patient wants the analysis to be the place where the forbidden and unacceptable can be lived, and the analyst himself is tempted by his own propensity to give in. Truthfulness and the ability to stick to what one knows to be right are the analyst's yardsticks. The consciousness of having stood up to the pressures and seductions, of having acted out of his moral and professional integrity, are the analyst's main reward.

The patient comes to the analysis and expects his fantasies to come true. The analyst firmly guides him on a process which will, if successful, lead to the point where the patient is willing and able to remain true to himself no matter whether his wishes are fulfilled or not. Dignity more than anything else is the reward the analysand is to gain from the process of reeducation an analysis constitutes. Freud quite often stressed that the goddess of fate is an irreducible force in human lives (e.g., 1930, p. 101). Psychoanalysis cannot bribe her; it can only help the patient to stand up to her in a dignified manner.

The philosopher Paul Ricoeur has described the attitude of psychoanalysis as a hermeneutics of suspicion

(1970). Freud rarely accepts what the patient says at face value. In the interest of true maturity the patient must be helped to recognize and withstand the manifold ways in which the pleasure principle undermines his personality. Excessive altruism is often nothing but a reaction formation against sadistic wishes, shrill moralism a defense against threatening sexual desire. Too much of what looks sublime is really covert fulfillment of infantile wishes. Psychoanalysis for Freud is the relentless pursuit of the truth about ourselves, the penetration beyond appearances to reality which was once too threatening to face.

This is why Freud recommends that the analyst take the attitude of a surgeon toward the patient (1912). Freud has respect for true maturity, but he has no feelings for the unconscious part of the mind: his aim is to know the unconscious because it is the enemy of rationality. Freud expects no romantic secrets, no treasures to be found in the patient's unconscious. What will be discovered in the painstaking detective work of the analysis is another perverse wish, another infantile sexual theory, and more murderous wishes toward those whom the patient consciously loves.

The analyst should have respect for the adult part of the patient. The mature part of his ego is the ally of the analyst in the battle against the darkness of irrationality. But the analyst must beware of feeling anything toward the patient. The patient's unconscious is always intent on seducing the analyst into gratifying his wishes. Hence the respect for the patient should be mitigated by the professional neutrality and suspicion of the patient's motives.

In the classical vision, the analyst's identity is a combination of the fearless, wise man who has no illusion about human nature, and the patient detective. The analyst is not afraid of the dragons of the unconscious. No human perversion is repellent to him, no murderous wish arouses moral condemnation. But the analyst is also a tireless detective: he knows all the ways in which human beings try to hide their true motives, and no manifestation of the pleasure principle will evade his searching eye. Ultimately the analyst is the ambassador of human enlightenment who carries the banner of rationality into the darknesses of the unconscious.

Freud's mind is, as Philip Rieff's classic study shows (1959), that of a moralist. But it is important to grasp the morality involved: it is one of maturity and dignity. The grimness of Freud's vision resides in his emphasis that humankind cannot achieve fulfillment at a low price. The dreams of childhood about a frictionless reality are seductions which ultimately lead to suffering rather than to happiness, a motif central to the French school of psychoanalysis as expressed in the work of Janine Chasseguet-Smirgel (1984). The long road to mental health knows no shortcuts, and effortlessness of existence is not among the constituents of mental health. Only true adulthood can save us, and toward the end of his life, Freud (1937) was painfully aware about how precarious and vulnerable true adulthood is.

Before proceeding to the presentation of the romantic vision in psychoanalysis I should point out once again that I have tried to isolate one particular, albeit central, streak of Freud's thought. Freud has his romantic moments as well, but the emphasis of the presentation was on the classic essence of his vision which is not mild and accommodating, but austere. As Rieff has pointed out, the use which has been made of Freud's *oeuvre* to support the utopia of an erotized culture (e.g., Marcuse, 1955), involves reading Freud against his grain.

The greatness of his intransigent demand for maturity and truthfulness resides in the perspective he opens toward a way of life governed by more integrity and less inner division. Freud never saw analytic therapy as geared toward the promise of happiness. The only road he saw for analysis was the road to health qua maturity. He did not deem it to be the task of psychoanalysis to tell to what extent this health will lead to happiness, joy, and fulfillment.

THE ROMANTIC VISION IN KOHUT

Heinz Kohut's later works are the strongest expression of the romantic vision in psychoanalysis, and I think that the intense controversies which have arisen around his ideas are probably at least as much a function of the vision, the ideology they embody, as they are reactions to their explicit theoretical content. Again the picture to be presented is somewhat purified in order to create the ideal type of the romantic vision in psychoanalysis.

For Heinz Kohut the newborn infant is not a pure pleasure ego, and the essence of mind is not to seek pleasure. The central striving of human beings is to achieve a sense of oneness, cohesiveness, and purposefulness. The self is formed in a series of developmental steps. First the infant needs to acquire a sense of the unity of his body, then a sense of being at the center of his own volitions. He then gradually acquires a sense of industry and competence and a grasp of what is good and valuable in life. The highest stage of development of the cohesive self is a structure which is composed of ideals which are experienced as intrinsically valuable and the ambition, the belief of the individual in his ability to realize his ideals.

The process by which the mature self develops is complex and hazardous. The child has no inner resources to maintain a sense of cohesiveness of his body. He needs the care and love of his parents who give him the feeling that his bodily presence is enjoyable. In this manner he can form a basic sense of his core self which is positive. Later on the child needs a sense of what it is like to do things which are meaningful and valuable. Again he does not have the resources to create this structure of ideals himself. This is why he needs his parents to provide the ideals which give him a sense of meaning and vitality.

In the classic view, idealization is either the result of immature cognition or a defense against aggression. In Kohut's view, idealization is an essential process in the child's development. If he cannot idealize his parents he will not acquire a sense of meaningfulness in his life. The idealized parental imago is the first experience of the child of something which is intrinsically valuable, something worth striving for which gives life meaning and direction.

The cohesive self is thus a bipolar structure: on the one hand it includes the experience of oneself as lovable, worthy, and capable, and on the other hand it includes the values which give life direction and meaning. The first pole is called by Kohut the pole of ambition and exhibitionism, the second that of ideals and values. The healthy self is characterized by a steady stream of energy from the pole of ambitions to that of values. The person is drawn toward realizing the values he experiences as meaningful, and he feels that he has the ability and the intrinsic worth actually to realize them (Kohut, 1977, chapter 4).

The parental figures which are so essential to the development of the self are called selfobjects by Kohut. This name reflects Kohut's idea that the infantile self is not an autonomous structure. Its survival and growth depends on the selfobject's ability to function adequately. The selfobject's function is twofold: by enjoying the child's existence in all its aspects, the child's self acquires the sense of being valuable. The second function is to let the child participate in the parent's own activities which enable the child to admire the parent. By internalizing this imago of the parent's sense of directedness, competence, and being valuable, the child can form the rudiments of his own value structure (1977, chapter 7).

If Freud's basic polarity is that between the pleasure principle and the reality principle, Kohut's basic polarity is that between joy and vitality on the one hand and depletion and depression on the other hand. The vicissitudes of development largely hinge on the parental ability to sustain the two poles of ambition and ideals in the child's self.

If the parents are not able to enjoy the child's presence and be empathic to his developmental needs, the child will feel lifeless, empty, and depressed. He feels that he is not valuable, not enjoyable and at worst feels not really alive. If the parents do not have a sense of their own worth and calling in life, the child will not be able to idealize them. The result will be a lack of ideals and values which make life worth living.

Kohut turns the Freudian theory of development upside down: for Freud, the instincts and the pleasure principle are the rock upon which everything else is built. The oral, anal, and phallic phases with their instinctual aims are normal parts of development and must be outgrown in the course of development. Adult perversion and neurosis are the result of fixation to one of these stages. The development of a mature personality is the result of renunciation and transformation of the original aims of the drives.

For Kohut, the most basic motivator is the formation and maintenance of a cohesive self. If a child is overly concerned with deriving pleasure from isolated bodily organs, Kohut sees this as the result of a failure of the selfobject. In optimal circumstances the child would not be preoccupied with his mouth, anus, or his genitals. Instead he would enjoy his whole selfhood and be oriented toward life. The Freudian psychosexual theory, Kohut claims, is not a theory of normal development. It is a theory which shows the disintegration product of a self which could not maintain its cohesiveness.

Kohut even questions the sanctum of classical psychoanalytic theory: he believes that in normal development the oedipal phase is not characterized by the intense conflicts around sexual and murderous wishes, guilt and anxiety, as Freudian theory assumed (1977, chapter 5). He thinks that if the parents can accept and enjoy the oedipal child's competition and sensuality, the child will enjoy it himself. But if the child's sexual stirrings and his aggression arouse anxiety, defense, and aggressiveness in the parent, they are not able to relate to the child as a whole, and they identify him with his sexuality or aggression. The result is that the child experiences himself as fragmented. His sexuality and aggression are dissociated from his total self-experience and this creates the intense murderous rages and sexual obsessions of the classical picture of the oedipal stage.

Kohut's ethic is romantic: sheer rationality is not enough. Without enthusiasm and joy, life is not worth living. For him, the central developmental task is not overcoming the pleasure principle but the development of a cohesive self. And a cohesive self is a structure which includes the joy about one's own existence and the striving for ideals. The later Kohut came to the conclusion that idealized goals are essential to every stage of life and not only for the child.

One of the main differences between the classic and the romantic modes of the analytic attitude can be related to the notion of therapeutic suspicion. Freud knows that the patient's tendency to deceive himself and the analyst is ubiquitous. His developmental theory leads him to the assumption that the manifestations of polymorph perverse sexuality are to be sought behind the patient's symptoms and rigidified character traits. Hence the classical analyst is ready to question appearances at any moment, and to seek for the rock-bottom phenomena of infantile sexuality in the interest of increasing the patient's truthfulness toward himself.

Kohut's patient comes to therapy because of feelings of depression and emptiness. He often has slightly perverse symptoms like masochistic masturbation fantasies, and he believes that he is empty and perverse. Kohut's attitude toward the patient is that these perverse wishes are not rock-bottom phenomena which are to be taken at face value. He looks for the human core behind them. His conviction is that he will find that these perverse fantasies and activities are attempts which the child developed to overcome a feeling of lifelessness. The child's original striving was to grow into a cohesive, strong, joyous self, but his parents could not sustain this growth because of their own psychopathology.

Kohut places much weight on the analyst's empathic function. He thinks that many of the distortions in the patient's functioning cannot be resolved by approaching them in a confrontational manner. The classical analyst is often distrustful of the patient's accusations against his environment and looks for the patient's unconscious wishes and fantasies instead. Kohut tries to understand the patient's inner world as a function of the external environment he grew up in. His case histories often show that he tries to help the patient to realize that his parents failed him, and that much of his self-hatred and self-deprecation is the result of the inability of his parents to enjoy him as a whole human being.

THE TENSION BETWEEN THE CLASSIC AND THE ROMANTIC VIEW

In the next chapter I will trace the motif of the classic and the romantic vision in the work of Winnicott and Melanie Klein. But now it is time to pause and to ask what these two views or moods are. Let me first juxtapose them in a schematic manner:

The classic view sees man as governed by the pleasure principle, and the development toward maturity is that toward the predominance of the reality principle. Neurosis is the result of the covert influence of the pleasure principle. The analyst's attitude toward the patient is a combination of respect and suspicion and the analyst takes the side of the reality principle. The ethic is stoic: maturity and mental health depend on the extent to which a person can acknowledge reality as it is and be rational and wise.

The romantic view sees man as striving toward becoming a cohesive self. Development aims at a self which consists of a continuous flow from ambitions to ideals, from a sense of vitality toward goals which are experienced as intrinsically valuable. Mental suffering is the result of the failure of the environment to fulfill the selfobject function, and the patient's symptoms are a desperate attempt to fill the vacuum in his depleted self. The analyst's attitude toward the patient is one of trust in his humanity, and the analyst takes the side of joy and vitality. The ethic is romantic: maturity and mental health consist in the ability to sustain enthusiasm and a sense of meaning.

THE TENSION BETWEEN CLASSIC AND ROMANTIC IN CLINICAL WORK

The vision or attitude of psychoanalysis is not just of theoretical importance. In clinical work we influence our patients by far more than the cognitive content of *our* interpretations. In fact there is growing empirical evidence that the human relationship between therapist and patient is far more influential than classical analysis previously thought (e.g., Garfield and Bergin, 1978, chapter 7). What the patient internalizes is not just a set of interpretations, it is no less than an attitude toward life and toward himself. This has, in fact, been recognized by those analytic authors who have claimed that an important aspect of the analytic process is the internalization of the analyst by the patient, i.e., the acquisition of a new introject.

As in the internalization of the parents by the child, the internalization of the analyst by the patient does not just include what the analyst says. The old idea of the analyst as a pure, undistorted mirror of the patient's unconscious has lost much of its appeal.

The patient internalizes, among other things, the analyst's basic attitude toward himself and human beings in general. And there is a great difference as to whether what the patient internalizes is the classic or the romantic attitude. The classical attitude contains an element of detachment, a certain irony which at its best is not biting and reductive, but wise and accepting. To take the classical attitude is to be willing to see the self-defeating and immature aspects of human action and character. It is the willingness not to be deceived by appearances, to be skeptical of human motivation in all its manifestations. It is to believe that a rich life can only be led in the light of truth and without illusions.

The romantic attitude is centered around the belief that enthusiasm and the search for full subjectivity are essential for human development. The emphasis is less on the extent to which man achieves a rationally based adaptation to his environment. Instead the focus is on the extent to which the individual could develop his individual essence and the intensity of his ability to experience.

It would be profoundly wrong to believe that the patient does not internalize such basic attitudes from his analyst at least as much as the explicit content of his interpretation. Actually the opposite is probably true: the analyst's basic stance toward life colors all his interventions: beginning with the slightest "mhmm" (which incidentally is a first rate therapeutic tool that has not received much attention); and ending with the longest interpretation.

This leads me to a major point: I have presented the tension between the classic and the romantic attitude in psychoanalysis and a distinction between different theories. This is in a sense misleading, although it is true that each of these attitudes has found paradigmatic expression in one of the theoretical frameworks I have presented above. I think that this tension is to be found in the daily clinical work of almost every analytic therapist.

The tension manifests itself in particular technical problems which can be exemplified briefly. A patient talks about the meaninglessness of his life, his lack of satisfaction and directedness. Should I express empathy for his suffering, for the dreadfulness of a life without joy? Or should I point out to the patient how he uses the lamentation about his depression to give me the feeling that nothing he ever gets—including the therapy—is good enough for him? Another patient talks loudly and quickly about all the situations she has gone through in the last days in which she felt that she was torn between sexual desire and a need to control and protect herself. Should I express empathy for her long-standing experience of her own sexuality as alien to her, and the suffering which goes along with the disunity of her self? Or should I point out to her how she not only refuses to acknowledge her sexual urges as truly her own, but also vents her anger at me by flooding me with a lot of details in a loud voice?

One answer would be that this depends on the context. If we had more context we could determine what the meaning of this patient's material is. This is true to a certain extent. But it would be wrong to believe that any amount of context would always settle the issue beyond any doubt. The idea that the patient's material lends itself to only one interpretation, if we look at it in a sufficiently close manner, is illusory. In fact, even classic psychoanalytic theory has recognized this through Waelder's concept of multiple function (1930). Every type of behavior, every utterance of the patient, can always be considered from a variety of points of view. Waelder focused on the ways in which conflict arises between the agencies of ego, id, and superego and the external world. Every action and utterance of a patient can be seen as a function of all these interactions.

My contention is that one such important point of view is linked to the tension between the classic and the romantic visions. We can look at every utterance, every action of the patient under the perspective of how truthful he is, to what extent is he able and willing to accept reality, inner and outer, without distorting it. To what extent does he take responsibility for who he is and what he does? This is to take the classic perspective, and it entails that we listen for the inconsistencies, the hidden meanings which are disavowed. It means that we must listen with a certain amount of suspicion, must always question the face value of what we hear.

We can also listen from the romantic point of view. We will then listen for the thwarted attempts to feel wholesome and alive, to feel enthusiasm and love behind the self-destructive, perverse, and unintelligible aspects of the patient's actions and words. We will try to understand why his development has been deflected from the path to true selfhood, and why his natural strivings took the twisted turns he enacts in life and in the therapeutic relation.

When taking the classic attitude, we tend to listen to the ways in which the patient's wishes and fantasies color his perception of his reality, past and present. The woman who complains of the seductiveness of her father may not admit the extent to which she wanted to be seduced. The man who complains of the competitiveness of others at work may not want to see the extent to which his behavior emanates from phallic exhibitionism. We tend to focus on the ways in which the pleasure principle acts both by creating unwillingness to abandon old wishes and by distorting the patient's perception through defense and fantasy.

In the romantic stance the opposite may often be the case. A patient is deeply convinced that his unhappiness is due to his basically disgusting essence. We may listen for evidence that the patient tries to protect his parents who failed him as a child and takes the guilt about his misdevelopment onto himself. A woman patient feels that she is just crazy because of her constant sexual preoccupation. We may listen for the ways in which her environment created unbearable tension in her which she could only contain by sexualizing it. We try to look for the healthy striving for wholeness and psychic survival behind what the patient experiences as irredeemably repulsive or perverse.

The decision between the two attitudes will be influenced by a variety of factors. One of them is the countertransference. This does not imply that the decision is purely subjective, as the countertransference is likely to be indicative of the patient's unconscious intention and feeling state. And the therapist should of course not act immediately on this countertransference but integrate it into a more general understanding of what is going on within the patient and between the patient and himself.

But there is no doubt that the analyst's personality will also play a role in the stance he takes. Detachment, irony, and the emphasis on rationality and wisdom on the one hand and an emphasis on joy, the belief in the importance of ideals, and an emphasis on full subjectivity on the other hand can be character traits no less than theoretical positions. The analyst's basic orientation toward life, his temperament and personality will influence his choice of general orientation and of particular strategies and tactics at every juncture of his therapeutic work.

Before, I simplified by presenting the classic and the romantic attitudes as aspects of different theoretical frameworks. Until now I have simplified again by saying that therapeutic interventions are either guided by the romantic or by the classic attitude. In point of fact the issue is more complicated again. The choice between the two visions is not an either-or matter. It would be *more* precise to say that every therapeutic intervention is characterized by the extent to which it is expressive of either attitude.

The French saying *c'est le ton qui fait la musique* captures a point which is of importance here. The same interpretation can be uttered in two entirely different ways. Take the simple intervention, "You are very angry with me for canceling the next session." The tone in which it is spoken can imply: "You are very angry with me, but you are not willing to experience your anger because you are afraid I won't tolerate it. But actually you are too sure that I cannot accept anger and ultimately you are harmed by your reluctance to feel and express anger consciously." It can also imply: "You are angry with me. It has been so terrible for you in the past when you felt rejected that you were filled with uncontrollable rage. You could not allow yourself to feel this rage because it made you feel like a monster, and your parents were not able to relieve your profound experience of yourself as monstrous. Therefore you cannot allow yourself to feel your anger with me consciously."

The way the interpretation is uttered can imply a combination of the two elaborations. It will not only be the tone which determines its connotations but the general tendency in the analyst's interpretive lines. The patient will experience every interpretation against the background of the general attitude that emanates from the analyst.

My own experience is that the choice between the classic and the romantic attitude accompanies clinical work all the time. Of course the alternatives as they present themselves are not formulated in terms of classicism and romanticism. They are encountered in questions of whether to focus on defensive structures and the element of disclaimed action which Schafer (1976) has placed at the center of attention, or whether to listen for the affective constellations and self-experience underlying the patient's mode of action.

A woman patient came to therapy because she felt diffuse anxieties she could not relate to anything, and because of a feeling of being overly vulnerable to small insults beyond what she considered reasonable. In the course of the therapy some aspects of her history which had had great impact on her development became clear. Her mother had been a very active woman, who was intolerant of weakness and sensitivity on the physical and mental level both within herself and others. The patient's younger sister was a more out- and easygoing girl than the patient herself, and her mother related to the sister more easily than to the patient. The patient was often criticized for both her moodiness and sensitivity, and her successes, based on an artistic gift which was to flourish later in her life, went unappreciated.

The patient's way to deal with the constant psychic pain generated by this situation was to develop the fantasy that she had something very special within herself which other people could not perceive, but of which she herself could be very sure. This fantasy nourished her development as a creative artist, but it also perpetuated her feeling of being basically lonely and the anxieties associated with this loneliness. In addition it did not allow her to understand her vulnerability which had lost its intelligibility behind the fantasy of uniqueness.

In therapy, this constellation expressed itself in a persistent, very subtle devaluation of whatever I said. One function of this mode of action was that the patient thus reversed the relationship with her mother by constantly

evaluating my interventions without every letting them
resonate. On another level it helped her to perpetuate the
fantasy that her inner world was too delicate and special
to be captured by words, and certainly not by words which
were appropriate for the feelings of people less creative
than herself. But finally it also protected her from the
unbearable, intrusive criticism which she felt was implied
by any of my interventions.

The main work of the therapy consisted in gradually
resolving the deadlock which this constellation created.
The point pertinent for the present context was that I
was faced with a constant need to oscillate between two
perspectives on the patient's material. For a while I took
an attitude mostly directed by the romantic vision and
tried to be primarily in empathic touch with the unbearable pain of generally not receiving positive mirroring and
being constantly criticized instead, and the corresponding
need to protect herself. It took me a while to understand
that the patient did not make use of this empathy because
she subtly made it irrelevant by concerning herself with
the evaluation of whether I was right or wrong in what
I said.

When I started to interpret this pattern consistently,
taking a stance more akin to the classic vision, I began to
feel that we were getting out of the deadlock. Instead I
was at times struck by her sudden pleas that I should understand how terribly exposed and vulnerable she felt at
moments in which I was unaware of how naked and fragile
she felt. The therapeutic process at that point could only
be kept going by striking a careful balance between keep-
ing the patient conscious of her ways of making the therapeutic work useless and constant monitoring of the
patient's self-state in order to alleviate her dread of being
intruded upon, and at the same time give her the experience of not being in total isolation in her pain.

The difference between the classic and the romantic
attitude is often a matter of degree. In this particular case
the main difference in taking one or the other stance was
primarily a matter of where to place the emphasis: what I

called the more classical approach focused on the way she was dealing with the therapeutic relation. In terms of the classical theory of technique this was analysis of resistance and character analysis. Here the main emphasis was on making her conscious of a subtle but pervasive character trait, namely her ways of not letting people get too close to her, in order to protect herself from the expected, unbearably intrusive criticisms.

The interventions guided primarily by the romantic approach focused on her self state. It consisted in trying to find words for the sense of loneliness, rage, and humiliation she experienced when her mother reacted to her first artistic attempts with a dry wholesale dismissal, and the sense of impotence she experienced when her sister was able to receive mother's praise easily whereas she herself felt that all ways were closed to her.

In terms of an ideal type characterization, the classic approach tries to make the patient maximally conscious of his ways of acting in order to allow him to take more responsibility for himself. The romantic approach focuses on factors in the patient's environment during his development which did not allow him to flourish, thus trying to mobilize frozen intrapsychic constellations which developed as a result of these intrusions.

Many good interpretations are combinations of the two attitudes. They confront the patient with what he does, desires, believes, and how he distorts his perceptions of himself and others. This helps the patient to improve on his really testing, and it opens new options to understanding and experiencing himself and others. But they also enable him to see that there has not been another way for him to deal with particular aspects of internal and external reality, they help him to see the human core behind what has seemed irreducibly perverse and revolting to him. This enhances the patient's empathy for the disavowed aspects of his self. Ideally, interpretations both allow the patient to step back and understand his feelings and behavior from a more objective point of view and allow him to come closer to aspects of himself which were experienced as intolerable before.

In the case mentioned above, such an interpretation would sound something like: "You keep anything I say away from you by busying yourself with assessing its plausibility, and thus subtly devaluing it. You cannot help doing so because you are so convinced that my interpretations are just ways to point to your defects and show you what you are supposed to be. This is because you experienced your mother as unable to appreciate anything in you, and you felt that she could only point out to you in what respects you were supposed to be different."

I do not want to imply, though, that there is a golden mean which can be taken as a measure at all times. Depending on the patient and the particular state he is in, differential emphasis on the classic and the romantic attitude may be in order. At times patients will be helped most by a firm insistence on the truth about themselves, including the ways they have to evade this truth. At other times the best way to help the patient to grow is to take their perspective from within to a higher extent than they do themselves; e.g., if they overly identify with a sharply critical voice they have internalized. But experience shows that it is difficult to reach agreement in every case as to what the right attitude is.

There may be many practitioners who feel that they try to strike this balance intuitively, and that therefore the point I am making is moot. And in fact I believe that most analytic therapists do deal with the dialectic between the classic and the romantic attitude even though they will not call it that. But it seems to me that several of the central disputes in present-day psychoanalysis are really expressions of the tension between the classic and the romantic vision. The most prominent current example is the issue between Kernberg's approach to narcissistic personality disorders (1975, 1976), a paradigmatic embodiment of the classic attitude, and Kohut's (1977, 1984), which exemplifies the romantic stance in its purest form.

The controversy between Kohut and Kernberg has, I think, to some extent been obscured by the fact that they are largely referring to different types of patients when they speak of narcissistic personality disorders. In my experience there are patients with a more quiet, introverted type of pathology who tend to develop the kind of idealizing transference Kohut has described (cf. Strenger, 1991, chapter 5), and there are those in whom the dialectic between narcissistic injury, rage, devaluation, and idealization described by Kernberg is more prominent.

Beyond this it is clear that they advocate profoundly diverging therapeutic strategies, and they have very different views about what is curative in psychoanalysis. For Kernberg, the main curative factor resides in the process in which the patient can gradually undo the splitting mechanisms weakening his ego, and deal better with his rage. Integration of the personality is therefore seen as a function of the extent to which the patient can tolerate aspects of his own mental life. Enhanced self-esteem and capacity to enjoy will be an (albeit crucially important) epiphenomenon of this process. Hence the analytic cure is seen as deriving from the enhancement of the patient's way of dealing with inner and outer reality in a more mature way.

Kohut interprets the process of analytic cure in the use the patient can make of the analyst's empathy to allow self-structures to grow and consolidate themselves. The analyst does not primarily aim at making the patient conscious of his own defensive strategies. His primary function is empathic resonance to the points at which lack of such resonance (''mirroring'' in Kohut's terms) fundamentally impaired the patient's development. Kohut does not try to weaken the impact of grandiose fantasies and idealization by interpreting them. His hypothesis is that they will disappear when the patient's ability to have a fuller flow from the pole of ambition to that of ideals will be restored. That is, the improvement in the reality testing is seen as epiphenomenal to the process of growth and self-structures.

The difference between the two approaches seems to me to derive largely from the general vision they presuppose: Kernberg's assumption is more classical in that he thinks that the prime mover of development and therapeutic change is the mutual interaction between drive maturation and the development of the ego. Therefore his well-known and widely used diagnostic scheme (1975) of three levels of pathology emphasizes structural considerations. As opposed to this, Kohut sees the development of a sense of being alive and having something valuable to strive for, the bipolar self, as the core of development. This romantic view leads him to focus on the cohesiveness of the self as the crucial determinant in diagnosis (1984, chapter 1).

In an important paper, Wallerstein (1988) has argued that what unifies psychoanalysis is the empirically testable clinical theory, whereas the value-laden metaphors of the developmental views are not to be seen as part of the necessary core of psychoanalysis. The present reflections imply that the state of affairs is more complicated: the Gestalts of the classic and the romantic visions have important repercussions both on specific questions of technique and on the whole question of how psychoanalysis cures (Kohut, 1984). At the present point there are strong disagreements not only about etiological hypotheses and the type of metaphors to be used, but also about the very nature of the psychoanalytic process. It seems to me that even in this respect there is a great deal of conceptual and empirical work to be done, and that at the present stage we are in the dark about many crucial questions in clinical psychoanalysis.

THE TENSION AS A BASIC FEATURE OF HUMAN LIVES

Is the tension between the classic and the romantic attitude to be resolved somehow? Is it possible to show the superiority of either the classic or the romantic vision? Or is it possible to provide a decision algorithm telling us when to adopt which of the attitudes?

Such questions assume that the tension between the classic and the romantic vision is a technical problem which can be resolved by technical means. I think that it is important to see that the tension between the classic and the romantic stance is not a purely technical problem. It cannot be resolved through amassing more knowledge about curative factors in psychotherapy. We are faced with it not only as psychoanalytic therapists and theorists, but as human beings.

The essence of the tension between the classic and the romantic attitude is ultimately the tension between identification with one's own perspective and the detachment from it. It is the expression of the fact that as human beings we have the ability to experience ourselves from within and to reflect about ourselves from without.

On the one hand we are able to take a distanced, ironic stance toward all our values and motives. At any moment we can ask ourselves: "Is this *really* valuable?" or we can reflect "Is this *really* what I want, or am I fooling myself?" Such questions are the expression of our ability for self-reflection, and this ability is essential to our humanity. What makes us different from other animals is self-consciousness, the ability to take a reflective stance toward ourselves. We are not just what we are at any given moment, but we are self-reflexive, and this ontological split within ourselves cannot be closed. We always have the possibility of questioning and taking an objective stance toward ourselves.

On the other hand, we cannot be in a constant state of self-reflection. Perpetual self-questioning and self-evaluation would leave us with nothing to live for. If we *only* step back and watch ourselves from outside, nothing can ever acquire value and meaning. Reflection is essential to the critical evaluation of who we are and what we do, but it cannot lead to the creation of value and meaning. Critical

reflection can create knowledge and correct biases, inconsistencies, and incoherences in our desires and values, but
its activity must be based on basic desires which are not
of rational origin.

We have a profound need to take ourselves, our values, and our desires seriously, and to *live* them rather than
to *think* about them. Only if we can experience certain
activities and goals as intrinsically valuable, do we have a
sense of meaning in our lives. As human beings we can
and must identify with our perspective from within, we
must be able to let our selves thrive as the romantic tradition has always emphasized. But if we never question ourselves we become impulsive, nonreflective, and often harm
ourselves and others. An essential process in maturation
is the development of the ability to step back from our
immediate perspective, reflect, and evaluate.

As the philosopher Thomas Nagel (1971, 1986) has
emphasized, this tension between the perspective from
within and the perspective from without cannot be resolved, it is part of the human condition. And it is also at
the core of the psychoanalytic endeavor. Our patients are
not willing to step back and look at what they are doing.
They want to continue their pursuit of infantile wishes
without reflection and without renunciation and thus
blindly perpetuate the same self-destructive patterns. But
patients distrust their own motives and their desires completely; they maintain a constant detachment from and
control of themselves, and are therefore unable to live a
fulfilled life.

It is possible to place different pathologies on this
spectrum from complete impulsivity to total self-detach-
ment. At one end we have the impulsive, hysterical, and
borderline, at the other end the schizoid and obsessive
personalities. But most patients show a constant oscillation
between overidentification with their own perspective and
excessive distrust and detachment from themselves and
their desires and values.

I think that it is one of the permanent tasks of the
analyst to listen to the dialectic of unwillingness for self-
reflection and inability for full and direct experience. The

choice between the classic and the romantic attitude is not to be made once and for all. It must depend at every moment on an assessment of where the patient is in this respect.

If the patient is locked into a perspective on himself and others which he is not willing to question, the analyst's classic attitude will lead him to self-reflection. If the patient experiences all human relations as dangerous competition or mutual exploitation, every enjoyment as the return to a nourishing breast, and work as the proof of his phallic integrity, he must be helped to recognize this tendency such as to enhance his freedom to create optional modes of experience.

If the patient is not able to take any of his motives and feelings seriously, if he is not able to sense and feel fully because of a basic distrust of his own nature, the analyst's taking the romantic attitude will gradually allow him to come closer to himself. He will start to understand how a reductive and critical stance of the significant others in his life led him to distrust himself, made it impossible for him to experience himself as valuable, and to develop a sense of vitality and joy.

I do not propose therefore to make an exclusive commitment to either the classic or the romantic attitude. Some of the great authors of the psychoanalytic tradition have painted their vision of human reality exclusively from one of these two perspectives. It is the nature of great thinkers to push ideas to their utmost consequences, and this enables us to see where these ideas lead. But we should not feel ourselves compelled to embrace one of the visions in its totality.

It is our task as analytic therapists no less than as human beings to bear the tension between the perspectives on ourselves from within and without, and hence between the classic and the romantic attitude. Many of the moral problems which we are faced with in life stem from the tension between our subjective point of view and the taking into account of other perspectives as well. A famous case exemplifying this tension was Gauguin's decision to leave his family and to devote himself to painting by going to Tahiti (cf. Williams, 1981, chapter 2). Was his decision right or wrong? The romantic vision will emphasize that his decision was the only way he could actualize his self-hood completely. The classic vision will point out that he did not stand up to the responsibility he had taken upon himself when he had created a family, and that he failed to transcend the narrow viewpoint of his own subjective desires.

In morals the point is that real dilemmas exist, i.e., situations in which there are conflicting sources of value which make demands on us. Often these conflicting sources are the perspective of our own needs and desires and a more detached, objective point of view. These are the points at which choices must be made, and at times we cannot hide behind some theory which tells us what is right. Our choices will define what type of human beings we are.

Psychoanalysis is, in this respect, part of what the British philosophical tradition used to call the moral sciences. It is an illusion to think that the analytic therapist can be neutral in the sense of not taking any stance. He is taking an attitude by the very fact that he sets emphases in his interpretations, and that he indicates a point of view by his tone. Any attempt to avoid this will of necessity end up in a paradox, or worse in artificial aloofness.

This is not to deny that one of Freud's major achievements was that of formulating the idea of the analytic attitude and analytic neutrality, and there is much work to be done in rethinking the idea of analytic neutrality (cf. Schafer [1983], for a sustained attempt to do so). One of the contentions of this chapter is that analytic neutrality cannot possibly mean neutrality *tout court,* i.e., neutrality in every respect. The tension between the classic and the romantic attitude is but one of the many choices to be made within the analytic attitude, albeit a crucial one.

The fact that there is no algorithmic decision procedure to decide what stance to take at every given moment, certainly means that there will always be a certain amount of room for subjective judgment. But this is not all that surprising because psychoanalysis is an activity performed by human beings who must use their own humanity in their work. One of the central goals of analytic training is to arrive at a disciplined use of subjectivity. The more conscious we are of the constant necessity to choose between the two attitudes toward our patients, the more likely we are to make decisions which, even though not right in any absolute sense, will reflect more than just the therapist's mood of a moment or an unconscious character trait.

The same holds true for the choice of one's vision in theory. One of the claims of this chapter is that the classic and the romantic visions are not just empirical theories. They are ways of looking at and experiencing human reality. As such they cannot be simply true or false. They can, rather, be more or less rich, useful, complex, and embracing. The classic and the romantic vision each enable us to see an aspect of the human condition more clearly. Embracing one of them exclusively might make things easier, but such a choice will blind us to the richness of the interplay between the classic insistence on rationality and maturity and the romantic emphasis on joy and ideals.

4 THE CLASSIC AND THE ROMANTIC VIEWS OF INDIVIDUALITY: KLEIN AND WINNICOTT

INTRODUCTION

In this chapter I will explore further the tension between the classic and the romantic visions in psychoanalysis. I will show that these visions are developments of a central Leitmotif of psychoanalysis, namely the mediation of inner nature and external reality.

I will clarify the deep structure of this motif by casting it into a vocabulary I developed in *Individuality, the Impossible Project* (1998) that makes it more visible. The sense of authorship will be defined as the phenomenological correlate of an individual's experience that he or she lives life according to inner nature and desire. The sense of fatedness is the sense that inner or outer limitations do not allow for authorship to develop. Finally, I will call the strategies of rebellion against the aspects of reality which are fateful, the ontological protest of subjectivity.

This vocabulary allows for a concise definition of classicism and romanticism: classicism is the position which sees fatedness as an inevitable aspect of the human condition. The development of a sense of authorship hinges on the ability to come to terms with fate. Romanticism sees fatedness as the result of avoidable impingements and failure of the human environment. The sense of authorship can only develop if the noxious aspects of fate are fought against or undone.

By means of a presentation of some basic themes in the work of Melanie Klein (an extreme classicist) and Donald Winnicott (an extreme romanticist) I will argue that each of them has a distinct ethical view about how life should be lived.

INNER NATURE AND OUTER REALITY

The deepest, most consistent underlying motif in psychoanalytic thought is the question of how inner nature and outer reality meet. Psychoanalysis has approached this question by formulating developmental psychologies. These psychologies always revolve around some basic themes: it is assumed that the infant does not have an adequate representation of external reality, or has no such representation at all. One of the questions asked is: how does the infant come to accept that there is such a thing as an external world, independent of her desires and needs?

Of course psychoanalysis has always assumed that the meeting of inner nature and external reality is difficult. If it were not, psychoanalysis would not exist, because individuals would not suffer so much. The developmental stories of psychoanalysis are therefore stories about the difficulties of mediating between the inner and the outer. These difficulties largely depend on what inner nature is, and classic and romantic psychoanalysis diverge in their accounts of this nature.

Classicist psychoanalysis tends to view the inner nature of human beings pessimistically. Freud sees the basic outfit of humans as a set of drives which is not in any way geared toward external reality. Instead external reality forces itself upon this set of drives. In the language of structural theory, we are born pure id; the ego develops through the frustrating encounter with external reality. The pleasure principle is only very gradually replaced by the reality principle, and every personality retains areas which remain under the aegis of the pleasure principle. For Melanie Klein the infant is, in Deleuze and Guattari's (1972, chapter 5) happy formulation, a *machine désirante*, full of greed, envy, and an inexhaustible supply of aggression. The infant's rage and envy is triggered by the very fact that good things are external, and not part of her own nature.

In other words, classicism assumes that inner complexity is an inevitable given of our existence. It is our fate to live lives fraught with pain, frustration, and limitation. Human nature is not made for a life that is easy and effortless. Fatedness, the encounter with the recalcitrance of inner and outer reality to our desire and our need, is intrinsic to life per se.

The romantics assume that inner nature and external reality are not as sharply opposed as the classicists say. Their view of inner nature is that the infant is not just a bundle of raging desires, but that its most basic strivings are to feel alive (Winnicott), to be in contact with the other (the "object," in psychoanalytic parlance; Fairbairn, Bowlby). Since the romantics take the view from within, they assume that the movement which will mediate between the inner and the outer is not just a movement of adaptation of the subject to the outer world, but also a movement of the outer world to the subject. In other words, the romantics try to delineate the conditions caretakers must create to make it possible for the infant's inner nature to maintain aliveness and yet build contact with external reality.

For the romantics fatedness is not an inevitable given, it is a function of the extent to which external reality has accommodated itself to the child's needs. The romantics assume that there is a possibility of a life of plenitude.

Fatedness takes the form of impingements and failures. The romantic tales of fatedness generally focus on parental psychopathology. In this manner, the romantics express their belief that under certain conditions the individual could have flourished, and that acquiescing in fate is not an option the individual can take if he is to live fully.

CLASSICIST PSYCHOANALYSIS: PERSONALITY AS THE SEDIMENT OF FATE

The basic question of ethics is how we should live our lives. The classicist answer is that life must be lived under the aegis of truth; truth about one's desires, truth about one's limitations, and truth about one's place in the world. This truth is often painful, and always dissatisfying in that reality clashes with one's desires. The one way to live with this is to curtail one's desires. Once the truth about them has surfaced, the individual must see that many of them are inconsistent with natural and social reality, and that there is no way to live other than by renouncing what cannot be had. Life is not about happiness, but about the dignity achieved by truthfulness and by overcoming one's own nature by acquiring the discipline necessary to master the complexities of adulthood.

Classicist psychoanalysis is largely a stoic interpretation of life. Its eye is geared toward the ways in which life is intrinsically complex, painful, ridden with guilt and anxiety. Freud's model of personality is centered around the idea that the acceptance of reality is in itself a highly difficult undertaking. In order to see things as they are we must be able to accept that very little in the order of the world is geared toward the fulfillment of our desires. In that respect Freud is heir both to the modern scientific tradition and Stoic philosophy. His world is governed by iron laws, both natural and social, and the individual's task is to accept this world as it is.

Let us call the experience of living an autonomous life, of being directed from within rather than being at the play of external forces, the *sense of authorship*. The classicist view of the sense of authorship is centered about taking responsibility for the person one has turned out to be. The sense of authorship cannot evolve by fighting fate, because the self is not something over and above what fate has made us into, but the result of the blind workings of chance.

In Freud's thought fate looms large. One of Freud's delights is to trace the intricate chains of associations of his patients. These chains are reflections of the multiple contingencies of their personal development. What would have happened if the Wolf-Man had not witnessed his parents' intercourse *a tergo*, if the rat man had not heard of the form of punishment involving the insertion of rats into the anus?

The question for Freud is moot: individuality for him is not the development of an inborn essence which can be fostered or hindered by fate. Freud sees fate as constitutive of individuality. Character, he says, is primarily the sediment of early object relationships. For Freud seeks no dignified events in life which shape the individual's personality. Whatever happens is what shapes the individual, even if this event is something as ephemeral as witnessing one's parents practicing *coitus a tergo* at the age of $1^1/_2$ years, as in the case of the Wolf-Man. Freud is the anti-Aristotelian par excellence. He considers the very idea of authorship qua asserting oneself against fatedness as an illusion. If anything authorship can only be based on the insight into the causality of fate. The human ability to understand is our one saving grace, the only possibility we have to counteract the causality of fate. Otherwise we are governed by nothing but the contingencies of life.

Fate permeates individuality both from within and from without. The Freudian ego is largely reactive; a mediator between demands, squeezed between the pressures of id wishes and the recalcitrance of an external world which won't yield. The household economy of libido reflects this:

the ego does not have any energies of its own. The individual is, literally and metaphorically, moved only by id energies. At best the ego manages to transform, fuse, sublimate
those energies. This transformation, in turn, is not initiated by any independent impulse of the ego. The demands
of the external world, the unpleasure generated by actions
purely emanating from the id, force the ego to take steps
which can mediate between the hammer of the id and the
anvil of external reality.

Hence personality is purely a matter of fate. There is
no self, no active striving toward the fulfillment of individual destiny. The ego has no plan; it just tries to find its
way through the maze of pressures which fate presents.
The individual's sense of direction, the sense of authorship which we may acquire, is the result of successful transformation of id impulses. The individual is ultimately
composed of impersonal forces. It is, so to speak, just a
lucky coincidence if those forces in the end lead to something more or less coherent.

Freud at times left some room for factors which could
not be explained by the psychoanalytic reconstruction of
the vicissitudes of the contingent meetings of the inner
and the outer, of drives and their objects. In his study of
Leonardo da Vinci, after having shown how crucial elements of Leonardo's personality—his curiosity, his irrever-
ence, his distaste for sex—are due to the constellation of
his early years, Freud says that he cannot explain Leonardo's genius, that psychoanalysis cannot really touch
upon an individual's creativity, since this is a matter of
biological nature.

Yet he ends with the following passage:

> But may one not take objection to the findings of an en-
> quiry which ascribes to accidental circumstances of his pa-
> rental constellation so decisive an influence on a person's
> fate—which, for example, makes Leonardo's fate depend
> on his ilegitimate birth and on the barrenness of his first
> stepmother Donna Albiera? I think one has no right to do
> so. If one considers chance to be unworthy of determining

our fate, it is simply a relapse into the pious view of the
Universe which Leonardo himself was on the way to overcoming when he wrote that the sun does not move [1910,
pp. 136–137].

Freud saw the blindness of fate and the sheer fatedness of existence as an inevitable consequence of the
modern, scientific view of the world. Not only could he
not see any place for a benign external force overseeing
our existence, but he could not see any reason to ascribe
to human nature an inherent directionality beyond the
contingent play of biological drives and their objects.

ROMANTIC VIEWS OF THE SELF

Psychoanalytic romanticism has an Aristotelian view of the
self: every individual has an inner nature. Life is about this
inner nature realizing itself in the spontaneous gesture,
in striving for what one values, in the experience of rich
interpersonal relationships. Because of the total dependence into which each of us is born, the development of
inner nature can only take place if the caretaking environment fulfills the individual's inborn needs. The question
of what makes life worth living arises when this environment has failed to provide the care which makes full selfhood possible. Hence the answer to the question of life
consists in the therapeutic provision of an environment
which allows the individual to resume development where
it has ceased because of environmental failure.

Winnicott, the archromantic of psychoanalysis, is
thoroughly Aristotelian. He thinks in terms of an individual essence which can either come into actuality or remain
a pure potentiality. His primary question is whether an
individual has a sense of this underlying essence, or what
he calls his true self. What could be meant by a true as
opposed to a false self?

A self can be true or false only if there is an inner, individual essence which resides in the organism as a potentiality to be realized. The notion of a self that is false implies that not all directions of development are equally close to a preexisting essence. Various circumstances will either foster or hamper the development of the personality in the direction of the telos it should arrive at.

The romantic model of the person is centered around a sense of authorship expressed in the experience of unique individuality. The environment can either foster or throttle this individual essence. As opposed to the classicist model, individuality is not simply the configuration created by the contingent forces of fate. For a classicist it does not make sense to say that an individual is not himself: he is simply what he happens to be at every single moment. For a romanticist it is possible to say that an individual can be more or less himself. Not all developmental possibilities are equal in the extent to which they let the individual's essence develop.

The sense of authorship can develop in either of two ways: ideally the individual does not have to fight to develop his sense of uniqueness, but the environment provides whatever is needed for the self's development. Under more adverse circumstances the sense of authorship evolves as the painful sense that true selfhood has remained a perpetual possibility that has never been actualized.

FATE AS ADVERSITY OF CIRCUMSTANCE

Interestingly enough neither Winnicott nor Kohut, the two most important romanticists in the history of psychoanalysis, have made use of the central narrative possibility of the romantic tradition, the self's individual struggle against fate. Winnicott's story line of the true and the false self emphasizes the individual's retreat from the external world to maintain at least the possibility of authentic self-hood. Kohut only talks about the self's depletion and fragmentation as a result of faulty selfobject functioning.

Romanticist psychoanalysis thrives on a central narrative line: that of an adversity of fate which has not allowed the individual to become who he could have been. Hence the two masters of romantic thought, Winnicott and Kohut, largely see psychoanalytic reconstruction as telling the history of adversity of fate. Kohut says explicitly that self psychological reconstruction should focus on the pathogenic factors in parental psychopathology.

Hence the notion of fate acquires a new weight: fate is the environment's intrusion into a course of development which should have taken place. Fate is what inhibits the development of the *spontaneous gesture,* to use Winnicott's term. Winnicott's metaphor for an environment which is not fateful, which allows the individual essence to emerge is that of the good-enough mother. This environment-mother is defined by allowing the essence of the child to evolve.

Kohut gives Hartmann's notion of the "average expectable environment" an almost moral weight, one similar to that of Winnicott's good-enough mother. The good-enough selfobject is the type of environment which gives the self the possibility of developing into what it can be. Neither Winnicott nor Kohut go so far as to postulate the existence of an inner essence, a telos of individual development. But their whole mode of thinking is based on the idea that the individual would have developed into something it *should* have developed into if circumstances had been different.

Of course romantic psychoanalysis does not return to a premodern view of the world. It does not assume that providence should provide for our needs. It replaces the notion of providence by that of the *family.* Romantic psychoanalysis is based on the narrative that development can either go right or wrong, and that the environment is responsible for this either happening or not.

This mode of thinking reflects a central experience of human beings: we all have a view of what we would like our life to look like. The more an individual's actual life diverges from the image he has of what he wanted his life to be, the more the individual experiences his actual life as somehow the "wrong" life. If life does not turn out the way the individual wanted it to be, some aspects of life are experienced as fateful, i.e., as an impediment for life as it should have been. Romanticist psychoanalysis, like psychoanalysis in general, tends to search for the crucial determinants of development in early childhood. Since early childhood is largely governed by the parents, they become the embodiment of fate itself, and, at least for Kohut, psychoanalytic reconstruction becomes reconstruction of parental psychopathology and its impact on the individual's development.

DESIRE AND NEED

There is an interesting semantic difference between classic and romantic accounts of the personality. Classicists tend to formulate the dynamics of personal development as a function of the individual's ways of dealing with the conflict between desire and reality. Desire is the unruly core of the personality, the part of the self which refuses to be curbed by civilization. Freud's theory of development is about the ways in which we mediate between desire and reality, and about the manifold ways in which we refuse to do so. The neurotic for Freud is someone who develops the art of having his cake and eating it. Consciously he accepts the limitations reality imposes on desire by refusing some of the legitimacy, and by making the fulfillment of others impossible. Unconsciously he adheres to his deepest desires and the mind finds ways to fulfill them symbolically through symptoms and character traits.

The work of maturation is to recognize the desires which continue to live in the personality, and to acknowledge that reality is always stronger. Ultimately the only way to live a life without neurotic suffering is to renounce the desires which cannot be fulfilled.

Romantics like Winnicott and Kohut rarely speak about *desires;* their favorite term is *need.* Their developmental stories are about how certain needs of the individual must be fulfilled by the environment to facilitate healthy development, and the malformations which occur if these needs are not met. Correspondingly, romantic developmental stories are about the extent the environment does or does not meet the individual's needs. The focus is moved from the individual's way of mediating between desire and reality to the ways in which the caretakers (generally the parents) succeed or fail to provide the minimum an individual needs for development. This tendency comes to its peak in Kohut's view that psychoanalytic reconstruction must focus on the psychopathology of the parents and the ways in which it thwarted the individual's development.

The semantic connotations of desire and need are quite different: "desire" implies that we want something which we can renounce. "Need" implies an organismic state which must be fulfilled, because the individual has no way to renounce it. The frustration of a desire seems bearable, whereas the frustration of a need is not.

CLASSICISM AND ROMANTICISM ON PATHOGENESIS

The psychoanalytic tradition has always interpreted personal development as the process of mediation between inner nature and outer reality. The classicist tradition—Freud, Klein, American ego psychology—has thought about this process of mediation as the transformation of basic, biologically based, drive wishes into desires which are socially acceptable and can be fulfilled in the social order. The romantic tradition—Ferenczi, Winnicott, Kohut—conceived of development as the process in which the individual's inherited potential is gradually actualized through the environment's meeting the individual's developmental needs.

Thus two basic narratives of pathogenesis emerged: the classicist narrative is that of fixation to a particular point in psychosexual development and growth of the ego, and regression to that point when the individual reaches an impasse in his life which he does not succeed in overcoming. This narrative sees the prime reason for fixation in the unwillingness to give up earlier pleasures, or the inability to bear the complexities of life.

The romanticist narrative is one of developmental arrest and deficit: the individual needs a certain minimum of environmental facilitation in order to support her maturational processes (Winnicott, 1965). If this minimal degree of environmental support is not provided for, the self will in some way become incapable of developing further. The romanticist tale uses the term *need* instead of *desire,* and, as I argued above, this choice of term has a deeper reason: as the romanticist position takes the patient's subjective point of view, its focus is on judging the environment's facilitation of the self's development.

PSYCHOANALYTIC TREATMENT

Both classicism and romanticism understand the clinical situation as a microcosm in which the developmental drama of the individual is enacted again. Classicism, with its objective point of view, sees the frame of psychoanalytic therapy as given. Its rules and regulations are representative of reality at large. Since neurotic problems are seen as the individual's failures to accept reality as it is, the classicist clinician is geared toward the deciphering of the ways in which the patient refuses to accept the frame of psychoanalysis.

Psychoanalysis for the classicist is about finding out, about insight. Everything the patient does which is opposed to that goal is understood as resistance—hence for the classicist, psychoanalyzing is almost coextensive with analysis of resistance. The patient wants to turn psychoanalysis into a game of seduction, power struggle, phallic competition, control through projective identification, restoration of omnipotent completeness, and the like. The analysis, as Schafer (the most sophisticated modern representative of classicism) says, comes to an end when the patient wants it to be nothing but an analysis.

The enemy of analytic insight is gratification of wishes. Since the classicist sees the analytic process as a struggle between the pleasure principle and the reality principle, since the fight is between the patient's wanting to hold onto illusion and fantasy, and the analyst's trying to help him to live in reality, the precondition of analytic treatment is frustration of the patient's desire. In Freud's words, psychoanalysis must be conducted under conditions of abstinence.

Romanticism, with its subjective point of view, sees the patient's needs as given, and it tries to find ways in which these needs can be met. Hence romantics like Ferenczi and Winnicott were always willing to change the frame if they thought that they could help the patient in ways not allowed by the classicist rules and regulations.

The romantic psychoanalyst thinks that there are ways in which the analyst can take on developmental functions the patient's early environment did not fulfill. Since he does not think in terms of desires, but of needs, he does not think of his fulfilling these functions ("holding," "selfobject function") as gratification, but as the provision of necessary conditions for growth. The enemy of romantic treatment is not gratification but retraumatization. The greatest danger in the analytic process is for the patient's being misunderstood again, and for vital needs not to be fulfilled again.

The classic and the romantic visions in psychoanalysis are ethical visions of the relationship between authorship, fate, and the ontological protest of subjectivities. Their deep differences in emphasis reflect their different perspectives: the classicist sees the subject from without, the romanticist judges the world from within the subjective point of view. As we will see, each of the strong authors of psychoanalysis developed his or her own story of how a sense of authorship could be achieved.

MELANIE KLEIN: MYTHOLOGIST OF ENVY AND GRATITUDE

Melanie Klein's Hells of Infancy

Infants, Klein says, are born with a capacity to love and a capacity to hate. Everything they want is out of their control, and everything that is good is outside of themselves. Hence they are desiring machines (Deleuze and Guattari, 1972), whose only way to react to the world is in fantasy (Isaacs, 1948).

And fantasize they do: they are flooded by destructive impulses which, according to Klein, only partially depend on external events and frustrations. Their feelings are polarized between love and hate, and they polarize their perception of the world correspondingly: their image of the breast is split into the image of the good breast (gratifying, satisfying, giving) and the bad breast (withholding, cruel, and frustrating), which in fantasy they maim, destroy, and spoil. The stage in which the perception of the breast (world) is polarized according to basic affective categories is called by Klein the *paranoid–schizoid position*.

Then, at the age of about 3 months the infant begins to integrate the image of the good and the bad breast into one image. It turns out that the breast loved and the breast hated are the same. The result according to Melanie Klein is not primarily relief but a crippling sense of guilt on the infant's part at the fantasied destruction inflicted on the breast, and a deep need to provide reparation. As the infant is not yet capable of realistic reparation, all that can be done is to deny the damage in a rush of manic defense. Yet the only way really to live with the destruction inflicted is to accept the guilt—hence this developmental phase is called the *depressive position.*

These two positions exhaust Kleinian developmental theory, if two points are added: first, in the paranoid–schizoid position intense envy is aroused by the fact that the breast contains everything that is good (Klein, 1957). This envy is not just a reaction to frustration but to the very fact that there is something good outside which is not part of the infant. Second, in the depressive position the Oedipus complex is actualized. The Oedipus is not a reaction to perceived, actual parents, but an inborn fantasy structure in which parental intercourse is imagined, with the father's penis being potentially wonderful, pleasurable, and creative, and the mother's belly being full of children. The oedipal primal scene from which the infant is excluded again arouses intense envy and mobilizes massive destructive fantasies in which the penis and the maternal womb with its babies are attacked and destroyed.

Klein's assumption is that these contents are inborn cognitive–affective structures, and that every human being begins life equipped with these unconscious fantasies. In fact these fantasies are taken to be the mental expression of basic bodily contents and drives, and thus, so the Kleinians think, are ubiquitous and unavoidable.

Kleinian theory has had very little impact on developmental psychology as it is currently practiced. Most empirical research on infants and later development works with a much richer motivational and cognitive armamentarium, and the enormous importance Klein attaches to aggression is not reflected anywhere in the field (e.g., Kagan, 1989). She has been criticized for having an unrealistically limited view of the interaction between infants and parents (Stern, 1985, chapters 9, 10). Most of all, the Kleinian view gives no room at all for a richer view of selfhood. Why then has the Kleinian view managed to entrench itself as one of the more established psychoanalytic schools with a remarkable following all over the world?

The Myth of the Struggle between Good and Bad

Stripped of its developmental psychology Melanie Klein's narrative is a powerful myth about the human condition, a myth remarkably akin to old cosmological and religious myths of the struggle between the forces of light and the forces of darkness, the forces that build and those that destroy, the forces of good and bad. This motif has returned again and again from Indian mythology through Empedocles' philosophy to Manichean theology; its historical recurrence reflects the power it has over the human mind. Melanie Klein takes this myth and places it inside the human mind instead of projecting it outwards. This does not make it into less of a myth, but one with a strong attraction.

Human life according to Melanie Klein is about the struggle between love and hate, creation and destruction. He whose world is ruled by hatred will live in a hateful world. He who is ridden by envy will not enjoy anything the world has to offer. Only gratitude and love can redeem us. And in order to receive grace we must confess to our sinfulness. The psychoanalytic process à la Melanie Klein is a hermeneutics of the impact of hatred, destruction, and envy on the patient's life. As long as the patient does not own up to the badness of his nature he will unconsciously be governed by it.

Once the destructive side is acknowledged and once the patient can bear the accompanying guilt, will his mind be opened to the possibility of gratitude. He will finally be able to use his analyst's interpretations; use and integrate the wisdom he is being offered. He will be able to see the good in what he has received and not be ruled by his resentment at the grievances he suffered at his mother's breast.

The Ahistorical (Paranoid–Schizoid) Position

Klein's thought has inspired a variety of reinterpretations of her concepts. As T. S. Eliot has said, classical works are characterized by their ability to generate new interpretations which are relevant for future generations, and so far Melanie Klein stands up to this criterion. My account here largely follows Thomas Ogden's (1986, chapters 2–6) interesting rethinking of Klein's notions of the paranoid–schizoid and depressive positions.

I think that the paranoid–schizoid position is best understood as the description of a mode of experience of the world in which the individual is incapable of perceiving the world as independent of her needs and desires. An object, another human being, has no existence, outside the question, "Do I want it, do I love it, do I hate it?" Hence, there is no representation of the object as it is in its own right, according to its own nature, but only insofar as it affects the individual in her desires. In the ahistorical mode the individual has no differentiated understanding of the self and its place in the world. There are only immediate, intense experiences which, correspondingly, fill the experiential world completely. Hence the world becomes a titanic struggle between the good and the bad, the sense that there is love and lovability and that there is hatred and hatefulness—and nothing beyond that.

The result is chaos: with the shifting states of desire, repulsion, love, hate, satisfaction, and frustration the world changes its color completely. There is no distance between the subject's state of desire and the object, and the object is nothing beyond how it affects the subject. To the extent a human being loves, she lives in a lovable world. To the extent she hates she lives in a hateful and hating world. It is this war between love and hate which determines what a life will be like.

It might be preferable to replace Melanie Klein's term *paranoid-schizoid position* with its problematic implicit assumptions by the term *ahistorical position,* thus elaborating on a proposal by Ogden (1986, p. 82). Most characteristic of this position is the subject's inability to give historical depth to her view of the world, which is based on nothing but the present state of desires. This has been poignantly depicted in Bret-Easton Ellis's *American Psycho* (1991) which could be used as a textbook exemplification of the ahistorical position.

There are in fact human beings who, even as adults, have very little ability to experience anything like continuity in their view of themselves and others. If they feel good, everything is great, but if they feel bad, it feels as if this state has been there forever, and will never go away. If they feel hurt by someone, they have no ability to experience their hatred while maintaining consciousness of the common history with the other in their perspective. If they love, their love is boundless, and without regard for the other's needs and desires—until this love will switch again into hatred.

Hence Klein says that the relationship is to a part object rather than a whole object. She chooses this term because she thinks the object is seen ("split") either into an all-good or an all-bad object. The prime characteristic of the ahistorical position is that there is no integration of object representations over time and over affective states of the subject. Of course he may know abstractly that others have an existence over and above how they affect him, but experientially this does not make a difference.

All of us at times fall back into the ahistorical mode of experience which presents us with the most intense experiences human beings are capable of. As opposed to Klein it does not seem to me that the ahistorical mode requires an active splitting of self and object. All it takes is a loosening of historical integration of complexity which allows for highly intense experiences to occur. Klein has emphasized the horrors of the ahistorical mode of experience, but it is also responsible for the moments of greatest plenitude: they range from intense desire through ferocious hatred to orgasm. Hence, as much as the historical mode of experience is an achievement, the transition from the ahistorical to the historical mode entails a loss of plenitude.

In my experience of reading and teaching Melanie Klein's writings it turns out to be useful to replace the term *breast* by the term *world*. This substitution highlights

CLASSIC AND ROMANTIC VIEWS OF INDIVIDUALITY   155

an interesting feature of her thinking. In many ways the ahistorical position does not differentiate between the world's intrinsic nature and our wishes to gain satisfaction from it. Individuals who experience the world as something which owes them and which often withholds gratifications, live in a constant state of rage and frustration. They lack a differentiated understanding of the simple fact that the world and other human beings have a nature which is independent of any individual's wishes. The ahistorical position is ultimately based on an inability to see the world (and this includes other human beings) as it is, independently of what we desire from it.

Individuals functioning primarily on the ahistorical level have not evolved a representation with a sufficient degree of objectivity to allow them to see that the world can be viewed from perspectives other than their own. In particular they do not have, or temporarily lose, the ability to truly understand that other human beings have a perspective, desires, and needs of their own. In other words, the ahistorical position is that it is a view of the world *sub specie* the individual's desire, which is why it provides the most intense experiences of which we are capable, for better and worse.

This point of view was developed in great detail by Spinoza in his *Ethics*. Human bondage is a function of the individual's unwillingness or incapacity to understand that nothing that happens in the world is specifically geared in favor of or against himself. As long as the individual views the world from the subjective perspective of desire, the impact of external events on his state of mind is indelible, and the individual has no resources with which to withstand strain and frustration without rage and anger.

Spinoza's metaphysics paints a picture of the world as an immutable structure with laws of its own. The condition of freedom is to understand that the world is what it is, and that our emotions are nothing but the reflection of the world's impact on our biological nature. The true internalization of this picture liberates the individual from being at the mercy of events which impinge on him by his seeing their intrinsic necessity. Spinoza's ultimate goal, *amor dei intellectualis,* the intuition of the world as a causal chain of events which unfolds according to its inner laws, is the way in which the individual can overcome the limitations of his personal perspective and come to accept and love reality as it is. I do not think that Spinoza's solution is structurally similar to Klein's emphasis on the development of gratitude. Nonetheless the juxtaposition of Spinoza and Klein helps us to see how Klein's idea of the ahistorical (paranoid–schizoid) position can be understood as the description of a mode of experience based on subjective desire.

The Historical (Depressive) Position

My interpretation of Melanie Klein's concept of the depressive position is again inspired by Ogden, and again I want to disconnect it from the context of her developmental scheme. The most important characteristic of the historical position is the development of a more abstract representational medium by which the individual can represent and understand the world and his own place in it. The most important impact of this more objective point of view is that the experience of the object is not totally colored by immediate affective intensities as it is in the ahistorical position. In Kleinian terms, the breast is finally seen as both giving and frustrating, gratifying and withholding, and the breast-mother is experienced as something with an existence of its own.

The historical mode allows a more complex integration of aspects of experience. Other human beings are not just perceived in terms of their immediate impact on the subject's state of desire. They are seen to have a history of their own, needs, desires, and aversions, in short, an inner life of their own. Moreover, the individual acquires a historical perspective on his own relationship with the Other. This allows relationships with their web of emotions, attitudes, obligations, and expectations to survive the onslaught of immediate emotional impact generated by disappointments, frustrations, pains, and limitations inevitable in human relationships. The common history of individuals and groups creates a structure which does not depend as much on desire as it depends on symbolically mediated forms of experience. The bond of friendship is one of the best examples. We expect friends to be there for us even if their immediate desire would be to do something more enjoyable. We expect history to carry a weight which goes beyond the fluctuations of states as fluctuating and instable as affect and desire.

Klein's use of the term *depressive* position is based on an important intuition. The sense of guilt reflects the fact that the historical mode of experience is equivalent to the introduction of a moral sphere into experience. Once the individual begins to experience moral demands generated by the very fact that the Other has needs, desires, expectations of her own, this means that his experience has been decentered, that he has come to see the existence and validity of perspectives other than his own.

Kleinian Ethics

Klein's interpretation of the dialectics between authorship, fatedness, and ontological protest of subjectivity is based on an image of the individual (baby) as a totally passive and helpless recipient of gratifications over which he has absolutely no control. This situation of necessity leads to rage and envy which in turn weaken the individual's ability to enjoy whatever gratifications the breast-mother-world can provide.

It is of interest to note that the Kleinian view leaves very little room for the individual's more active strivings, and the desire for autonomous individuality. Kleinians would probably argue that they do not deny this aspect of human nature, but that mature selfhood can only be based on the individual's realistic acceptance of his limitations and dependencies. Nevertheless the individual's desire to express an inner nature (Bollas would say, to develop his *idiom*) has no significant place in Melanie Klein's scheme of things.

This is reflected in Kleinian analytic technique. The patient is generally seen as a helpless victim of his unconscious fantasies, and the analyst as the dispenser of analytic wisdom. One of the most frequently found locutions in the Kleinian literature is "I succeeded in showing the patient . . .," or "I finally interpreted to the patient. . . ." Much of the Kleinian narrative centers on the patient's inability to accept the analyst's analytic ability or creativity, on his attempts to destroy it enviously, and on his avoidance of making productive use of the insights he is being offered (e.g., Segal, 1994).

Klein's ethics is therefore one centered on the importance of gratitude and the ability to bear guilt. It is an interesting revival of the doctrine of original sin. In Klein's version original sin is the rage and envy the individual feels about not having his needs completely satisfied—or as she says, the individual's grievances at the breast. Like original sin, neither rage nor envy can be eradicated, they can only be acknowledged. The individual's salvation is a function of his ability to bear the guilt of having wanted to destroy the life-giving breast-mother-world. Only bearing this guilt without falling into fantasies of omnipotent reparation enables the individual to develop the final saving grace; gratitude for the good things the world has given him.

DONALD WINNICOTT: ROMANTIC MYSTIC

Winnicott's main story takes up an age-old theme, that of the true and the false self (Winnicott, 1960). His version of the true self is that in essence all of us are playful artists, seeking creative expression and the possibility of meeting the world on our own terms as a playground which allows freedom within cultural constraints. The infant is born with pure spontaneity; its nature reaches out to the world. The infant invites the world to dance with her. The spontaneous gesture, the smile, the desire for realizing her inner nature, her true self in interaction with the world is what drives the infant.

The fate of the true self, this pure spontaneity, will be sealed by the extent to which the world accepts the invitation to dance. If the primary caretaker (generally mother) is capable and willing to adapt herself to the infant's needs, the true self will stay out in the open, and the child will truly live.

If she is not, the child will begin to adapt to outer pressure too early, and lose any sense of true spontaneity. This adaptive shell which is purely reactive rather than spontaneous gesture Winnicott calls the *false self*. This reactive layer is a defensive structure which tries to prevent the true self from being overly traumatized by painful impingement of the external world.

Winnicott developed these theories through analytic work with individuals whose prime complaint was a sense of lifelessness, a sense of not really being there and just going through the moves, whether in conversation, making love, or pursuing a profession.

As a result Winnicott came to say: "What I say does affect our view of the question: what is life about? You may cure your patient and not know what it is that makes him or her go on living. It is of first importance to us to acknowledge openly that absence of psychoneurotic illness may be health, but it is not life" (1971, p. 117).

Winnicott's Poetics of Subjectivity

Winnicott's main theme is how the meeting between the inner nature of the individual and the external world can occur without leading to the abolition of subjectivity. His basic idea is that acceptance of externality must be gradual; the infant needs first a stage of the illusion of omnipotence. Without knowledge of the externality of the mother the infant must find the object of desire (generally called "the breast" in psychoanalytic parlance) in a way which makes it possible to maintain the illusion that desire has created the breast.

The next stage is the creation of an intermediary realm—the transitional realm, as Winnicott calls it—in which there is a tacit understanding between the mother and the baby not to question whether a particular object is external or has been created by the baby. This transitional realm is maintained throughout life in art and religion.

If acceptance of the externality of the world is forced upon the infant too early, too harshly, the infant begins to live on a purely reactive level, adapting itself to the rhythm of the caretaker rather than maintaining its own. It develops what Winnicott calls a false self, a superficially successful adaptation to the demands of the environment. The false self is a defense: if every manifestation of the true self is encountered by impingement, the false self tries to create a fortress behind which the true self can hide, waiting for the opportunity to emerge, should circumstance permit it.

At times the true self is so deeply hidden that the individual loses any conscious contact with it. And at times the false self comes to the conclusion that there will never be an opportunity for authentic living, and hence decides to protect the true self from further pain by arranging suicide.

Winnicott sees subjectivity not as something beyond nature, but rather as a manifestation of it. His concept of the *psyche-soma* (1949) is meant to show that psychic existence is essentially natural, formed by the structure of the body. Not unlike Sartre, Winnicott tries to maintain the dialectic between *en-soi* and *pour-soi* by constantly taking into account that the structure of subjectivity is a reflection of the body.

Nevertheless Winnicott would probably have seen Sartre's (1943) pessimistic view of the impossibility of interpersonal relationships which do not limit freedom, as a reflection of the experience of unbearable impingement.

Schizoid withdrawal should not be a necessity, according to Winnicott. He has a utopia: it is called the good-enough mother (a modest title for a utopia. . .). The good-enough mother need not be perfect; she must just be capable of protecting the child from impingement which breaks the child's capability of maintaining its own natural rhythm, its true self.

Winnicott on Therapy

Winnicott's views on psychoanalytic therapy are an extension of his views on the mediation between individual nature and external reality. The therapist must be able to create an environment in which the patient's true self can get in touch with reality again. This environment he calls potential space, a space in which the dialectic of the transitional is recreated: where there is no need to maintain the defense of wounded subjectivity against intrusion, since no intrusion is to be expected.

Winnicott's model of potential space is close to the ideal of free improvisation, the jam session: "Therapy takes place in the intersection of two areas of play: that of the patient and that of the therapist." It is to be an approximation of the Leibnizian dream of monads which reflect each other without intruding into each other's essences. Each overture is taken as a proposal; each motif an offer for playful, improvisational elaboration.

Winnicott emphasizes the individual's need to be left alone. He says: "I am putting forward and stressing the importance of the idea of the *permanent isolation of the individual* and claiming that at the core of the individual there is no communication with the not-me world either way, "The over-all fact remains that the primordial experience occurs in solitude" (1963, pp. 189–190). Winnicott restitutes the yearning for true solitude as one of the most legitimate, most needed experiences of the individual. The terror of having to communicate has been described by Winnicott with the strongest expressions I have ever found in his works:

Rape, and being eaten by cannibals, these are mere baga-
telles as compared with the violation of the self's core, the
alteration of the self's central elements by communication
seeping through the defences. For me this would be the
sin against the self. We can understand the hatred people
have of psycho-analysis which has penetrated a long way
into the human personality, and which provides a threat
to the human individual in his need to be secretly isolated.
The question is: how to be isolated without having to be
insulated? [1963, p. 187].

Winnicott's target here is the technical approach in
psychoanalysis, which considers good analytic work to constantly address the patient's presumed preoccupations
about the analyst. Winnicott's goal in these remarks was
to restitute the legitimacy of the individual's desire to be
taken as a subject in his own right whose contents as a
human being go far beyond preoccupation with the
object.

Regression to Dependence

How can one deal with the patient's lifelessness? How is
it possible to somehow get behind the patient's false self
and reach the hidden, true self?

Winnicott's answer was a new version of the myth of
rebirth. His label for it was *regression to dependence* (Winnicott, 1972). The narrative structure behind it was simple
and compelling: the false self had begun to develop at a
point at which environmental provision to the infant's
needs had been insufficient. Hence the only way to reach
the true self was to let the patient regress to the point
where the true self had gone underground.

Such regression could not be forced, it could not even
be initiated by the analyst. The patient's protective false
self had to test the analyst in order to make sure that he
was suitable for taking care of the true self without damag-
ing it as it had been damaged in infancy. Such testing

could go on for years, until the false self gave its approval for the analyst to take over.

Once the true self came into the open, the analyst was in for a very strenuous period. The true self of the patient necessarily was at an infantile stage, and hence the analyst's care had to be quite concrete. During such periods the patient needed to be taken care of physically, and the analyst had to be willing to accept the patient's total dependence on his care. Winnicott's metaphor for such provision of care was that he had to *hold* the patient (which quite often entailed physical holding as well).

From this point on, where the true self could finally come into contact with the external world through the analyst, a renewed development could take place. The true self could gradually find ways to relate to the outside world on more mature levels without having to retreat behind the protective layer of the false self again.

The myth of regression to dependence is powerful; so is that of the true self as pure spontaneity. The role of the analyst as the trustworthy figure who will allow the patient to regress as deeply as needed to come back alive has all the moving qualities of the stories of real saints and of individuals who are willing to sacrifice themselves for the sake of others.

The problem of Winnicott's myth is that it caters to the fantasy of the possibility of a life of plenitude; a life in which spontaneity reigns and all the painful moments of lifelessness, of being a spectator rather than a protagonist in one's own life, disappear. Furthermore I cannot help thinking of all the descriptions in the history of religion of individuals who felt reborn, finally found their true self in conversion. Winnicott's narrative of the regression to dependence is in many ways a secular version of the myth of rebirth, and his clinical practice a ritual which can help individuals to find ways of experiencing themselves anew.

Some individuals feel that they can enter Winnicott's symbolic universe and some don't. The first case is poignantly illustrated by Margaret Little's account of her analysis with Winnicott. She had been partial to the idea of regression to dependence from the beginning, and she entered Winnicott's universe enthusiastically (Little, 1985).

The second case is exemplified in Winnicott's book length case history *Holding and Interpretation* (1972). As Stephen Mitchell shows quite convincingly, the patient obviously does not feel touched by Winnicott's metaphors of regression to dependence, and voices his discomfort feebly but audibly (sufficiently so to come through in Winnicott's account) time and again. It is both funny and exasperating to see how Winnicott continues his interpretive line as unperturbed as an ocean liner disregarding the patient's protestations as ripples which do not bother his line of thought (Mitchell, 1993, pp. 70–73). Winnicott at his best is one of the most enthralling poets of the psychoanalytic tradition, but he had his moments of disregard for the patient's subjectivity, and could stick to his myth stubbornly, continuing his ritual of reaching the patient's true self without listening too much to the patient's protestations which, after all, were only those of his empirical (as opposed to the true) self.

MELANIE KLEIN AND WINNICOTT COMPARED

It is a useful exercise to briefly compare the myths of Melanie Klein and of Winnicott. Melanie Klein sees infants as quite nasty beings, totally egocentric, destructive, and aggressive. She thinks that the innate degree of destructiveness, and envy on the one hand, and innate level of frustration tolerance on the other hand will be largely responsible for the infant's (and later adult's) fate.

It should be remembered that Melanie Klein's theories were developed at a time in which it was indeed habitual practice to see infants as nasty. Manuals of infant rearing quite often stressed that infants must not be spoiled, and that it was healthy for infants to cry. Therefore her theory was quite in tune with the spirits of the time.

Winnicott's development of his theories (1940s and 1950s) coincided with the beginning of a shift in views of good infant rearing. During this period the famous pediatrician Dr. Spock came to the conclusion that infants had no way to modulate their tension and need states and that there was absolutely no use in frustrating infants since this built no resilience to their character.

Klein's views are a development of the age-old theme of the wickedness of the human heart and the impact of this wickedness. She formulates her ethical judgment in terms of a developmental theory, as psychoanalysis usually does.

Winnicott's narrative is an extension of the idea that human nature is essentially innocent, and that society spoils this innocence by wrong practices. He is one of the purest Rousseauans of the twentieth century by elaborating to its utmost consequence the narrative of the true self as a creative well.

The clinical styles of Klein and Winnicott mirror their ethical stance faithfully. Klein relentlessly interprets the patient's destructiveness, envy, and hidden guilt, and sticks to the format of psychoanalytic ritual as closely as possible. Her stance is that of the grand inquisitor who will first bring the patient to a full confession of his wickedness, and finally get him to see the extent of his guilt in order to bring him back to true love.

The technique of the Kleinian analyst focuses almost exclusively on the presumed transferential implications of each of the patient's utterances. Their theory is that the patient, like the infant, is exclusively focused on the mother's breast as the provider of all the good things in the world: food, warmth, and protection. The infant's total dependence is supposedly recreated in the analytic situation, and so are the envy, rage, and destruction the Kleinians think to be ubiquitous in the infant's mind. From a Winnicottian perspective Kleinians make the mistake of delegitimizing the patient's ontological protest completely. This protest is mistaken either for an attempt to destroy the analyst's analytic capacity, or for an omnipotent denial of actual dependence.

Winnicott is committed to salvaging the patient's true self. He shuns no toil to adapt himself to the patient's needs. When once asked how such flexibility allowed him to maintain the schedule of an analytic practice he mused: "Maybe one should nor treat more than one patient at a time."

The comparison of Klein and Winnicott is instructive because they are at opposite ends in their understanding of the interrelation between authorship and fate. For Klein the individual's fate is the extent of his inborn aggression. Authorship is achieved by integrating and overcoming this aggression to the point of being able to love. For Winnicott fate is the extent to which one's mother is good enough in the provision of infant care; the restitution of the self is achieved by achieving a sense of creativity.

DANGERS OF CLASSICISM

Classicism is ultimately an ethics of austerity. The demands it imposes on the individual are high. Its ideal of the well-analyzed person is to live a life beyond illusion. Its emphasis on a dignified acceptance of fate, i.e., the multitude of factors which determines an individual's life without being in his control, is both lofty and grim.

The beauty of classicism resides in its refusal to give in to the human need for images of redemption—total love, self-realization, creativity. Classicism always traces them back to some infantile fantasy of some sort, since nothing but total lucidity will do.

The problem with classicism is that by driving toward total lucidity it may leave the patient with nothing to live for. By reducing the patient's idealizations to defensive attempts at avoiding the truth about his own envy and aggression, the patient can end up bereft of any image of a life truly worth living.

Winnicott's implicit critique of Kleinian analysis is contained in his careful attempts to maintain a space of illusion, an intermediary area in which the patient can negotiate the tensions between his wishes for a life worth living and the structure of actual reality. Classicism, with its inexorable identification with the objective point of view, takes the risk of smothering the patient's subjectivity. If the goal of analytic clinical work is the restoration of a sense of authorship, classicism can fail to achieve this end by pushing the patient to the point where the sense of fatedness becomes overwhelming.

DANGERS OF ROMANTICISM

Romanticist psychology has finally found a reasonable foundation for the individual's claim that reality must be attuned to his needs, and for moral outrage if it isn't. Romanticist psychotherapy has found the ritual for restoring the hurt self: we must have the individual regress to the point where the damage was done, and thus reach the patient's true self. From there a sense of authorship is regained. Finally the romantic vision provides a useful interpretation of the sense that there must be more to life than meets the eye, that there must be some hidden meaning. This meaning is relegated to the lost paradise of the times in which the individual was still in touch with his true self, mostly infancy.

This narrative has tremendous appeal, and it provides many individuals with a powerful interpretation of their sense of being disconnected from the possibility of truly living their lives. However the romanticist interpretation faces many problems:

1. There is the conceptual difficulty of specifying the true self which is supposed to be reached. Why should reclaiming the inner child make an individual more capable of dealing with life's hardships? What form should the unadulterated true self take?

2. This narrative can lead into a malignant therapeutic stalemate: as long as the individual has not reached a sense of aliveness and plenitude, the romantic view takes this to mean that the regression achieved is not sufficiently deep. Hence the patient and the therapist can get stalled in a grotesque version of *Waiting for Godot* where Godot would represent the emergence of the mysterious true self (Beckett, 1952).

3. The next point does not pertain to romanticist psychoanalysis, but to some of the popularizations of the romanticist viewpoint in the therapeutic market. It is the creation of class consciousness of victimization, a danger very concretely embodied in the current appalling tendency of a vast number of American therapists to coax their patients into believing that they have been victims of child abuse (a tendency not endorsed by romanticist psychoanalysis itself). The patient then gets stuck in a position of being eternally bitter for the injustices done to her. By this I am not trying to deny that child abuse occurs, nor that it can have terrible consequences, but to teach patients the language of victimization as a solution to the problems of life is simplistic and often harmful.

4. The romanticist interpretation can feed into the fantasy that if only conditions for the emergence of their true selves were obtained, life would flow effortlessly. This is reinforced by the romanticist use of metaphors taken from early infancy which inevitably lead to the feeling that the true self is pure, unmediated spontaneity. The result reinforces the *Waiting for Godot* effect.

CLASSICISM AND ROMANTICISM AS ETHICAL VISIONS

Classicism and romanticism are expressions of two different experiences of life. Late modern skepticism with respect to theories of human nature makes the question of which of them is right somewhat moot. I think that their validity is to be sought in the extent to which individuals can recognize their lives under these descriptions, and the therapeutic effectiveness of the therapeutic approaches based on these visions.

One of the questions then is, what therapeutic climate is created by the use of each of these approaches? In the United States romanticist approaches have been gaining ground rapidly in the last few years. Self psychology and intersubjectivism emphasize environmental failure in their theories of psychopathology and advise the clinician to try to meet the patient's needs for empathy. They argue that greater emotional availability and a more relaxed atmosphere are crucial for better therapeutic work.

Stephen Mitchell (1993, chapter 1) has argued that there has been a change in our understanding of what patients need. There is less and less emphasis on the patient's coming to accept unacceptable impulses. He argues that the overriding need of the typical present-day patient is the development of a richer subjectivity. This view would go along with sociological accounts which argue that most developed Western societies are less characterized by repressive measures and rigid normative conceptions. Instead there is the pressure on the middle-class individual to make a successful career of his life combined with a lessening of parental resources to provide the type of stability and safety which helps people to do so. Communities are less tightly knit than they used to be, and hence the emotional high-pressure atmosphere of traditional societies which tended to generate the psychopathologies Freud centered upon are less likely to be met with today.

If the patient's problem is primarily to create a stable identity and coherent sense of self in a society which is largely indifferent to him, therapeutic strategies which provide him with the emotional support that helps him to do so are more likely to be useful.

Pragmatic considerations of this sort do not in themselves constitute an argument for the romantic vision. They would, if substantiated, constitute an argument for a particular clinical approach, the creation of a type of

therapeutic atmosphere. The inference from the success
of a therapeutic strategy to a theory of pathogenesis is, as
has been convincingly shown (Grünbaum, 1984; Strenger
1991, chapter 1 and passim), a non sequitur.

Psychoanalysis has always tried to link developmental
psychology, ethics, and clinical practice into unified visions. This has been an essential constituent of its beauty,
its powerful cultural impact, its attraction to both clinicians and patients. The classic and the romantic visions of
human reality are two clusters of such visions. The fact
that they have persisted for centuries only shows the extent
to which they reflect a human need to make sense of life.
In particular it shows how the metaphysical and theological question of whether human beings are essentially good
or bad has an inexorable hold on our imagination.

I believe that it is impossible to divest clinical practice
of such considerations. The semimetaphysical, value-laden
Gestalts by which we give expression to various ways of
experiencing life seem to be an integral aspect of how we
live. Attempts to eradicate the element of Weltanschauung
and ethics from the domain of psychoanalysis have back-
fired. Instead of making psychoanalysis value neutral, they
have obscured the fact that many of the heated disputes
which seemed to be about developmental psychology are
really about ethics.

As much as each school would like to base its ethical
preferences on grounded knowledge, this seems to be an
illusory undertaking. The fact that the fights have been as
heated as they were in the past only proves the extent to
which they have not been about developmental psychology
but about views of what it means to live a good life, and
why it is so difficult to do so.

As I have argued in chapters 1 and 2, clinical schools
are always based on ideals of accomplished individuality.
For many decades psychoanalysis has coached these ideals
as conceptions of maturity which were presumably descrip-
tive and scientific. My proposal is to accept that these ideals are cultural constructs which try to provide a sense of
direction to the formation of the self. Individuality is, as

Foucault has argued, much more a work of art than the achievement of a biologically predetermined developmental goal. As therapeutic practitioners we cannot but adhere to some ideal of accomplished individuality and a practice of the discipline of the self. Being aware of the fact that any discipline of the self is but one form of life is the one guarantee we have of not indoctrinating both students and patients, and instead allowing them to make up their minds about how to live their lives.

PART III

CONFIGURATIONS OF INDIVIDUALITY

5 FREEDOM AND BONDAGE: REFLECTIONS ON SELF-CREATION AND SADOMASOCHISM

A PERSONAL JOURNEY

In doing psychoanalytic work one encounters, of necessity, one's own limitations and blind spots; that much we know since Freud. What has changed since then is that in contemporary culture much of what was once repressed by most members of the middle class, and could only be reached through arduous work, is often to be found today in established lifestyles.

A very good example is sadomasochism (S&M). Once relegated by psychoanalysis to being a side-effect of anal fixation, S&M has become a cultural phenomenon. In the 1970s S&M clubs flourished in San Francisco's Castro district, and soon spread to other cities as well. Masochism became a performance art as in the work of Owen Flanagan (Juno and Vale, 1993), that attracted significant audiences, even though it remained a fringe phenomenon. The iconography of S&M reached the fortresses of high culture through the work of the photographer Robert Mapplethorpe.

The uninitiated tend to react to the imagery of S&M with a mixture of disgust and thrill, but generally refrain from trying to understand the phenomenon from within. In many respects the psychoanalytic literature kept its distance from S&M. Even writers, like Masud Khan (1979), who wrote sympathetically and profoundly about perversions somehow kept their distance from the phenomenon. Learned disquisitions about the pervert's inability for close object relations, and his or her need to keep a distance from the object, left the phenomenon ultimately obscure, and failed to make it fully human.

This chapter is meant to report on a personal journey: until a few years ago, I kept my distance from the phenomenon of S&M. My knowledge of its culture was scant, my understanding of it, I now think, zero. Then two prolonged and deep encounters led me to a deeper interest in it and forced me gradually to overcome my prejudice and fear and to try to understand S&M in its own terms.

The first encounter, in 1988, was through reading, when I was on the faculty of the philosophy department at Hebrew University. Until then I had a rather vague acquaintance with the work of Michel Foucault, and was curious to know more. At a lunch with a colleague of mine who is a philosopher of science it turned out that, like myself, she was interested in Foucault, but didn't know him well, and we decided to teach a seminar together. We prepared over the summer, and enjoyed the seminar greatly (I hope the students did, too).

At the end of the seminar I felt a curious sense of unease. I had more of a grasp of Foucault's work, but felt that I was missing out on something essential. I had a vague premonition that behind the scintillating, impersonal prose and the brilliant historiophilosophical analyses there was a deeper, demonic level of the man. Only knowledge about this level would make his work truly intelligible to me. I sought biographical material. At the time only Didier Eribon's (1987) biography was available. I read it, but it left me unsatisfied. Somehow the dry facts that Eribon related did not touch upon the level that I vaguely felt to be the true motivation behind Foucault's work.

In the early nineties a second encounter began. An extraordinary woman I will call Tamara asked for a rather unusual type of work. She did not live in Israel, but her work as a filmmaker made it possible for her to come and see me rather regularly. She did not want therapy in any standard sense of the term. She wanted to talk, to be listened to, and be accepted and understood on her own terms. I have given a full account of our encounter over the years in *Individuality, the Impossible Project* (1998), and will present some of it here.

Tamara was (and presumably still is) a sexual masochist, and she has taken great risks in the pursuit of what to her is the deepest pleasure she knows. The encounter with this deeply intelligent and creative woman did not allow me to keep my clinical, classifying gaze on S&M, and I gradually had to widen the limits of my imaginative empathy and lower the defenses that psychiatric diagnosis so easily maintains on our minds.

In 1993 I came across James Miller's seminal *The Passion of Michel Foucault* (1993). Miller's work is a masterpiece of biographical writing. His understanding of Foucault's work and his ability to show its deep structure is remarkable. But what makes reading this beautifully written work into an inspirational experience is Miller's uncanny ability to unify the perspective on Foucault the man and Foucault the intellectual.

As I had vaguely felt all along, it turned out that Foucault had been haunted by deep-seated fears throughout most of his life. He hovered between madness and suicide throughout his twenties. His work on madness, incarceration, medicine, and sexuality was an attempt to cure the deep traumas of his life. It also turned out that Foucault was deeply involved in the world of S&M. It was probably in the clubs of the Castro district that he contracted the HIV virus that would put such an untimely end to the life of one of the great intellectuals of this century.

Miller is generously open about his own motivations and the process that he underwent in writing *The Passion of Michel Foucault*. He began his investigation after hearing the rumor that Foucault continued to frequent S&M clubs after he knew that he was HIV positive with the express intent to infect others. Miller came to a conclusion that there was no basis to this rumor, but by then he had embarked on the process of deciphering the demonic fears and forces that drove Michel Foucault in his life and work. Miller himself had to overcome the type of judgmental distance that separates most of us from the world of S&M, but his admiration for and interest in Foucault led him to seek a deeper understanding of the phenomenon.

One of Miller's sources in trying to understand Foucault was the work of Robert Stoller, one of the foremost psychoanalytic authorities on perversion. Reading Stoller's work I saw that Stoller underwent a fascinating process himself that was tragically cut short by his premature death. In his last works Stoller felt compelled to leave the psychoanalyst's armchair and to investigate the worlds of pornography and S&M on their own terms from an anthropological perspective. Stoller wrote that the more he investigated human sexuality, the less he felt that there was a sharp difference between "normal" and "perverse" sexuality.

Throughout this time I continued to work with Tamara and we gained a progressively deeper understanding of her project of self-creation, her complex gender construction, and her sexual masochism. This understanding did not lead Tamara to change any of these features. She felt that all of them were essential to her identity, and she adhered to them out of her free choice.

At the end of 1993 I began to write a book. For three years I wrote rather obsessively and I did not quite know as yet, what I was up to.

The first theme I was dealing with was the experience of protest against features of life and the world that are subjectively experienced as unbearable. I found this phenomenon in people I worked with, in philosophy, art, and religion, and in my own personal experience. I called this *the ontological protest of subjectivity*. I assumed that this rejection of reality could be both a source of great creative achievement and the reason for existential deadlock. I wanted to find out more about this.

The second theme was the need many people feel to recreate their selves if they feel that their past is unbearable. This desire for self-creation was powerfully exemplified in the lives of Tamara and Michel Foucault, and they became two of my most important examples for the process of self-creation.

The third theme was my own desire for a more open, pluralistic and truly tolerant version of psychoanalysis. I had felt for years that psychoanalysis was in the grip of what I came to call *developmental moralism*. The psychoanalytic universe was organized along a developmental story that differentiated between the higher and the lower, the mature and the immature, thus rationalizing its preference for particular styles of life.

I ended up with a huge manuscript that had to be reorganized and cut into two in due time. The first part was *Individuality, the Impossible Project*, and the second one is the present book. I feel that this process has gradually crystallized into a more or less coherent position, and I also feel that a growing number of psychoanalytic authors have evolved in similar directions.

Foucault's life was a protest against the wounds social categorizations can inflict on human subjectivity. In his case the major trauma was that his homosexuality turned him into a deviant. Tamara's life was a protest against the violence with which women are forced into a mold that does not fit the desires and needs of many of them. Both Tamara and Foucault were ardent in the assertion of their right to create their selves according to their own sexual, ethical, and aesthetic preferences.

This chapter recounts the process I underwent in moving from the idea that there are developmental steps that you have to undergo to become mature, to the idea that culture should be the space that allows individuals to structure their selves according to their own desire.

PERVERSION OR NEOSEXUALITY?

Sexual perversions, or the neosexualities, as Joyce McDougall (1995) has felicitously called them, have been investigated from many points of view. In the Freudian tradition they have been interpreted as a reflection of castration anxiety by Freud himself (1927), as the inability to accept the difference of generations and the sexes (Chasseguet-Smirgel, 1984), or as the attempt to master early trauma (Stoller, 1985, 1991). Object relational approaches have emphasized the way in which neosexualities put a distance between themselves and the object (Khan, 1979), and self psychological authors have interpreted them as the disintegration products of incohesive selves (Goldberg, 1995). Sadomasochism in particular has been interpreted as reflecting the incomplete subjectivity assigned to women in patriarchal societies, and has been placed in a sociopolitical context as well (Benjamin, 1989).

I should like to offer an additional interpretive hypothesis. In *Individuality, the Impossible Project* (1998) I have argued that there are individuals who are less willing than most of us to accept that we are not self-created. They are involved in what I have called an ontological protest of subjectivity against the constraint of externally imposed fate. As a result they try to recreate their selves in ways that reflect their own desires.

In this chapter I will investigate individuals whose temperamental disposition leads them into conflict with their early environment. They feel that the constraints imposed on us by upbringing, culture, and socially entrenched gender roles impinge on their human right to form their own selves. For them Nietzsche's injunction "be who you are" is a categorical imperative that defines a life worth living. They are highly conscious of their own project of self-creation, and of the biographical determinants of their project. They feel that to be fully human they must have the freedom to create their selves as works of art; otherwise they experience themselves as passive victims of an externally imposed fate. They want to have a sense of authorship over their lives.

The two examples on which this chapter will focus are Tamara and Foucault. Tamara from early on was an extremely independent and strong-willed child, and could not accept the limitations of her conventional upbringing. Michel Foucault was basically at odds with his conservative, Catholic environment because he was homosexual. Both experienced painful tensions with their environments, and both made early existential choices of not giving in to pressures. Both Tamara and Michel Foucault became involved in the world of S&M. Both celebrated their sexual choices and saw them as an integral part of their identity. My interpretive proposal is that S&M for them became a way to master their experience of painful conflict, and to turn it into an integral part of the work of art that was their self.

As has been pointed out by many authors (e.g., Chodorow, 1994), the classical literature often assumes that individuals who recreate their selves, genders, and sexualities are of necessity ill, driven, and unconscious of their motivations. I think that examples like Tamara and Foucault indicate that, at least in certain cases, such choices are made by emotionally and cognitively highly differentiated individuals who might, in fact, be more conscious than other people of differences and qualities of all sorts. If anything, individuals like Tamara and Foucault are driven by an excess need to allow for individuality and differentiation, not by the need to turn everything into an undifferentiated pulp.

The topics of self-creation and sadomasochism are intertwined in the lives of these two people. For both early trauma was something to be met, mastered, and transformed actively rather than to be borne passively. In this

respect both of them lived according to the heroic narrative of fighting fate rather than bearing it passively. This
heroic narrative is often associated with immature romanticism in classical psychoanalysis, because acceptance of
reality rather than the fight against it was the telos of the
classic Freudian and Kleinian developmental narratives.

One of the classical versions of psychoanalytic theory
was formulated by Bion, who thought that the ability to
bear mental pain is crucial to the development of the mind
(Bion, 1961). As we will see Tamara and Foucault raise
the interesting possibility that there are various ways of
suffering mental pain. The heroic narrative of self-creation constitutes an interesting alternative to the
Freud–Klein–Bion narrative of growing through the acceptance of the past as it was, and settling into the limits
of human existence.

The goal of this chapter is not to glorify either S&M
or transgression. It is to investigate narrative possibilities
of understanding and of existential transformation. The
spirit of pluralism that governs late modern culture has
had a growing impact on psychoanalysis lately. It allows us
to play between narratives rather than forcing us to decide
which narrative is the one, correct description of human
nature (Mitchell, 1997). This increases our chances of accommodating our narratives to the experience of individual patients rather than fitting their experience to our
favorite theory of human nature.

TAMARA, THE WOMAN WHO KNEW NO LIMITS

Tamara was on a two-week visit in Israel, filming a docu-
mentary on a Chassidic group known for its extreme initia-
tion rites. I met her at a social occasion, where we spoke,
among other things, about the question of whether psychoanalysis was supposed to normalize people. Subse-
quently Tamara asked me for a consultation. I asked her
whether she was aware that there was little I could do for

her in the brief period of her stay. She answered that she did not want a therapy, but an occasion to talk and to be listened to. Thus we embarked on a series of encounters which lasted for several years at a pace of six to eight consultations a year, which Tamara organized around her trips to various parts of the world.

Tamara related the facts of her life with pride. She was a sexual masochist, and she took great risks in fulfilling her desires. She would pick up men in raunchy bars, and her criterion of choice was whether she thought they could deliver the rough games of bondage and domination which gave her the deepest pleasures of her life. She also had innumerable lovers with whom she engaged in more conventional sex.

She lived on the edge in most respects. She had achieved a world-wide reputation through her documentaries, and she was known for thriving on impossible assignments. She was willing to face great physical danger to get precisely the shots she wanted. She had filmed on every continent, and proudly told me that she had lovers on each of them.

She played with all types of drugs. Speed, grass, and Ecstasy were her daily bread. She had also experimented with LSD and other hallucinogens. She had also taken great risks: she had tried heroin, and even crack, because she wanted to prove to herself that she could do so without becoming addicted.

For the first meetings she primarily presented the image of an infinitely tough woman who knew no limits. Her philosophy of life was that she should be able to do whatever she desired. Nevertheless I felt that behind this presenting image she was a sensitive, even fragile woman. This impression was strengthened when she asked me to see a video version of a low-budget feature film she had written and directed some years earlier.

The film was about a preadolescent girl who had gotten lost in the rough life of a big city. She was picked up by a drug dealer who turned her into a Lolita-ish lover. Many scenes revolved around her desperate attempts to

please him, without quite understanding what exactly she
had to do or why it was supposed to be pleasurable.

There was one island of humaneness in this chilling,
heartbreaking universe of cruelty and senselessness. The
protagonist spent some days in the apartment of a group
of drag queens, who were portrayed as both pathetic and
deeply human. They shared the feeling that the world was
a dangerous place, without pity and feeling, and they tried
to turn their apartment into an island of solidarity and
mutual protection. The film ends with the protagonist's
return to the drug dealer.

This film led to an important aspect of Tamara's life,
her deep involvement in the male gay community of the
West coast city in which she lived. She felt safer with them
than anywhere else. She identified with the gay community's experience of being, and her close friends were male
gays, with whom she had deep, lasting playful relationships. One of her favorite games was to have her friends
dress her up as a boy, and to join them on their outings.
This gave her the powerful feeling that she could eventu-
ally be a boy if she wanted to.

It soon turned out that this film also reflected Tamara's deeper experiences. Throughout a series of widely
spaced consultations Tamara began to unravel her biography. She was the third child of a Czechoslovakian Catholic
immigrant who had made a fortune quite early in his life,
and whose project had become to achieve social respectability. This was difficult because the WASP establishment
of the East coast town where he had settled considered
him to be nouveau-riche. He pursued his project relentlessly by trying to turn his children into well-bred examples
of WASP culture.

Tamara's elder sister fitted the mold: she was a sweet
girl, and became her parents' darling. Her brother, the
middle child, severely disappointed his father, because he
was not tough. His father soon withdrew from him, and
gave him nothing but material assistance. Tamara was 6
years old when this happened, and she remembered how
she thought that she could make a much better son for

her father. This thought was particularly compelling because she felt that she could and would never be as sweet and compliant as her elder sister.

Tamara remembered the precise moment when she became a masochist. At the age of 6 years, on a summer day, her father was screaming at her because she had not followed one of his orders. She was furious and scared to death, and ran away. Then, suddenly a thought crossed her mind: "If I enjoyed the pain, I will be at one with father, and he could never hurt me again."

Tamara's life thus became an extended project in self-creation: she tried to prove that she could be a boy. She tried to square the circle by maintaining her sense of individuality vis-à-vis a father who was intransigent in his demands that his family be molded according to his desires or lose his love. She did so by turning pain into pleasure, and thus merging with him.

She also tried to heal the wounds of her childhood terrors. The most important part of her masochist scenarios was that after inflicting pain for hours, her lovers would nurse her and become warm and caring. After years in which we explored her soul, she came to the conclusion that these scenarios were her magic attempt to turn her father into a warmer, more caring parent, and thus to undo the pain he had inflicted upon her.

I tried to convince Tamara several times to enter a therapeutic relationship in her home city. She refused to do so for several reasons: first, because she had been terribly hurt by an analyst she had seen in the past, who had interpreted her sexuality as phallic fixation and incomplete femininity. Second, because she was not sure at all that she wanted to change. Her identity was deeply tied to her relentless fight against social norms and conventions. She felt that to cease this fight would obliterate all she was. To the best of my knowledge, Tamara continues to live according to her preferences, even though she may be calmer and feel more wholesome about the choices that made her into who she is.

MICHEL FOUCAULT'S PHILOSOPHICAL LIFE

On his deathbed the French philosopher Michel Foucault told a young writer, Hervé Guibert, three memories that haunted him throughout his life.

The Amputation: At age 8 he was taken by his father, a Roman Catholic doctor, to watch a leg amputation. This was supposed to help him become a man.

The sequestrée de Poitiers: In his home town, Poitiers, there was a house connected to an uncanny story everybody knew, but that was only talked about secretly. Years ago the authorities had found a woman there, almost blind, living in her own excrement and in rotting food. She had been locked away by her family when she was 17 because she had become pregnant, and she lived in these conditions for twenty-five years.

The deported Jews: Paul Michel Foucault was the star pupil of his class, until Jews who had escaped from Paris came to Poitiers. Since the standards in Paris were much higher, Michel lost his star status immediately. He hated the Jewish boys and wished them dead. Shortly after the Nazis came, the boys were deported to concentration camps and died.

To these memories one should add the cumulative trauma of his life: Michel Foucault was gay, and he knew it from early on. In the small Catholic town of Poitiers, he had no cultural frame of reference except the conservative culture into which he grew. His childhood was lived with a sense of rottenness, the unnamable guilt connected to being deviant, and the constant fear that he was going to be incarcerated for his sexual and moral depravity.

Michel Foucault could never forgive society for the fate of living the life of a deviant. His life work was to be no less than to show that the social categories, values, and theories that had condemned him to the status of a pervert were completely unfounded. In his work he tackled the notion of madness (1961), the medical gaze (1964), the very idea of human nature (1966), the penal system

(1975), the notion of sexuality (1976), and finally turned to the Greek notion of care of the self as a source for a modern ethics (1983).

His strategy was to recount the genealogy of these notions and theories. He would show how they had come into being by blind historical processes, circuitous routes, and social forces that had nothing to do with rationality and scientific research. By showing the "humble roots" of our present conceptions of normality, health, and maturity, Foucault creates the uncanny experience of seeing oneself from a point of view that makes it difficult to maintain the self-satisfied certainties that make us intolerant and judgmental.

Foucault was very careful not to make the mistake so many other intellectuals made. He never proposed a utopia of his own. He did not believe that previous "truths" about madness, health, sexuality, and the good life had to be supplanted by new dogmas. Instead, he believed that only continuous reflection on the genealogy of our beliefs could create true freedom. For him the completion of Kant's Enlightenment project to allow humanity to come of age was not to be achieved through positive knowledge. Humans could be free only if there was a cultural space that allowed them to shape their selves according to their desire and aesthetic preference.

In an interview Foucault said that the starting point of *The History of Sexuality* was his aggravation while listening to a radio interview in which a psychoanalyst talked about sex. The very idea that there was someone who claimed to be an authority on sexuality, and could therefore say what was "healthy" and what was not, struck him as absurd.

One of Foucault's surprising theses was that the twentieth-century discourse on the liberation of sexuality was a hoax. He argued that the eighteenth and nineteenth centuries created endless discourse about sex, and that the twentieth-century continuation of this discourse was no less coercive than earlier forms. Foucault's deepest and surprising thesis was that the very notion of sexuality was

a form of power-knowledge and normalization. By classifying certain pleasures as sexual, we place them in a grid
that pushes toward normalization. Foucault wanted no
classification: he wanted there to be bodies and pleasures
that could be put together according to the individual's
wish.

This wish becomes more intelligible once we know
the great importance of S&M in Foucault's life. Miller
writes about the surprise and unease of some of the philosophers at Berkeley whom Foucault asked for information
about the S&M clubs in the Castro district. When he discovered them during his first tenure at Berkeley he felt
that he had found something he had looked for throughout his life.

For him S&M was a deep form of complicity and
friendship, in which consenting partners formed a bond to
explore the limits of pain and pleasure, terror and delight.
Here was a form of human contact in which all boundaries
broke down: the inner and the outer, self and nonself,
horror and bliss merged in the theatrical enactments of
consensual S&M.

On a deeper level S&M was a way to encounter the
ghosts that had been buried in Foucault's soul for a lifetime. The images of punishment, mutilation, and incarceration that were condensed in the three memories he told
Hervé Guibert about during the last days of his life were
ineradicable. The rituals of S&M, the encounter with pain
in a setting that was both controlled and protective, provided the opportunity to meet one's deepest fears without
disintegrating.

TWO MODES OF BEARING PAIN

From Freud to Bion psychoanalysis has assumed that the
only way toward psychic maturity leads through developing the capacity to bear psychic pain. Neurosis and psychosis are unavoidable concomitants of trying to avoid

psychic pain in all its forms. In neurosis the psyche tries to avoid consciousness of impulses and affects that are linked to shame and guilt. Psychosis is an attempt to destroy the parts of the psychic apparatus that are in touch with painful realities.

Perversions, Chasseguet-Smirgel (1984) and McDougall (1983, 1995) have argued, are also attempts to evade pain. Sexuality is inherently traumatic, in that it confronts us with limitations: we cannot be both woman and man, nor can we be our own progenitors. If Freud thought that perversions like fetishism are attempts to deny the fact of female castration, McDougall argues that perversions are encoded scripts that both preserve and try to abolish the trauma of separateness and gender.

Tamara and Foucault raise the issue of the importance of bearing psychic pain in a very interesting manner. In the case of Tamara I am able to state with some conviction that neither her dramatic life nor her sexual practices served the function of denying the psychic pains of her past. One of the defining characteristics of Tamara's mental structure was an extraordinary capacity to remember details of her life from early childhood onwards, including their affective contents. Her ability to bear affect was also reflected in her intense, close friendships.

Tamara felt that bearing pain was essential to the possibility of leading a complete life. Sexual masochism for her was a way of meeting pain time and again, but in a way very different from what has been prescribed by classic psychoanalytic theory. She did not suffer pain to accept loss, but to prove to herself that it could not get the better of her. The suffering of pain had to be integrated into the work of art that was her life rather than be left as an unnegotiable facet of her early life.

It might be argued that the result of her mode of dealing with early pain precluded her from achieving full genitality. Such an argument would be the logical implication of two psychoanalytic narratives: first, that genitality is the one, healthy outcome of mental development; second, only if we can accept and suffer mental pain can we keep our minds from fragmenting into disconnected parts. There is an inner logic that connects the two narratives. If the goal of development is acceptance of the strictures of society, the pain these strictures impose must be borne in order to bend the self to the measures prescribed by society.

The narrative of the heroic fight against the limitations of fate leads to a different conclusion: pain must be borne in order to turn the meeting with fate into a source for creativity. Therefore pain must not simply be borne to be accepted, but it must be faced to be transformed and overcome. Correspondingly, this narrative gives rage another place from that assigned by the classical narrative. Instead of seeing rage as an infantile reaction against the order of nature, it tries to channel rage into becoming a source of creative transformation.

REFLECTIONS ON SELF-CREATION, FREEDOM, AND BONDAGE

As Bion (1970) pointed out repeatedly, psychoanalysis, like any other form of depth psychology, always needs myths, narratives that organize psychic reality. The myth of epigenetic development toward genitality has been one of the defining myths of psychoanalysis from the beginning of its history. Only in the last decade has Freud's narrative in the *Three Essays on the Theory of Sexuality* begun to lose its hold over some major psychoanalytic movements. It has become possible to rethink neosexualities in terms other than a regressive avoidance of oedipal conflicts or schizoparanoid distintegration of the psyche.

What other narratives can we use to understand individuals who refuse normative modes of life? The way I have narrated Tamara's and Foucault's lives is inspired by the myth of the heroic fight against the limitations of fate.

This myth, which is at least as old as the myth of Prometheus, has been reformulated in terms of humanistic psychology by Ernest Becker in his seminal *The Denial of Death* (1973).

In this account, the Oedipus complex is not primarily a story about forbidden love for the mother or father and competition with the father or mother. It is an ontological project of self-recreation. The oedipal problem is how to come to terms with the fact that each of us is the result of a sexual act between a woman and a man we have not chosen to be our progenitors. At its extreme, the oedipal desire is not just to sleep with one's mother and to kill one's father, as Diderot said, but to be the cause of one's own being, to be *causa sui.*

Causa sui has been one of the terms by which medieval scholastic philosophy defined God, who is the cause of his own being. The logical conclusion of this train of thought is that the human desire for individuality and authorship culminates in the desire to be self-created, and hence to be God.

How can this desire manifest itself without leading into straightforward psychosis, given that the most obvious fact of existence is that we are *not* self-created? One possible answer to this conundrum is provided by another myth, that has been a powerful presence since the inception of European romanticism. The self is seen as a source of artistic creativity and thus becomes a creator ex nihilo. Harold Bloom (1973) has shown, convincingly, how the history of English romantic poetry can be read as a reflection of the *anxiety of influence,* the fear that the history of poetry does not leave any space for anything radically new to say, and radically new ways of saying it.

What happens if we add the myth of the need for self-creation to the psychoanalytic myths of Oedipus and of the need for environmental support? I think that it enriches our narratives by a new dimension. We would be capable of seeing a need for aesthetic form and for a sense of authorship in neosexualities.

This would, for example, shed completely different

light on the lives of people like Owen Flanagan, the masochist performance artist who died some years ago (Juno and Vale, 1993). Flanagan was born with cystic fibrosis and from early childhood onwards he had to undergo painful and frightening medical procedures in which excess fluids were drained from his lungs. Early in puberty he found out that his true sexual kick came from inflicting pain upon himself or having it inflicted upon him. A book length series of interviews with Flanagan (Juno and Vale, 1993) shows that his masochism and his art were a conscious, reflective attempt to transform the cumulative trauma of the fear of death and the pain of intrusive medical procedures into sexual pleasure. By turning his masochist practices into performance art he pushed this transformation to its utmost conclusion: he turned a cruel fate into a source of creativity.

The lives of Tamara and Foucault can be viewed under a similar light. Both refused to accept early trauma and later stigmatization by society as a fate to be endured passively. Instead they turned their suffering into a source of intellectual and artistic creativity and sexual pleasure instead. Even though they could not recreate their selves from scratch and undo the pain of their early lives, they applied their considerable creative talents to transform their fates into the material for their own will to form.

Their choice of the themes of dominance and bondage as their prime sources of sexual pleasure is but a logical continuation of the theme of self-creation. Both were traumatized by the constraints of social sexual morality and gender construction, and both were unwilling to leave the scars of trauma as sediments of fate that had to be accepted. Instead they chose sexual scenarios that fused sexual pleasure with the feeling of triumph at being able to meet and overcome traumatic pain.

THIS IS NOT A NEW THEORY OF PERVERSION

I want to make one thing as clear as possible: I am not putting forward a new theory of the perversions. It has

been one of the persistent illusions of our profession that
we can arrive at definitive formulations of the deep structure of the mind on the basis of clinical observation
(Strenger, 1991). The most we can do is to formulate narratives that have heuristic usefulness in trying to make
sense of our patients' biographies and mental lives. Arguing for the exclusive rightness of one particular narrative is nothing but an attempt to impose one's preferred
Weltanschauung and lifestyle onto others.

    Chasseguet-Smirgel (1984) sees perversions as the re-
sult of an analization of experience. She assumes that the
perverse mind inevitably flattens out contrasts and lives in
an undifferentiated universe. This may hold true for some
individuals who have opted for neosexual solutions, but it
certainly does not hold for others. Joyce McDougall assumes that neosexualities inevitably carry an obsessive and
driven quality (1983). Again it seems to me, along with
Nancy Chodorow (1994), that any such generalization is
irresponsible. Any exclusive adoption of the view that neosexualities are regressive and characterized by drivenness
implies that one prefers settled, bourgeois lifestyles to unconventional risky modes of life.

    Conversely an uncritical adoption of the heroic narra-
tive of neosexuality as self-creation against all odds is no
less unpalatable. Some perversions (as well as many standard heterosexual solutions) certainly have an obsessive
quality, and deaden the psyche's potential for deeper experience. Exclusive adoption of the heroic narrative of
self-creation boils down to a glorification of deviance and
is equally unsuited to a differentiated understanding of
individual lives as its more conservative counterpart. My
point is that only a detailed examination of individual lives
and psychic textures can tell us what is suitable for whom.

    I think that it would be a mistake to try to argue
exclusively for one rather than the other narrative. Such
argument assumes that our narratives can reflect the ultimate structure of human nature, an assumption that has
been undermined very effectively during the last decades
of postmodern cultural criticism. Foucault's contribution

to this process has been substantial. Psychoanalytic narratives must be judged by the extent to which they contribute to the elucidation of individual lives. The idea that one such narrative—Freudian, Kleinian, Winnicottian, self-psychological or other—will turn out to be equally useful for all of them is one of the illusions that we carry from the past.

My claim is far more modest: I argue that two particular individuals, Tamara and Foucault, were not involved in a battle against nature. Pace Chasseguet's thesis, they were not trying to deny the difference between the generations and the sexes. If anything they were fighting the social constructions that are grafted onto natural differences and they denied society's right to stigmatize those whose sexual and aesthetic preferences do not correspond to the mainstream. Their rebellion carried a distinctly political flavor which, in Foucault's case, was both explicit and to some extent successful.

I try to show that the combination of two narratives—of self-creation and of protest against the social order—is useful in trying to understand these two lives. Given that these narratives are also quite fruitful in interpreting other patients and some cultural phenomena like body-building and Cartesian philosophy (Strenger, 1998), I offer them as additions to the narrative tools which help us to do our daily work of making sense of people's lives and experience.

THE POSSIBILITY OF THE PHILOSOPHICAL LIFE

Two thousand four hundred years ago an Athenian court condemned Socrates to death because he had dared question beliefs cherished by the majority of the polis. Millennia later the vast majority of humankind is still busy condemning and persecuting people because they believe in another religion, have another culture, or another race. As Julia Kristeva (1982) has shown, the history of expelling the other from the domain of the socially legitimate is endless and its impact is still with us. Even in the age of the global village there are still large groups who believe in anything from white supremacy, the superiority of Judaism or Islam, through the absolute rightness of Christian family values, to the need to cleanse areas of other ethnic groups.

The biologist Jared Diamond (1991) has made a powerful case for the idea that xenophobia is a genetically entrenched trait. Biological evolution had no sophisticated ways to keep the gene pool of the group from being harmed by faulty genes. Therefore it programmed us to hate what looks, feels, talks, and believes things different from our own group.

The counterpart to xenophobia is the panic of being excommunicated (cf. Strenger, 1998, chapters 5, 6). If biological nature pushes us toward conformity and uniformity of the group, the individual must have an inborn panic at the possibility of being different, and therefore being expelled.

Clinically we encounter this phenomenon daily. Patients are terrified of "not being normal." So much so, that they often cannot even ask themselves what they really want. If often takes years of work until it dawns on them that they may have asked the wrong question by constantly wondering why they are abnormal.

Psychoanalysis has been one of the important humanizing factors of the twentieth century. Freud grew up in a climate in which degeneracy was the standard medical and anthropological explanation for anything from hysteria through criminality to perversion (Gilman, 1993). By arguing that we are all polymorphously perverse at least unconsciously, Freud opened up the possibility of a discourse that would unite human beings in solidarity rather than looking for rationalizations that would justify claims of superiority of some group.

Notoriously, Freud did not go all the way. It would indeed be irrational and historically naive even to expect him to. We are all historical beings, and there is a limit to the extent to which anyone can detach himself from his historical determination.

The notion of degeneracy continued to exert a hidden, but powerful impact on Freud's thinking and the history of psychoanalysis. Perverts were fixated to a particular form of pleasure, and neurotics were hidden perverts. Their sin was not to have fully grown up, and psychoanalytic developmental theory could tell us where they were fixated. This theory created a great chain of being, an ordered universe of developmental phases and correlated mental disturbances. Ultimately the psychoanalytic theory of neuroses is still a theory of character weakness. It is the story of those who do not want to, or cannot, fully grow up and accept reality. They cannot fully face the "difference between the generations and sexes," and are therefore condemned to destroying the natural order in fantasy and their rituals.

My encounters with Michel Foucault and Tamara were two significant experiences that showed me how wrongheaded and limiting this ordering of the human universe can be. With the risk of being repetitive, I want to emphasize that I am not taking the position of being a new authority on sexual perversion. If anything, I try to question the very idea that such authority is either desirable or possible. Maybe a fruitful psychoanalytic position would rather be to deconstruct the very idea that there must be someone who knows what sexual (or other) pleasures are right or wrong.

People like Tamara and Michel Foucault are rare. They had the determination, the strength of character, and the sheer talent that allowed them to turn their protest into a project of self-creation that not only succeeded ethically and aesthetically, but gave them fame and status as well.

They also felt that their sexuality was part of their project of self-creation. Foucault felt to the end of his life that S&M had given him the ultimate fulfillment of his desires. In the last months of his life, under the shadow of death, he worked feverishly to complete the work that elaborated on his idea that the self was there to be created as an aesthetic creation, and he did not regret the course his own creation had taken.

Even after extensive investigation of the roots of her masochism, Tamara felt that she did not want to change. It was *I* who had to change. I had to renounce some of the certainties that made me believe that I knew in which direction Tamara had to evolve. If I helped her, it was because of my, sometimes reluctant, willingness to remain sufficiently open for our dialogue to continue.

In his last years Foucault investigated the possibility of living a truly philosophical life. He called this view an aesthetics of existence. He sought an ethics that would allow people to form their selves according to their values and tastes rather than striving for "health" or "normality." He thought that he had found a precursor to this view in the Hellenistic schools of Stoic and Epicurean philosophy.

Foucault's historical interpretations have been disputed by several authorities on the topic (cf. Hadot, 1995; Nussbaum, 1995). It seems that both Epicurean and Stoic philosophies were based on the idea of living according to a universal nature that the philosopher had to come to understand in order to live a right life. Foucault may indeed have imposed his twentieth century, postmodern sensibility (and wishes) onto his material.

Even if it was a misunderstanding, it was a creative misunderstanding. Foucault seriously opened the question of whether in our times a serious meaning could be attached to the idea of the philosophical life; a life based on serious examination of the self and based on conscious decisions not necessarily in tune with accepted lore. Tamara and Foucault for me exemplify this possibility of the philosophical life. In Tamara's case I have first-hand evidence for the process that structured her life down to the details of her gender construction.

We live in an age in which most people keep anxiously looking for authoritative statements about how to live their lives. The space of play that has been opened by postmodern thought and practice has failed to liberate many people from the terror of having to be like everybody else.

Psychoanalysis, I believe, stands to gain from moving into this space of freedom. I am not making Tamara and my encounter with her into a paradigm for therapeutic work. Hard cases make bad law, as lawyers say, and extraordinary cases cannot teach us directly what to do with others who seek our help. Nevertheless I feel (and hope) that my encounter with Foucault, Tamara, and the process of reflection and widening of narrative empathy has opened my mind and soul for others whose lives are not necessarily lived on the edge.

6 FOUR CHARACTERS FIND THEIR AUTHORS: CONTEMPORARY PSYCHOANALYTIC VOICES IN WRITING AND CLINICAL DIALOGUE

INTRODUCTION

The contemporary literature is replete with important insights into the therapeutic uses of the analyst's subjectivity. I feel, though, that while subjectivity has received a great deal of attention, therapeutic *voice* (or *presence*, or *character*; I will use the terms more or less interchangeably) has been less investigated. The vignettes that illustrate therapeutic uses of the analyst's subjectivity often center on fleeting moments and temporary affective status. This can make us forget that these states of subjectivity are always organized by more coherent, long-term character traits, beliefs, and attitudes.

Psychotherapists need voice that allows the patient to internalize a more or less coherent presence, because one of the most important agents of therapeutic change is probably the internalization of a new form of dialogue.

The therapist's voice in the patient's mind should, presumably, become a benign presence that counteracts the condemning, sadistic, intolerant introjects that have accompanied the patient for most of her or his life.

Therapeutic presence is an amalgam of temperamental propensities, modes of interaction, styles of interventions, modes of thought, and guiding values. It evolves through the interaction of the therapist's life experience, therapeutic training, personal analysis, ethical and social values, lifestyle, and theoretical views. This presence is internalized through a dialogue in which the analyst's subjectivity is an active, felt participant.

The history of psychoanalysis has taken an interesting trajectory. Throughout the final decades male and paternal metaphors have permeated theory and writing. Interpretation *uncovered* the hidden. The analyst was the *phallus,* the patient desired. Then female and maternal metaphors began to take over the field. The analyst *held* the patient. The patient envied the maternal–analytic *breast.* The analyst was to be the *container* of the patient's psychic contents.

It seems that we have now entered a phase in which parental metaphors of the analytic interaction are finally giving way to more egalitarian conceptions. In Adam Phillip's (1995) words one might say that the ideal state of analytic work is having a fruitful conversation. Analytic interaction is most certainly a very special type of conversation, but it is nevertheless a conversation, and conversations are most definitely a two-way process. Hence the growing emphasis on an, albeit nonsymmetrical, mutuality as a central characteristic of the analytic interaction.

These statements can, I think, be taken to reflect a consensus of late modern psychoanalytic writers in the 1990s. This is in itself rather remarkable, because it shows the extent to which psychoanalysis has changed in outlook in the last decades. Most authors in the various classical traditions would have argued that the analytic therapist's personal predilections are not only irrelevant to the therapeutic process, but that their interference is positively noxious. From the sixties onwards it was legitimate and useful to be aware of one's feelings, but only to the extent that they constituted objective countertransference, i.e., reflected the patient's psychic contents in one way or another.

Today it has not only become commonplace to believe that analysts cannot be neutral, but that they should not try to be. The present-day climate makes previous vices into virtues: awareness of one's subjectivity is not there to neutralize countertransference, but in order to put this subjectivity into disciplined use in therapeutic processes.

I certainly do not want to imply that psychoanalytic individual voice is an invention of the last decades. Throughout the history of psychoanalysis there have been clinicians with unmistakable voice and presence; Ralph Greenson is one of the prime examples. Even though his technique was rather orthodox, Greenson's juiciness can be felt in almost every clinical vignette, and his patients comment upon it rather often, sometimes happily and sometimes with some fear of being overwhelmed.

Contemporary psychoanalytic discourse certainly provides more space for individual voice than there has ever been before. Even though many of the traditional clinical virtues have retained their importance, a new element has been added to our understanding of the analytic clinician's role. It has become of crucial importance to know how to be an individual with a distinct subjectivity within the analytic situation. This is reflected in psychoanalytic writing. Papers are not expected to be neutral, sober, and distanced. An element of poetic voice has become rather positively viewed.

Existentialists and Jungians might, of course, sigh, "Didn't we tell you so for the last eighty years. . . ." Indeed it seems that recent developments in psychoanalysis have made the discipline more open toward ecumenical trends. It is far more common nowadays to find reference to Jung and Jungians. This goes along with a renewed interest in the spiritual dimension of the therapeutic process: Freud's determinedly antireligious stance has ceased to be good

etiquette, and a positive attitude toward religious experience is reflected in a number of recent psychoanalytic writings (Eigen, 1992; Spezzano and Gargiulo, 1997).

The *rapprochements* to other traditions have not diluted the fact that the current search for therapeutic presence is distinctly psychoanalytic in character. What makes
this search particularly complex is that as clinicians our
voice is not supposed to impress, to carry away by enthusiasm, or generate unbridled admiration. It is supposed to
be the counterpoint that allows patients to find *their* voice.
Therefore the question of how the psychoanalyst can find
an authentic voice that has its roots in her deepest personal experience becomes so urgent.

What characterizes voice in the consulting room and
in writing at the end of the twentieth century, then? This
chapter attempts a number of portraits of clinical presences as they are reflected in the recent literature. The
selection neither purports to be representative, and certainly not exhaustive. It centers on Nina Coltart, Christopher Bollas, Adam Phillips, and Michael Eigen who have
become distinct presences in contemporary psychoanalytic discourse, and whose voices have distinct individuality. Their characters shine through every paragraph they
write, and they seem to have found ways of being themselves in the analytic situation as well. While Coltart, Bollas, Phillips, and Eigen have very distinct voices, they never
come across as gurus. They are truly engaged in dialogue,
and they let their patients become themselves rather than
trying to turn them into pale copies of their therapists.

The following portrayals are not concerned with the
authors' theoretical contributions in their own right, but
rather with their voice. If psychoanalytic therapy is an intensely personal undertaking, voice may be no less important than explicit theoretical contribution. Each of
these authors has presented us with their distinct ways of
being individuals within the clinical exchange. They show
that there are ways of using one's subjectivity that do not
impinge on the patient's psyche, but present unique possibilities for this psyche to evolve.

A word on methodology: these portraits are based on these authors' written *oeuvre*. We all know that written communications and actual practice can diverge, even though today's more personal ways of writing may lessen this distance. At any rate written accounts have great influence on what happens in consulting rooms throughout the profession, since they define the professionally acceptable domain. Therefore the investigation of psychoanalytic voice as reflected in the literature can certainly be said to capture important trends in the contemporary psychoanalytic scene.

One more word about selection: this chapter was essentially finished when I came across Anthony Molino's (1997) beautiful *Freely Associated: Encounters in Psychoanalysis with Christopher Bollas, Joyce McDougall, Michael Eigen, Adam Phillips and Nina Coltart*. It was a striking experience to see the convergence in the selections, particularly as I had thought of including Joyce McDougall as well. I refrained from doing so because I felt that I had less of an integrated response to her than to the other four. I have included some quotations from Molino's marvelous volume, and am happy to offer this piece as a resonance to something I had no knowledge of.

SOME CHARACTERS OF CONTEMPORARY PSYCHOANALYSIS

Nina Coltart: Both a Buddhist and an Analyst

Nina Coltart (1992, 1996), with whose portrait I would like to start, is a somewhat unlikely member of a group that characterizes contemporary clinical voices. Nina Coltart was a training analyst at the British Institute in London from the early seventies to the early nineties. What she considered, and unfortunately turned out to be her last book, *The Baby and the Bathwater*, appeared in 1996 when she had largely retired from analytic practice. On purely historical grounds she would have to be reckoned as being part of the generation before the one that creates the contemporary atmosphere.

Nevertheless, I would like to write about her in the present context for two reasons. First and foremost, because I think that her voice constitutes an interesting, viable, and potentially important paradigm for the contemporary clinician. Coltart's is a unique, idiosyncratic voice that one may not be able to emulate, but that constitutes an ideal that we may at times want to approach. The second reason I put her into the present context is because, ahead of her time, Coltart succeeded in exemplifying some of the virtues present-day psychoanalysis has come to cherish.

Coltart's writing is remarkably nontechnical, as a brief look at the index of *The Baby and the Bathwater* shows immediately. "Projective Identification," "Selfobject," "Alpha-Elements," "Internal Objects," and many other theoretical terms do *not* figure in the index. As opposed to that "inspiration," "jokes," "laughing," "smell, patients who," and "vocation" do. Coltart first and foremost tells stories, second of all muses about them. She does so in a way that allows almost every interested layman to follow her thoughts.

Reading her books evokes the presence of a woman who is capable of making therapeutic use of openness, surprise, rage, laughter, intense concentration, obvious liking, and intense dislike. Coltart works and writes in an intensely personal way, and is nevertheless unobtrusive. Her mind becomes a reflection of her patient's human realities. She openly expresses her horror at the destructivity of a patient headed for suicide, and does not hide her dismay at the impossibility of reaching this man who seems to want nothing more than to head for disaster. But neither her judgment nor her dismay are strident and moralistic. They are expressions of her human sensibility that is sufficiently honed never to become a hindrance for the reader in reflecting upon Coltart's experience.

Coltart's voice is in many ways an heir to the distinguished tradition of British humanistic writing from David Hume and Samuel Johnson to Michael Oakeshott and Isaiah Berlin. This tradition has always valued thought and writing that expresses a distinctly personal point of view that nevertheless lets the object of writing shine through rather than covering it up. David Hume's *History of England* (1762) was condemned by all parties when it was published, because it was not partisan history. It was written with the distinct voice of dispassionate skepticism in the service of liberating humanity from the throes of stifling dogma. Coltart brings this quality into the consulting room and into her writing about clinical practice and living a life.

The empiricist sensibility of their British lineage is reflected in the ways in which Coltart brings her medical background to bear on her clinical judgment. Psychoanalysts often write as if the psyche was devoid of embodiment, as if nothing but fantasies mattered. Even though the body seemingly looms large in psychoanalytic theory, it is more often a fantasized body than the actual observable body with its kinesthetic, aesthetic, and medical characteristics. I often sorely miss descriptions of physical presence in psychoanalytic writing (I don't think that this is primarily due to respect for the patient's privacy, important as it may be). With Coltart physical being-in-the-world receives the attention it deserves, whether from the medical or from the existential point of view.

Another salient characteristic of Coltart's presence is what I should call an unobtrusive, calm spirituality completely devoid of preaching quality. A practicing Buddhist for decades, her writing and clinical style have a quality of selflessness that has nothing to do with suffering self-sacrifice, or moral masochism. It is rather that she seems to be object-related in the best sense of the word. She can use her thoughts, her emotions to let human realities, whether general or of particular patients, shine through.

Yet again her selflessness is not to be confused with a lack of personal voice. After several pages the reader becomes acquainted with a very distinct voice and perspective. Coltart is modest, but she has sound, strong judgment that she is not afraid to make heard. Her spiritual perspective is a prism that helps us to see rather than a set of beliefs that blinds.

Coltart makes sparse use of theory, and this again is one of the reasons why her writing is so transparent. While knowing her psychoanalytic theory, she does not feel compelled to cling to it. She writes in terms that are acceptable to all. When she asks what people are gifted for analytic work (both as patients and as therapists), she answers the question in terms that are devoid of jargon. In this respect she connects to the Scottish tradition of commonsense philosophy. Coltart shows that psychoanalysis at its best need not be hermetic and obfuscating, but can be a sophisticated use of humane and literary intelligence.

Coltart is prematurely late modern in one distinct sense: she loves psychoanalysis for being a cultural form of life that allows people to find out about themselves. Yet she has very little respect for the pompousness of transcendentalized conceptions of psychoanalysis. For her analysis is the ability to maintain a type of relationship and to conduct a type of conversation that might open people to their own experience. Her writings attempt to pour out the bathwater of pomposity and pseudoknowledge, without losing the baby of the distinctly psychoanalytic ways of listening and being helpful.

Her attraction to and admiration of Bion is not so much geared toward any particulars of his theory, but to Bion's constant striving to open both psychoanalysts and their patients to experience. This is where her analytic identity, her British empiricism, and her Buddhism merge: at the end of all exploration there will be no dramatic insight, but rather the disappearance of cloggedness of the mind.

In an interview with Anthony Molino, the transcript of which she endorsed days before her untimely death, she said about herself: "Well, I suppose it's rather a contradiction in terms, but I would like to say that if I have been consciously sensitive to my place in the psychoanalytic tradition, it's been as the most independent representative of the Independent Group. I couldn't possibly have belonged to anything but the Independent Group. And I suppose if my message has been anything, it's been to follow your gift" (Molino, 1997, p. 177).

The Independent Group arose to begin with because of the need of a number of members of the British Society not to swear allegiance to either Anna Freud or Melanie Klein. Nevertheless Coltart ended up leaving the Psychoanalytic Society because she could not bear the warfare between the various groups and the religious fanaticism of some of its members (Molino, 1997, p. 170).

She obviously had no taste for the infighting necessary to maintain an individual voice in an environment that was hostile to it, and therefore found that she could more easily breathe outside the Society. By refusing to get involved in the fight about the right doctrine and administrative power, Coltart foreshadowed what is becoming one of the most important characterizations of the emerging contemporary psychoanalytic culture. She enjoyed and cherished her individual voice rather than seeing it as a threat to unified doctrine.

The other three examples of contemporary psychoanalytic voice are men. Nina Coltart is not a distinctly feminine voice in the sense that she is not part of the current feminine and feminist contribution and presence so important to current psychoanalytic discourse. Nevertheless there is a yinlike quality to the transparency of her voice, an almost complete effortlessness that allows her voice to just *be*. There is no sense that she had to shape it.

Coltart said in an interview: "While not easy to formulate, part of my attitude to producing books has been to write the way I speak and teach, as well as the way I analyze. Patients of mine who've read my books say they hear me all along in them. This pleases me, because I don't have to tell you that an awful lot of analytic writing is extremely heavy, turgid, pompously theatrical, and quite boring . . ." (Molino, 1997, p. 165).

This effortless unity of personal, therapeutic, didactic, and written voice is an important aspect of Coltart's gift to psychoanalytic culture. An important part of what psychoanalytic therapy is meant to impart to its patients is a more authentic, less compartmentalized way of being. Coltart shows us how the rapprochement between the various levels of being can be a lived reality for the psychoanalytic clinician and writer as well.

CHRISTOPHER BOLLAS: THE NECESSITY OF BEING A CHARACTER

If Nina Coltart shows the virtue of being an unclouded mind, Bollas (1987, 1989, 1992, 1995) exemplifies the virtue of allowing oneself to be a character. Steeped in psychoanalytic theory, literary theory, and the experience of living with literary texts and musical works, Bollas does not shy away from living the contents of his mind to the fullest.

Bollas's major theme is how the self evolves through the use of objects. His metaphor for the true self is *personal idiom*. He develops Winnicott's idea of the true self and its use of objects in an original way. Like Winnicott, Bollas points out that the self cannot evolve without using objects, and that there is an aspect of experience in which concern for the other can be noxious to the self. In an apt example Bollas shows how the self must be centered on its possible futures (1989, pp. 41–44) in the choice of a partner. Since objects are the medium through which idiom can evolve, the choice of the wrong object can leave the self in a static state, and therefore we must be ruthless in major choices. Concern for the other as an overriding ethical value may be laudable, but at crucial junctures altruism can have destructive consequences.

Bollas (1992) sees the self as an aesthetic that strives to come to the fore, and to realize itself. The inborn potentialities do not contain specific contents. These evolve through generative object use. The results are what Bollas calls *psychic genera,* aspects of the psyche-soma that strive for further encounter with objects that allow them to evolve, differentiate, and crystallize further. Bollas's writings abound with subtle analyses of the structure of everyday experience. His ear is geared toward the ways in which the psyche is in constant interaction with the outside world to generate and modify personal meanings. Bollas's view of the psyche is that essentially it seeks neither pleasure nor attachment to objects. Its primary goal is a constant process of becoming and evolving.

"The dream is an intelligence of form that holds, moves, stimulates, and shapes us. When I enter the world of dreams I am deconstructed, as I am transformed from the one who holds the internal world in my mind to the one who is experientially inside the dramaturgy of the other." This randomly chosen passage from *Being a Character* (1992, p. 14) shows one of the most salient features of Bollas's voice: his way of writing mirrors the experience he is trying to capture.

Bollas tries to follow the minute ways in which the psyche strives to constantly elaborate itself through making use of objects and in the ways it generates and structures experience. The psyche is depicted as undertaking a constant search for evocation. Objects are sought that evoke psychic genera, and Bollas's way of writing is a constant exemplification of the very process he talks about.

He presents vignettes of personal experience which make this process tangible. He shows how his own psyche seeks different objects throughout the day that will reverberate with different aspects of his experience. The sports page resonating with experiences from childhood onwards, may awaken the "phantom-self" of the athlete he chose not to become. Brahms's Fourth Symphony allows a sensuous form of melancholy feeling to evolve. Taking care of his son makes him wistfully aware of the ruthlessness with which the self seeks the objects that present opportunities for idiom to evolve further.

Bollas refrains from using a standard diagnostic vocabulary, and instead coins terms of his own like *normotic*

personality, antinarcissist, or *ghostline personality.* In doing
so he does not try to add further diagnostic options to the
next edition of the DSM. His intent is rather to sharpen
our vision for ways in which individuals are trapped in
modes of being that do not allow them to make an object
use that allows them to develop their personal idiom.

One of the main extensions of this view of the self
and its evolution is Bollas's very original understanding of
the therapeutic process (1989, chapters 1, 2). He differen-
tiates between deconstructive and elaborative functions of
psychoanalytic activity. The first comes close to what is
traditionally called analysis of transference. In it rigid, paradigmatic uses of the analyst are understood in order to
make room for what Bollas considers to be the most important part of the analytic interchange.

The patient ultimately turns to analysis because she
has not found the objects that would allow her self to
flourish. Impingements, disappointments, and failures of
the environment to support the self have led the patient
either to protect herself by not using objects at all, or to
endlessly repeat interactive modes that are not conducive
to growth.

Bollas directs our attention to a quiet, undramatic,
and yet essential layer of analytic work, what he calls the
elaborative function of the analysis. The analyst must know
how to be an object that allows the patient's idiom to
evolve. Bollas's central thesis is that in order for the analyst
to constitute such an object, he needs to know how to be
a subject within the analytic situation. The analyst who is
afraid of spontaneous reactions like laughter, anger, and
seemingly unrelated associations will not be capable of
providing the patient with the type of object she needs to
evolve as a subject.

This is a crucial departure from the classical psychoanalytic image of the analyst as a transference figure or
container of split-off parts of the patient's self. These images assumed that the analyst's actual subjectivity is not of
any importance, because the very idea of the elaborative
function of analysis had not come to the fore.

By emphasizing how the analyst's actual subjectivity provides the object the patient needs in order for her idiom to evolve, Bollas makes an important contribution to the late modern efforts to understand the personal element of the analytic process. Bollas provides the practicing clinician with a tool to understand processes many of us have been dimly aware of, but may have felt vaguely guilty about. Clinicians with open minds have always felt that there are many little interchanges that seem very important to the patient even though they do not constitute "analytic work" according to classical models. Bollas's view of the elaborative function of analysis allows us to focus on the ways in which our subjectivity provides an indispensable object to the patient's growth.

Bollas does not shy away from writing about the idiosyncratic ways in which he uses personal associations, his own elaborations of classical theories, and his own affective responses in relating to the patient. He does not argue that each of these details has been "put into him" by the patient. He presents them as what they are: his own subjective responses, but he also provides a theoretical rationale for the therapeutic use of these responses through his narrative of the patient's true self use of the analyst's subjectivity.

Nevertheless it is important to differentiate between Bollas's understanding of this process and emphasis on mutuality characteristic of current New York based relational thinking. For Bollas the patient's true self use of the analyst's subjectivity is not characterized by mutuality. His guiding metaphor is taken from Winnicott's idea of the provision of a facilitating environment that allows the patient's true self to emerge. By allowing his true subjectivity its place in the analytic process, Bollas elaborates on this theme, but he does not believe that mutual recognition is what will make the analysand grow. It is rather that the analyst's subjectivity fulfills an environmental function previously not recognized by psychoanalytic theory.

ADAM PHILLIPS: AGAINST PSYCHOANALYTIC POMPOSITY, OR THE VIRTUES OF THE UNCOMMITTED LIFE

On Kissing, Tickling and Being Bored (1993), *On Flirtation: Psychoanalytic Essays on the Uncommitted Life* (1994), *Terrors and Experts* (1995): Such are the titles of some of Adam Phillips's books, or more precisely, essays. In literature there is the genre of the novella, placed between the short story and the novel. Adam Phillips has become the master of the corresponding form of psychoanalytic writing. His essays provide a fascinating option for a psychoanalytic voice, an intriguing way of having a distinctly psychoanalytic perspective without the pitfalls of pomposity that have characterized psychoanalysis at many of its less enticing junctures.

Phillips does not strive toward an integrated theoretical contribution. His essays are loosely held together by some themes, and Phillips lets the writing take him where it leads rather than sticking to a tight argumentative thread. The reader is lured by an associative literary style, and the major enjoyment stems from often insightful aperçus rather than an elaborated thesis. Phillips's tone is conversational, he looks for enjoyment and interest rather than unity of exposition. What unites his rapidly growing *oeuvre* is ultimately voice rather than content, style rather than integrated perspective.

Phillips is, as yet, rarely quoted in the more strictly professional psychoanalytic literature. The reason for this regrettable state of affairs is that Phillips is truly subversive. As opposed to many authors who announce their subversiveness all over the place while making every effort to root their practice and discourse in the establishment, Phillips does not leave any space to tame his writing.

Phillips's most subversive, and to my mind most compelling, claim is that psychoanalysis is essentially a form of having helpful conversations. It would be against Phillips's own spirit and words to turn him into an expert about what psychoanalysis *really, essentially* is. If, as he says (1995, p. xvi), psychoanalysis is telling stories about stories, then his own story about psychoanalysis is one possible story. Nevertheless it is a story worth listening to at this juncture of psychoanalytic history. Once our pretensions that psychoanalysis uncovers the essence of the human mind have been shattered, the question is indeed how one can do psychoanalysis without usurping the role of an expert on a topic on which there is no expert knowledge to be had, namely how to live a human life well.

Phillips can be read as providing an interesting psychoanalytic voice for those who find the current tendency to look for experts on how to live their lives stifling and often laughable. He points out the ways in which psychoanalysis has turned itself into the opposite of what it once used to be. If for quite some time, psychoanalysis showed the self-possessed bourgeoisie how little they really knew about themselves, psychoanalysts for decades told candidates, patients, and the world at large, how much psychoanalysis knows about early infancy, the roots of suffering, and the goals of maturity. The result is aptly described in the following words: "Most psychoanalytic theory now is a contemporary version of the etiquette book; improving our internal manners, advising us on our best sexual behavior (usually called maturity, or mental health, or a decentered self). It is, indeed, dismaying how quickly psychoanalysis has become the science of the sensible passions. . . . " (1995, p. 87).

Possibly Phillips's most important contribution is to have pointed out that the pretensions of psychoanalytic knowledgeability can have the most antipsychoanalytic effect imaginable. Instead of making the clinician and the patient curious about how strange and interesting they and human life in general are, they can make them afraid not to correspond to some predetermined notion of what they should be like.

This danger is by no means a figment of the imagination of those who do not like the establishment. Otto Kernberg can certainly not be accused of being outside the establishment. Nevertheless he wrote a courageous and insightful paper about institutional problems in teaching psychoanalysis, in which he showed in detail how the structure of psychoanalytic institutes can have a paranoiagenic effect (Kernberg, 1987). The more frightened the practicing clinician is, the more likely is she to transmit her lack of inner freedom to her patients.

Phillips has a political agenda. He believes that the monopolization of the title "psychoanalyst" by a central institution does not serve the profession well. "From my point of view a psychoanalyst is anyone who uses what were originally Freud's concepts of transference, the unconscious and the dream-work in paid conversations with people about how they want to live" (1995, p. xiv).

No one should have the right to define what the right way to preserve Freud's legacy is. By now there is a century of psychoanalytic discourse and practice, and the interpretation and continuation of this cultural tradition cannot be institutionally limited.

Phillips, who has a lot of therapeutic experience with children, is acutely aware of the consequences of the tendency of psychoanalytic institutions to be run in terms of a family: authority becomes defined in generational terms, and can therefore be maintained by fiat. At least one psychoanalytic branch tends to define mental health in terms of accepting the difference between the sexes and generations, and has indeed used this supposedly objective diagnostic criterion to disqualify rival institutions based on perverse character structures.

Phillips is not interested in entering the power struggles within psychoanalysis. He does not publish in the central psychoanalytic journals. Most of his books are published by Faber, a venerable publisher primarily of fiction and poetry. If anything Phillips is trying to define some open space outside questions of legitimacy, normality, and purported mental health.

Within that space Phillips develops his own, idiosyncratic voice. His goal is to have conversations that help people to become curious about rather than frightened of themselves. His latest book to date, *The Beast in the Nursery* (1998), is an exploration of the unashamedness of curiosity and desire in childhood. While not idealizing children in a Rousseauan manner, Phillips refrains from providing a developmental narrative that shows how we are supposed to become sensible by giving up childhood illusions. If anything he points out the price paid for becoming too sensible and hence losing the ability to passionately desire anything.

Phillips carefully avoids the duality between a classicist suspicion of human nature and a romanticist idealization of it (see chapters 3 and 4 above). Correspondingly he wants neither to be in an attitude of suspicious search for hidden motives, nor of self-righteous identification with those who did not have good-enough parents. Instead he tries to maintain an attitude of ironic curiosity. For him psychoanalysis at its best says, "How funny that human beings should be that way!" He neither endorses nor condemns human nature, he actually doesn't have much use for the very notion of human nature.

A good psychoanalytic story for him is one that makes human beings interesting, primarily to themselves. A useful psychoanalytic dialogue would give patients (a term Phillips dislikes) a perspective on themselves that makes them into people whose story is worth telling. He tries to make us see the interest in the small manifestations of human life without dramatizing them.

Phillips does not give a great deal of clinical illustration. I should imagine, though, that people working with him would gradually internalize an attitude of puzzled curiosity. They would gradually cease trying to find out what the right thing to do or say is, and instead accept that the sheer factuality of existence is of far more importance than any normative conception of mental health. In one of his most beautiful pieces of writing (1992, chapter 1), Phillips shows that the ability to simply accept the contingency of human lives is an important achievement. We do not like coincidences, because they undermine our sense that the world is somehow attuned to our needs or desires. Nevertheless the inability to accept coincidences leaves those obsessed with hidden continuity without the possibility of using contingency.

Phillips thus goes against the grain of the psychoanalytic tendency always to look for the deeper reason why something happened. The unconscious can often become a way to make people responsible for all that happens to them. Phillips neither wants to exculpate, nor to victimize. He just wants some open space where people can marvel at the fact that things just happened to be as they were. Accepting coincidences may indeed be the only way of trying to create beauty around them, as Kundera has pointed out in his beautiful meditation on coincidence in book 4 of *The Unbearable Lightness of Being* (1984). By accepting contingency we also, invariably, accept the limitations of our knowledge. Omniscient explanation gives way to the surprise of finding out about the inexplicable, and, maybe, to the possibility of making fruitful use of it.

Phillips is almost vociferous in his condemnation of all forms of psychoanalytic pompousness:

> Psychoanalysis, as theory and practice, should not pretend to be important instead of keeping itself interesting (importance is a cure for nothing). You would think, reading the professional literature, that it was psychoanalysis that mattered and not what it was about. It is not the future of psychoanalysis that anyone should be concerned about, but rather the finding of languages for what matters most to us; for what we suffer from and for, for how and why we take our pleasures. . . .

> But when psychoanalysts spend too much time with each other, they start believing in psychoanalysis. They begin to talk knowingly, like members of a religious cult. It is as if they have understood something [1995, p. xvi].

His distaste for pomposity and unwarranted claims of knowledge betrays a strong ethical commitment to human freedom. Phillips's message is that even if totalitarianism and the use of knowledge as power may not be avoidable in other contexts, at least the psychoanalytic consulting room should be devoid of it. Otherwise the psychoanalytic ethos of autonomy can end up being a thinly veiled form of coercion into conformity.

Phillips's celebration of the uncommitted life may not be to everybody's taste. Neither will all analysts think that someone who hasn't made a substantial, coherent contribution to psychoanalytic theory is really worth reading. If, however, we seek interesting voices, not in order to emulate them, but in order to explore the space of possibilities open to the analytic practitioner and thinker, to develop his or her own voice, Phillips's contribution is worth considering. Not because it is weighty, but because it helps us to see the existential, intellectual, and clinical virtues of lightness of touch.

MICHAEL EIGEN: IN SEARCH FOR PSYCHOANALYTIC SPIRITUALITY

For most of its history psychoanalysis (as opposed to Jungian analytic psychology and humanistic psychology) had no room for spirituality as a positive notion. The schism between Freud and Jung defined the position of warring factions for the better part of a century. Freudians looked at Jungians as murky obscurantists, Jungians looked at Freudians as soulless analyzers. The eighties brought a gradual blurring of these boundaries, and nowadays psychoanalysts can again talk about spirituality without having to dissect it in terms of some infantile illusion.

Michael Eigen is one of the most distinctive champions of this late modern rapprochement between the languages of spirituality and psychoanalysis. He relies heavily on Bion, the classical psychoanalyst whose concern with the spiritual bordered on the mystical. Bion very rarely presented clinical material that would have shown how the spiritual plays a role in daily work. Eigen transforms Bion's

spiritual concerns about psychic truth into dense, concrete, prose that is saturated with experiential detail.

Within two decades Eigen has published a remarkable
oeuvre that has established him as a powerful voice in contemporary psychoanalysis. Eigen's first book, *The Psychotic
Core* (1986), is a sustained meditation on the nature of
madness that is centered on Freud, Jung, Federn, and
Bion as theoretical inspirations. In it Eigen establishes a
style of writing that seeks to grasp madness not so much
as a manifestation of pathology, but as the inability to live
with human despair. Bion's idea is that in order to become
fully human we must be capable of suffering our pain;
and facing our psychic catastrophe looms large in Eigen's
writings, and he has returned to it repeatedly.

What makes Eigen's voice unique is not so much his
theoretical contribution per se, but his ability to make
Bionian notions like faith and catastrophe concrete and
sensible. Eigen's writings abound with clinical detail, and
the striving for integrity, spiritual wholeness, and human
meaning are taken out of the realm of resounding abstrac-
tions and become a lived reality.

Eigen is not afraid of putting himself on the line.
The Afterword to his collection of papers *The Electrified
Tightrope* (1993) is an intensely personal account of his
way toward inner peace and a sense of integrity. Eigen
makes explicit what holds true for all psychoanalytic writers: our theory is always an attempt to gain authorship
over our own lives (Strenger, 1998). Eigen does not turn
his writings into a *roman à clef* that requires decoding of
his motivations, but instead shows his own, complex trajectory as a person and a clinician. This does not detract from
his clinical and theoretical contribution, but provides it
with a stamp of authenticity.

In a touching description of an encounter with a
beautiful, suave, articulate, and elegant woman patient
Eigen relates his sense of unattractiveness vis-à-vis this
woman (1992, p. 65). He does not go on to interpret this
feeling as being the result of the patient's projective identification. Instead he simply relates his own attempt to find

the value of what he had to give to this patient. This is an instant of spiritual struggle. We all find envy, a sense of inferiority, and a questioning of the value of what we have to give in ourselves. More often than not psychoanalytic accounts of such feelings in the analyst tend to put the onus of responsibility onto the patient. The understanding is supposed to be complete when we understand how the patient has tried to put his or her unbearable shame/pain/envy/aggression into ourselves.

But what is more natural than for a man to wonder how a beautiful woman could ever find him attractive as a man and as an analyst (even though he knows that his contact with her will never be other than therapeutic)? And how can this painful question not have a radical impact on the way he will or will not be capable of being therapeutically useful to this woman?

Eigen's spirituality expresses itself nowhere more clearly than in the moments in which he asks these questions. They have a simple, existential urgency. He does not analyze away his own pain when he feels that a male patient lives the life he would have liked to live in his twenties; he just tries to bear it.

This is where Eigen links up to the great spiritual traditions that have always asked how we can live with pain, limitations, envy, and frustration without losing the joy of life and a sense of meaning. One of the classic answers has always been that we need to find something of lasting value in ourselves. Eigen shows in detail how the process of acquiring this sense of value is a constant struggle.

Patients force us to face our own catastrophe time and again. The most dangerous temptation is to accuse the patient as the source of one's pain. The notion of projective identification, useful as it may be at times, is particularly dangerous in this respect. Every unpleasant feeling is traced to the patient's attempt to rid him- or herself of it. Eigen does not succumb to this temptation. He knows that analytic work requires him to suffer his own pain if he is ever to be able to help patients to live with theirs.

The search for transcendence becomes a concrete, lived reality in Eigen's work. In order to live with pain and envy we must transcend our limitations as human beings. Transcendence reached is never a wordless, mystical unity for Eigen; it is the ability to truly experience joy on a different level. Even though Eigen hardly uses the notion of sublimation, his writing and clinical experience make the idea of sublimation tangible. By finding ever new ways of overcoming emotional deadlock and living through the pain of unfulfilled desire, Eigen provides concrete instances of the human ability for transcendence.

Eigen's spirituality is specifically psychoanalytic. Even though he likes analogies with religious thought, in his clinical work and writing this spirituality gains its psychoanalytic dimension by being linked to bodily and affective experience. Eigen explores the depths of primordial experience in Bion's tradition, but, I dare say, he reaches a precision and richness of nuance that Bion never achieved.

Thus Bion's transformation from catastrophe to faith becomes a lived reality. In the moment to moment descriptions of affective states, their stasis, and transformation, Eigen comes fully into his own. In Eigen's descriptions psychoanalytic writing reaches the heights of poetry, and when Eigen says, "Nowadays, I think of psychoanalysis as an aesthetic, as a form of poetry" (Molino, 1997, p. 104) his writings turn this saying into less of a metaphor than one would assume at first glance.

Eigen's writings at times remind me of the tales of the great Hassidic rabbis (Wiesel, 1984). Like them he knows that life's hazards can easily make us lose faith in the goodness of God and of life. And like them he does not settle for enlightened understanding of the limitations of life. Nothing but true joy will do as a reason to live. As in the Hassidic tales, Eigen puts great emphasis on depth of experience; adaptation to reality, important as it may be, often hides experiences of deadness and despair. Eigen is willing to thread on the path of Hassidic teachers like Nachman of Bratslav and Mendel of Kotzk: he travels the road from despair to joy time and again, because he prefers the hardships of this journey with its aliveness to the safety of compromise that often entails loss of soul.

Eigen is unique in the way in which he combines this ability for living with extreme affect with the psychoanalytic tradition of lucidity. This is what prevents his writing and his clinical work from sliding into the saccharine sweetness that characterizes some of the work in the humanistic tradition. He is never content to call upon his patients for self-realization. Instead he accompanies them in the search for psychic truth, in the faith that this will ultimately help them to move toward openness to experience and life.

FAREWELL TO ARMS: THE NEW CULTURE OF INDIVIDUAL VOICE

Coltart, Bollas, Phillips, and Eigen are very distinct voices. This is why I chose them to begin with. Nevertheless there are some themes that connect between them. All of them have little use for allegiance to schools and see the received institutional aspect of psychoanalysis as a hindrance to psychoanalytic thought, practice, and creativity. None of them has any ambition to enter the arena of political struggle, and they find their individual ways to fulfill their vocations.

They have little patience with those who fanatically believe in the unique rightness of their own approach. Tolerance for plurality and multiplicity is a virtue for them, both for analyst and patient. They do not believe in the ideal of the unity of the self anymore than they believe in the ideal of the unity of psychoanalytic theory and its organization.

They are not worried by the ways in which psychoanalysis is gradually turning into a loosely knit cultural movement rather than a tightly organized scientific organization. If anything they think that this is of advantage. All of them are defenders of the need for privacy of

the self, both of the analyst and the patient. They have
no need to turn out well-analyzed, normal, well-adapted
clinicians and patients.

They therefore celebrate individual voices rather than
theoretical tightness. Phillips and Eigen both explicitly say
that they are more interested in the analogies between
psychoanalysis and art, particularly poetry, than they are
in the relationship between psychoanalysis and science.
They are therefore far less interested in finding common
denominators and to generate consensus. You will rarely,
if ever, find diagnostic considerations of the standard sort
in their discussion of patients. What matters is the individual patient or the individual analytic writer or clinician.
Coltart is interested whether a candidate has true vocation
rather than looking for impeccable technique.

What we are witnessing is a new form of psychoanalytic culture that is interested in whether books, interpretations, and modes of thought are interesting and fruitful
rather than whether they are in line with some standard
practice. Analogously they are far more interested whether
the patient finds an authentic mode of being rather than
whether he fits some preconceived standard of mental
health. This new psychoanalytic culture will, I trust, in due
time do a lot of good for generations of clinicians and
patients alike.

There are differences between their voices, of course.
They put different emphases, and they put varying weights
on the different ideals that guide analytic thought and
practice. Isaiah Berlin has shown throughout his life work
how various ideals we have in the political sphere compete
with each other (1958). Our striving for equality and our
belief in liberty conflict with each other. The belief that
there is a state of affairs in which all ideals are fulfilled to
the same degree, what Berlin calls the belief in the final
solution, is one of the persistent illusions of Western metaphysical and political thought.

Berlin does not slide into the facile relativism so fash-
ionable in many quarters nowadays. He believes that there
are values that have objective validity. The problem is that

their claims on us conflict with each other. This is why political and ethical dilemma is not a function of lack of knowledge, but an inevitable feature of human reality.

I have tried to show elsewhere (Strenger, 1998) that Berlin's demonstration that not all ideals can be fulfilled at once, that adhering to one value may force us to sacrifice, or at least lose emphasis on, other values, holds true for psychoanalysis as well. Hence the development of an individual therapeutic voice involves choices and reflects the clinician's beliefs about what really matters both in life and in therapeutic processes.

In developing one's therapeutic voice, one is faced with dilemmas. The schools that thought that psychoanalysis uncovers one, preexisting psychic truth could fight about what this truth is. If psychoanalysis is a specialized form of conversation, and if the analyst's subjectivity and individuality have a crucial impact on how this conversation evolves, it is clear that the clinician's voice will be more helpful in bringing out certain aspects of the patient's subjectivity than others.

LIGHTNESS AND HEAVINESS

One such dilemma is exemplified in Milan Kundera's (1984) pertinent and fascinating question whether lightness or heaviness is to be considered good for human life. This question is highly relevant to clinical work. Of the four voices presented in this paper, Eigen's is certainly the heaviest and Phillips's the lightest. Eigen's belief is that the way toward being truly alive leads through the dire straits of existential despair, through meeting one's catastrophe.

Phillips, while obviously deeply appreciative of Eigen's work (cf. his Introduction to Eigen [1993]), would certainly not accept this as an unquestionable fact. He prefers a more deconstructive, ironical tone in his own writings. For him no form of drama reflects the intrinsic structure of life. If anything, he puts a premium on stories that are interesting and, if possible, he would probably prefer the patient to smile about the incoherences of her life rather than seeking the inevitable catastrophe lurking behind it.

What is better then: lightness or heaviness? Eigen tends to take his patients through the whirlwinds of their psychic lives, assuming that this is what will give them true strength. His patients are likely to experience a spiritual journey, and to feel that they have been to the abyss in order to reach heights that they looked for. They may gain an appreciation of the deeper recesses of their minds, and feel that after having been through their own hells, they are now capable of facing the hardships of life with more authentic strength.

But, one may ask, is there not a price to be paid for this? Are patients who have become honed to the depth of despair not prone to experience life in overly dramatic terms? Cannot the narrative of the spiritual journey through catastrophe to faith fixate patients to suffering rather than liberate them from it?

Phillips is more likely to see the advantages of a more ironical approach. He might point out that patients often tend not to dramatize their plight to begin with. He might want to evoke their curiosity about desire and its vicissitudes, to get them to accept that unconsciously they preferred passion over safety, and that they have never become quite as reasonable as they thought they were. As a result the patients might more often than not smile about themselves and the tenacity with which they refuse to give up the intensity of childhood experience.

Lightness of touch can have its dangers as well. Patients can often feel abandoned if their analysts do not accept their experience of catastrophe as they subjectively experience it. Irony can often bring relief, but it can also create a sense of unbearable loneliness when the patient feels that the analyst cannot empathize with his pain.

SATURATION AND TRANSPARENCY

Let us now look at another dilemma. Psychoanalytic voice can be more or less saturated with the analyst's subjectivity. Let me call this dimension *density of voice*. Coltart seems to be at one end of the spectrum; her voice is particularly transparent. While her presence is personal, it has a peculiar way of directing attention away from itself. It is, so to speak, a medium through which the human reality of the patient's psyche shines.

Bollas's voice is more saturated. This is not to mean that it drowns the patient's voice. It is rather that Bollas gives more space to the various levels of his psyche that are evoked by the patient's presence, the contents of the session, and the dynamics of the interaction.

Bollas rarely uses the term *countertransference*. Rather, he tries to show how the patient evokes responses inside the analyst's mind that are very idiosyncratically his. He does not think that these responses reflect the patient's in any direct ways. He rather thinks that the patient brings particular aspects of his, Bollas's, subjectivity to the fore. Hence the analyst's individual subjectivity is given a more concrete attention. The density of personal association that is deemed relevant by Bollas is higher than it is with Coltart.

Bollas may actually not be an ideal example for density of voice. Much clearer instantiation of dense voices are to be found in the Jungian and existentialist camps. Jung emphasized that every patient demanded the full engagement of all of the therapist's personality, beliefs, and values. Existentialists tend to emphasize the notion of encounter, and their presence in the consulting room is therefore by and large much more felt.

Density of voice will rather increase the patient's experience of his or her individuality as it evolves through an intense interaction. At its extreme this is exemplified through the tendency of existential therapists at crucial junctures to call upon their patients to take responsibility for their lives. The therapist takes a strong stance, not in order to impose a point of view, but in order to mobilize the patient as fully as possible. Another way favored by existential therapists is by telling their patients stories that come into their minds, thus trying to shift the patient's perspective.

What are the advantages and disadvantages of density of voice? Schematically speaking, I should say that the higher the density of voice, the more the patient will experience the therapeutic process in terms of dialogue with another human being. The more transparent the voice, the more the patient will experience the analyst's presence as a way to hear his own, the patient's, voice.

Dense personal presence, if it is therapeutic, and not simply the therapist's way of forcing his or her views on the patient, has a strongly mobilizing effect. It enables patients to develop their voices through dialogue. The therapeutic voyage becomes inextricably linked to the specific interaction between two human beings. The intersubjectivity of the process, that has become the focus of so much psychoanalytic writing, is more explicit.

Density of therapeutic voice is therefore rather a matter of emphasis on how the patient's voice will primarily develop. Metaphorically speaking one might say that dense therapeutic presence leads to a focus on personal interaction, whereas transparency leads to a more listening stance in both the patient and the therapist. Both listen to the patient's contents, and the atmosphere will tend to be more reflective, trying to make sense of what has been said. It is more likely to induce a sharper differentiation, between what ego psychology called the experiencing and the reflecting ego.

Lest I be misunderstood, I do not want to present Eigen, Phillips, Bollas, and Coltart as more monolithic than they are. I am sure that Eigen has moments of lightness and that Phillips can bear with patients in their moments of despair. Coltart (1992, chapter 10) gives examples of dense presence at crucial moments, and Bollas's voice has moments of lucid transparency. The false response would be to commit once and forever to one particular tone of voice for all patients at all moments.

Nevertheless choices must be made. At every moment the therapist must choose a tone of voice. Since there is no such thing as a neutral tone of voice, it is necessary to commit, to take a stance. This stance should be open enough to allow patients the freedom to find their own way of relating to themselves, but not choosing a tone of voice is as realistic an option as playing music without opting for an interpretation of the composition. One's choice should primarily be guided by one's assessment of the patient's needs. But, to continue the musical analogy, the instrument is a given; it is the analyst's personality. Coltart, Bollas, Phillips, and Eigen are good examples of the virtue of knowing how to use their instrument, or, to use Bollas's term, who have developed their *idiom* into a coherent voice.

A while ago a student of mine told me: "You offer your therapeutic personality for consideration, and at the same time you provide us with the tools that allow me to be critical towards it. I can pick what I agree with and discard what does not suit me." For me this meant that I had achieved what I had aspired to in the two-year course for graduate students in psychoanalytic theory and technique; namely, to offer my own therapeutic style as a concrete example while making it clear that I offer it for consideration rather than as the only possible way of doing things.

In this respect teaching and practicing therapy are analogous. If psychoanalytic work is achieved through a particular kind of conversation, it is unavoidable that the therapist is an individual in this conversation. This is not to imply that traditional virtues of the clinical craft have become obsolete. Stamina, the ability to contain the unbearable, and to contain powerful affects, listening for hidden meanings, providing a calming, stable environment certainly continue to be at the foundation of the clinical craft. The art of clinical individuality is to develop a presence that catalyzes individual development rather than stifling it.

One of the negative consequences of impersonal clinical styles is that it makes patients afraid of their own individuality. Even though ideally the patient is not supposed to imitate the analyst, there is no way to avoid the patient being influenced by the analyst's personal style. If this style exudes the analyst's fear of her own individuality, this will in one way or another have an impact on the patient. The art of psychoanalytic work is to find a way to be oneself that does not force one's character onto patients but allows them to use it to develop their own individuality.

EPILOGUE: TOWARD A NEW PSYCHOANALYTIC CULTURE

FROM UNIVERSAL THEORY TO LOCAL KNOWLEDGE

Since Plato Western philosophy and religion had tended to accept some version of the idea that the true world is hidden from the eye. *Real* reality can only be known if you have some very special knowledge. Psychoanalysis for most of its history has accepted the Platonic metaphor. For the world of ideas it has substituted the unconscious, and for philosophical thought it has substituted the rituals of analytic training. The unconscious, like God, is the source of truth about human life.

Monotheism needs singularity, if there is but one God and one truth, there must not be more than one story. The history of religion and philosophy has been governed for millennia by the search for the one right story. The desire for one truth has totalitarian consequences. In order to defend one's illusion of being blessed with the one true version of the world, holy wars have been, and still are, being fought, because the unbeliever is a perpetual threat to those who want certainty and redemption.

Only in the last decades has Western culture come to the point of truly exploring (and not being afraid of) the possibility that the plurality of stories about the world is not the result of ignorance, but an inevitable constituent of human life. The result has been beneficial. It has opened the vista of a world in which plurality is no threat to integrity, and that allows us to celebrate forms of life as expressions of human creativity.

This transformation has gradually begun to change psychoanalytic culture as well. I get the sense that we are moving from a hermeneutics of suspicion to a celebration of difference and creativity. Psychoanalysts have too often indulged in disqualifying rival interpretations of life as expressing the author's psychopathology. This has often created a climate of envy, hatred, and a stifling of creativity (cf. interviews with Coltart in Molino [1997]). Because different versions of psychoanalysis were taken to be competitors for the one truth, they could not enjoy each other.

Psychoanalysis has tended to be excessively concerned with its own continuity and identity. A remarkable number of publications have asked what makes psychoanalysis different and special. For too many years the ritualistic opening of psychoanalytic papers with the obligatory quotation from Freud has persisted and is becoming less and less fruitful. No one who, like myself, has been changed forever by the reading of Freud will stop admiring this man who has given us one of the most powerful sets of concepts and metaphors with which to make sense of human lives. But this doesn't mean that psychoanalysis must anxiously preserve aspects of theory and practice that have lost their vitality. Psychoanalysis need not be characterized by an eternal set of questions, or a particular set of theoretical dogmas. Like other cultural phenomena, from painting through poetry to philosophy, its continuity is created through overlapping themes that bear family resemblances to those investigated by its originators.

Psychoanalytic knowledge is neither eternal nor universal. It is derived from a very particular interaction with a very particular population. The psychoanalytic contribution to the discourse on human lives is not that it provides knowledge of the deep structure of the mind. I do not think that we should expect any lasting contribution about the nature of humankind to emanate form psychoanalytic consulting rooms. Such contributions are more likely to arrive from the neurosciences, evolutionary biology, and psychology.

The contribution of psychoanalysis is rather the creation of stories based on psychotherapy, the fascinating ritualistic interaction that has evolved in the Western middle classes during this century, in which one human being tries to help another one to make sense of her or his life, and to change it in fruitful ways. Notoriously, psychoanalysis only works for very particular strata of the population: you need a rather particular cast of mind to be receptive to the strange type of interaction that psychoanalysis proposes. That isn't too surprising either. These vocabularies make sense against the backgrounds of very particular forms of life: liberal, democratic individualism.

Psychoanalysis is, to use a distinction currently *en vogue* with philosophers of science, a form of *local knowledge*. It is embedded in a very particular form of life, and cannot be divorced from it. It is a form of practical knowledge. As every psychoanalytic educator knows, the essence of what makes a good clinician is transmitted primarily in interactions of apprenticeship, and far less through theory.

The two most influential philosophers of this eventful century were probably Ludwig Wittgenstein and Martin Heidegger. Both argued against the idea that meaning and mind can be divorced from practice and culture. Practices generate meaning, and culture is the repository of human mentality. The individual mind can never be understood except within the context of the culture that constitutes his or her mentality.

I think that psychoanalysis at this point in its history might fruitfully be understood as a culture of the mind. It is a practice that generates stories and rituals that enable people to both make sense of their lives and make them more meaningful. The question it can answer is: how can modern secular individuals whose lives are not governed by strong belief systems cope with the basic features of life? What are we to make of loss, anger, hatred, ambivalence, love, desire, violent emotion, restlessness, emptiness, joy, hope, and dread?

Now that it becomes clearer that we don't really do much theory (in the strong, scientific sense) anyway, we might as well reconceptualize the interface between psychoanalytic writing and practice. Primarily we might stop calling this writing *theory* and call it *writing* instead (as a number of psychoanalytic authors already do). I think that what characterizes contemporary psychoanalytic writing at its best (as exemplified by the authors I discuss in chapter 6) is that it is conscious of being writing (incidentally this has greatly enhanced the pleasure of reading these texts).

More than anything psychoanalysis is a love affair with the complexity of human life. It is the unwillingness to accept that living a life most efficiently is enough. As long as there are people who love plurality and paradox in human life, psychoanalysis will exist. If Western civilization ever moves toward a total pragmatism, we will live in a Brave New World in which there will be no clients for psychoanalysis—but no one with a passion for human complexity would want to live in such a culture anyway.

Once we accept that psychoanalysis is a culture, a form of life meant to generate meaning, we need not be afraid of plurality of interpretations. Instead, as in the arts, we can celebrate this plurality as an expression of the human ability to create ever new forms of life.

The current transformation of psychoanalysis enables it to live with the insight that has transformed postmodern culture in all its versions. Our stories of who we are and how we can live are groundless. They are not based on knowledge of the deep structure of human nature. If psychoanalysis comes to terms with the contingency of human lives, and with the contingency of its own history, we might get a story of psychoanalysis that is less orderly, but to my mind, both more compelling and more realistic. What kind of history of psychoanalysis would such a psychoanalytic culture that celebrates plurality and paradox need?

CELEBRATING THE WILD STORY OF
PSYCHOANALYSIS

There is still a tendency to find the humanity of Freud, Jung, and other depth psychologists shocking. Noll's *The Jung Cult* (1994) is a good example. It is very useful to the extent that it shows a strong affinity between Jung's work and the *völkisch* ideology and fascination with myth that characterized much of German culture of his times. In this respect Noll's book provides us with service similar to Sulloway's magisterial *Freud, the Biologist of the Mind* (1979). The book becomes less than useful once Noll tries to turn Jung into a fraud. Why should it be surprising that Jung really came to his conclusions without empirical evidence?

Of course Jung was not a dispassionate scientist any more than Freud was. Freud and Jung were cultural heroes. They would not and could not settle for less than an integrative account of human nature to make their own lives intelligible. Their cultural preferences differed widely: while Freud loved classical culture and the language of science (Gay, 1988), Jung was drawn to the neopagan revival that permeated German culture of the fin de siècle (Noll, 1994).

The history of psychoanalysis is very human indeed. The last decade has brought us some interesting biographical materials of some of its major figures: Phyllis Grosskurth's (1986) landmark biography of Melanie Klein, John Kerr's (1993) fascinating study of the triangle of Jung, Sabina Spielrein, and Freud, and Judy Cooper's (1993) brief but illuminating study of Masud Khan. They show how each of these writers tried to gain authorship over a complex life through psychoanalytic writing.

John Kerr's magisterial study of the fateful schism between Freud and Jung shows how both men needed the belief that they were onto the one, true theory of human nature. The result was that the history of psychoanalysis began with a schism. *Schism* is a term derived from the history of religion, and, like religions, psychoanalysis in particular, and depth psychology in general, fought for the privilege of being the one, true church. The fact that the wars were fought using a pseudoscientific vocabulary only obfuscated their true nature.

Freud's great existential problem was that fin de siècle psychiatry tended to put femininity, hysteria, and Jewishness into one great category of degeneracy. Freud was both Jewish and suffered from a variety of hysterical symptoms. Did this mean that he was an inferior human being and man (Gilman, 1993)?

Freud's thesis that all human beings are, at least unconsciously, polymorphously perverse and bisexual was a wonderful equalizer: the difference between the hysteric and the upright, "normal" man was not that the former was weaker and morally depraved. It just meant that one of them had stronger defenses than the other.

It was precisely the idea that the unconscious did not contain anything but repressed childhood wishes that was not acceptable to Jung. He needed a new myth that would replace the Christian myth he could not live with anymore. Because Jung, like Freud, wanted the authority of a scientist for his story, he needed a scientific version of the *völkisch* mythology that was resurrected in many German intellectual circles of his time.

It is certainly important to grasp the extent to which Freud and Jung (no less than Shakespeare, Goethe, and Joyce, or Galileo, Newton, and Einstein, for that matter) were children of their times. Authors like Sulloway, Noll, and Kerr make us appreciate their cultural struggles against a historical background, and thus make us more conscious of our own need to retell the dilemmas of our own times in our own terms.

The same holds true for other heroes of psychoanalysis. Grosskurth's work tells the story of a woman caught at the lower border of the professional middle class in a family beset by envy, bitterness, and a sense of deprivation. Melanie Klein grew up with a mother deserted by her husband, and lived through a great deal of failure and tragedy herself. Left by her husband and rejected by the great love of her life, she also lost a son, presumably by suicide.

Grosskurth provides an interesting hypothesis about why Klein needed a version of human life that projected everything of relevance into a mythological past. Grosskurth tells of an (as yet unpublished) autobiographical essay Klein wrote in the last years of her life. In it she describes her childhood and adolescence in idyllic terms. Instead of the family that was full of hatred, envy, and bitterness, we get a picture of warmth, mutual caring, and happiness. Grosskurth speculates that Klein could not deal with the terrors of her memories, and instead projected her real suffering into a mythological childhood that could only be recollected by "memories in feelings," as Klein said of the earliest periods of life.

Melanie Klein lived a tragic life, full of failure, loss, and pain, and she needed an account of it that would make it more bearable. Her myth of the dramatic fight between love and hatred, envy and gratitude, guilt and reparation gave her the possibility of forgetting how little joy her actual life had contained. Instead life became a mythological fight between primeval forces.

Heinz Kohut also needed a better story of who he was to maintain a sense of authorship in his life. The editor of his letters makes a strong case for the hypothesis that one of his most famous and gripping papers, "The Two Analyses of Mr. Z" (1979), is a veiled analytic autobiography (Cocks, 1994). Kohut's first analysis, and the Freudian account of who he was, left him with an intolerable feeling of being an immature, pleasure-driven man who had never given up the paradise of his early, blissful relation with his mother.

Kohut needed a different story if he was ever going to feel good about himself. Since he couldn't find one that helped, he created it himself. His narrative of selfobject failure made his own egocentricity (he says that for Mr. Z other human beings never became central), vulnerability, and irritability more bearable. He finally had a story

that didn't turn him into a misfit, but into a tragic hero
(he called his theory the "psychology of tragic man").

The list could, of course, be continued. Indeed, there
is nothing new in the thesis that the psychoanalyst's subjectivity crucially influences theory. Atwood and Stolorow
(1993) have made this a cornerstone of their understanding of the nature of psychoanalytic theory. In their analyses, they emphasize the ways in which Freud, Jung, Rank,
Reich, and others were limited through their own pathologies, traumatizations, and developmental deficits. Even Atwood and Stolorow, who are so open-minded and
nondogmatic, assume that there is such a thing as progres-
sion in psychoanalytic theory, and that earlier authors are
superseded by the later ones. They therefore assume that
each theory reflects, among other things, what its author
could not see.

To my mind that turns the heroes of psychoanalysis
into victims of their characters, rather than into the cultural heroes they are. I would propose not seeing the dis-
tinctness of each of these theories as a function of blind
spots and limitations.

The history of psychoanalysis is, I think, not really the
history of new discovery. I can attach no distinct meaning
to the idea that Melanie Klein "discovered" the paranoid–schizoid and depressive positions, or that Winnicott
"discovered" transitional objects and the importance of
early mothering. I rather think of them as creators of new
vocabularies, perspectives, and rituals.

Because psychoanalytic narratives, metaphors, and
stories need to make sense of an ever-changing human
and cultural reality, these stories must be told and retold
time and again. In that respect I think that it might be
interesting to rethink the history of psychoanalysis in
terms of cultural history, or the history of art forms.

This would, for example, allow for the intuition that
I probably share with many others, that Freud is the grand
master of psychoanalytic writing, not just because he
founded the genre, but because, like Shakespeare, the
quality of his writing and the richness of his vision has

remained unsurpassed. It would also explain why Winnicott is a more important psychoanalytic writer than John Bowlby, even though Bowlby has added immeasurably more positive knowledge than Winnicott.

The reason is that Winnicott's qualities as a writer, the richness of his metaphors, and the gripping quality of his narrative are by far superior to those of Bowlby. This is also why practitioners generally prefer to read Winnicott and not Bowlby, because as practitioners of a culture of mind we need evocative, suggestive, multilayered metaphors rather than precise empirical information (as valuable as this is in and of itself).

PSYCHOANALYTIC WRITING AND THE DESIRE FOR AUTHORSHIP

The story of psychoanalysis is the epic of men and women who struggled to make sense of their own and their patients' suffering, who competed with each other for fame, dominance, and recognition. The heroes of the story of psychoanalysis are strong characters (otherwise they wouldn't be heroes). They wanted stories that would turn their own lives into a good life worth living. Each of them came to the point where the only good story was a story they had written themselves.

Freud said in an *aperçu* that many psychoanalysts are frustrated novelists. One reason for this is that many of us who write psychoanalytic theory lack the talent for writing fiction. Another reason is that the psychoanalytic writer wants to write about actual life rather than fictional lives. This is why psychoanalytic writing is always at the border between literature and theory.

At the core of psychoanalytic writing there is the striving for authorship (cf. Strenger, 1998). That is not surprising, as the desire for authorship is the driving force of all writing. The solitary occupation of creating a story has always been one of the ways in which individuals have tried to both create and understand their lives. The reason I have chosen the term *authorship* to denote the striving for integrated individuality is precisely because this metaphor resounds on so many levels.

Having a sense of authorship means having the sense of originating one's life. The desire for authorship sometimes takes the form of the desire to be fully self-created. Freud saw this aspect of human mental life when he said that the oedipal wish to replace the father effectively means that one wants to be one's own father. When pushed to the extreme the desire for authorship becomes the desire to be *causa sui*, to have the cause of one's being in oneself.

Psychoanalytic writing is geared toward authorship in another sense as well. The goal of such writing is to gain citizenship in the exalted republic of letters. By creating an *oeuvre* the desire for authorship achieves a coveted goal: the author creates himself by literally creating his or her persona as a figure in the public space of culture, and participates in the cultural sense of immortality associated with the status of authorship.

Understanding has always been one of the ways certain human beings have had to overcome fatedness. When Sartre (1963) says (following Balzac) that by understanding the world he turns it into *his* world, he expresses the enhancement of the sense of authorship by intellectual grasp of the world's complexities.

Psychoanalytic writing is one of the attempts to make fatedness bearable by making it intelligible. The individual who can think his fate gains some control over it by this very thinking. The theorist's desire for authorship in life is manifested in the attempt to become the author of an accepted narrative of human life in general. Freud, Jung, Klein, Erikson, and others attempted to overcome fatedness not just by understanding themselves, but by trying to show that the vicissitudes of their lives exhibited structures of individuality which were universal.

This insight has found application in the history of psychoanalysis itself. From the first generation of psychoanalysts onwards the movement has been infected by a

vice. Analysts of differing persuasions have tried to disqualify each other's contributions by arguing that they are
nothing but the expression of the opponent's unresolved
conflicts. This rather unpalatable tactic is based on the
truth that psychoanalytic writers always try to gain authorship over their lives by writing.

This should not be used as a weapon in discussion,
but should be accepted as an inevitable feature of psychoanalytic discourse. The ineradicability of the analytic therapist's subjectivity has achieved growing recognition in the
last decades, and the intersubjectivist school has made it
into a cornerstone of its understanding of the genesis of
psychoanalytic theory.

Psychoanalysis cannot be impersonal. Its whole point
is to occupy the space between the subjective and the objective by formulating narratives which bridge the gap between the idiosyncratic and the field of interpersonal
validity. As Atwood and Stolorow have shown, it is perfectly
possible to write about the subjective determinants of psychoanalytic writing without entering the vicious circle
(pun intended) of mutual disqualification.

THE DESIRE FOR AUTHORSHIP AND THE ANXIETY
OF INFLUENCE

The dynamics of authorship and fate is doubly influential
in the history of psychoanalysis: first, because each of the
great interpretations of human life is an interpretation of
the interplay of authorship and fate, as I have suggested in
my rendering of Klein and Winnicott in chapter 4; second,
because the history of psychoanalysis is itself governed by
the dynamics of authorship and fate. The history of psychoanalysis exemplifies a dynamics to be found in art, and
more subliminally in the life of every individual. Following
Harold Bloom (1973), this dynamics can be called *the anxiety of influence* (see chapter 5 above).

Bloom has made a strong case for the idea that the
dynamics of romantic poetry was governed by a central

motif: poets were crucially preoccupied by the anxiety that their predecessors had left no room for truly new creation; that every poem worth writing had been written already; that nothing but epigonal status was left for the poets of the present.

Bloom distinguishes between strong poets and weak poets. Strong poets are those who feel that there is no value whatsoever in being a follower, to simply develop styles and themes created by others before them. They want to create *ex nihilo,* to feel that they have something to say which is utterly new, a creation coming completely from their own being. Weak poets do not mind being followers, developers of what has been created by others. They aspire to no more than writing good poetry.

Bloom's thesis would be easily applicable to other art forms as well. Since the eighteenth century the sense of individuality has been connected strongly with the notion of the genius who creates out of the depth of his own being, driven by an inspiration coming totally from inside, most artists were driven by the anxiety of influence in one way or another.

I think that the history of depth psychology in our century is governed by the dynamics of the anxiety of influence no less than the history of art was. There are three central reasons for this: (1) Theories of personality in their essence are much closer to works of art than they are to scientific theories. (2) These theories and the accompanying therapeutic techniques are depictions of ideal types of what a person should be like. (3) The founders of the various schools experienced their own personality as exemplifications of their theories, and so did their followers. The difference between the founding fathers and the followers is the same as that between the strong and the weak poets: the founding fathers were driven by the desire to be self-created. The followers felt comfortable with the sense of belonging to the clan of those singled out by having the one right theory, and to be competent analysts or therapists.

The desire for authorship in its extreme is the desire to be self-created, or at least to have a mind that is truly one's own. Like strong poets the strong authors of psychoanalysis want their creations to be truly original. In the history of psychoanalysis the metaphor of the sense of authorship comes close to becoming a literal description; authorship here means to be the author of a set of works which create a new perspective on human life.

PSYCHOANALYTIC HEROES

By becoming a psychotherapist you enter a force field; psychoanalysis and depth psychology is a cultural field polarized and structured by the major voices which define its ideal-type possibilities. The great authors are those which provide archetypal images of what it could be like to be a psychotherapist.

Of course the very definition of what a great author is, and who they are, is in itself a decision about what depth psychology really is. I have been told that in Oxford philosophy departments staff and students would express their view of what philosophy is by classifying the traditional authors into Major Deities, Minor Deities, and Great Philosophers (Avishai Margalit, personal communication). There would of course be major disputes about who belonged into which categories. The view was that a philosopher's list defined what type of philosopher he was.

In psychoanalysis the same holds true: Freud will be in everybody's list of Major Deities—for strict psychoanalysts he is in fact the only Major Deity, in an ontological category of his own (Foucault calls this a founder of Discourse). The style of an analyst will be defined by her list of minor deities: in some cases it might just contain one name, Melanie Klein, for example, or Jacques Lacan, or Heinz Kohut, or, for a growing number of people, D. W. Winnicott.

Or it might contain more than one name: Klein, Winnicott, Bion, might be a possible combination, which characterizes a certain style of British object relations orientation. Such analysts will favor maternal metaphors in their description of the analytic situation. Their therapeutic style will be concentrated on five-times a week analyses, and they will interpret a lot of envy and destruction. Some might add Fairbairn, thus indicating a preference for an admixture of outsiderishness and Scottish quaintness to their style. Masud Khan's combination was Klein, Hartmann, Winnicott, and Erikson (an unusual combination, but Masud Khan was an unusual man).

Today, some analysts, like Michael Eigen, hold to a postmodern mix: Lacan, Winnicott, and Bion for example. This indicates a certain sophistication of style, a willingness to take intellectual risks, and a preference for opaqueness in writing. The analytic style would be slightly enigmatic, with a knack for paradoxical formulations. It also indicates a worldview which shuns simplicity and clear pronouncements and aims to reintroduce spiritual concerns into psychoanalysis.

There is a growing number of self psychologists who have one major minor deity: Heinz Kohut. Their therapeutic style is characterized by a more informal type of warmth. Their reconstructions will center on the failures of the parents, and they see empathy as the major virtue and curative factor. The list, of course, could be continued. Its main point is to suggest a rewriting of psychoanalytic history as a history of personal and clinical styles rather than a history of discoveries.

OTHER DEPTH PSYCHOLOGICAL SCHOOLS

Once you move out of the boundaries of the International Psychoanalytic Association, the styles progressively diverge. There is a whole variety of therapists with a distinct New Age flavor: all of them have Jung on their list of major deities. Freud for many of them is their evil reductionist who does not understand the farther reaches of human nature. The niceties of their identity is, among other things, a matter of their distance from standard, more bourgeois forms of life. Some of them are more deeply involved in the growing number of people who combine psychotherapy with some kind of body-centered approach.

Others stick more closely to the identity of the depth psychologist as it has evolved since the beginning of the twentieth century: they often have a good grounding in classical studies, and they like to deal with mythology, medieval mysticism, and the like, of course paralleling Jung's own predilections. Erudition and unconventional writing are part of their identity. James Hillman (1989) provides a good paradigm for this search for a new spirituality.

On the other side of the spectrum there are those who look for a more scientific approach. They want more research and less metaphor; more outcome orientation and less ideology. They include the researchers doing work on the various psychodynamic forms of short-term therapy. Their books preferably contain schematas and strategies rather than myths and metaphors. Their jargon is drier, their habitus more scientific, their frame of reference is the academic community rather than any of the depth psychological schools (e.g., Garfield and Bergin [1978] for a sample).

The list could be continued almost endlessly. But by now the point should be clear: one's choice of heroes is an expression of one's identity. In the case of psychotherapists this identity is not just an issue of professional style, but pertains to one's deepest values and beliefs. It is not just a quaint sociological fact that you can identify a psychotherapist's style by looking at his clothing, listening to his diction, and having a look at the style of his consulting room, but an indication of how tightly personal and professional identities are interwoven in this field.

It is less surprising that you can find out about this style with a high degree of certainty by looking at his library, and leafing through the bibliographies of his papers. Depth psychologists live in a tightly knit community which spans the world and creates a microcosmos of its own. This community has its myths of identity, the myths of founding fathers and mothers, its rituals, heroes, and villains. In particular it has its "do's" and "don't's"; each subgroup has its own views of what they call analysis and what they consider just psychotherapy; each has its convictions about what constitutes the essence of psychoanalysis.

The mix of the identity of the healer, the confessor, the tradition of medicine, and its legal regulation in Western countries provides the analytic therapist with a professional ethics which has evolved throughout the century in which modern psychotherapy exists. By undergoing training, the depth psychologist acquires basic techniques and is initiated into the style of the school which he has chosen or gravitated to. Each individual depth psychologist must now find his own way of working. For a while he might be strongly identified with one or more of his teachers, and one of the major deities of the field, and his identity might coalesce around a banner, "I am a modern Freudian, a Kleinian, a Lacanian, a self psychologist."

FROM PATHOLOGIZING TO THE RETELLING OF LIVES

Within the psychoanalytic profession we may be coming closer to the point of *enjoying* the diversity of styles. Instead of pointing out each other's pathologies, we might see what is interesting, fruitful, and fascinating in other people's styles. This doesn't mean that each of us won't end up liking her or his style most and argue strongly for it. But the tone of the discussion would shift: it would be a joyful competition, and not vicious disqualification of alternatives.

This would fit well with contemporary rethinking of the tendency to pathologize our patients. The complexity of the current discussion of the meanings of "normality," "pathology," "maturity," and the like is enormous. The growing discontent with simplistic notions of normality has been centered on the questions of gender and sexuality (Chodorow, 1994). The discussion has dismantled the dichotomies which had been taken for granted for a long time: mature love versus compulsive sexuality, intimacy versus fantasy-based sex, normal heterosexuality versus pathological homosexuality. The strategy of developmental moralism has been deconstructed thoroughly, and it is gradually being discarded by many major psychoanalytic authors. The very idea that nature prescribes the right way of life is being emptied of its content.

This development has a highly beneficial therapeutic implication. The distinction of normal versus abnormal, healthy versus unhealthy seems to be primarily a tool in the maintenance of social order, and as such it is very difficult, if not downright impossible, to abandon. Every society has the need for standards of behavior which make communal life possible. In order to enforce such standards it is necessary to stigmatize deviant behavior in some ways, and modern society has replaced the vocabulary of moral depravity and sin with the vocabulary of normality and maturity.

Vocabularies of stigmatization generate a great deal of suffering. I am very impressed by the amount of anxiety patients experience about not being "normal" or not being "okay." Much of this anxiety is a function of internalized social pressures. These pressures begin at home, are continued by peer pressure, and perpetuated by social images of the "normal," "happy" individual. The internalization of these judgments is reflected by the intrapsychic analogue to excommunication: the individual experiences certain aspects of his personality as unfit for human intercourse. Guilt, shame, and the anxiety of being seen as inferior, different, or unattractive because of some deviance, become the guardians of these inner spaces of loneliness.

To the extent that clinical discourse is permeated by the judgments of society, the experience of excommunication is reinforced. The individual continues to experience himself as a misfit because of the very fact that he feels different. As Kohut has pointed out, the clinician's adherence to a morality of maturity becomes in and of itself, an impediment to the process of the individual's building of cohesive selfhood.

It is highly instructive to note the extent to which current developments in psychoanalysis take this into account. The intersubjectivist approach developed by Stolorow, Atwood, Brandchaft and their associates provides a good example. Their explicit aim is to clean the therapeutic interaction of attempts of the therapist to introduce "objective" knowledge. They do not believe that the clinician has such knowledge, and at any rate they think that anything but the exploration of the patient's subjective experience is therapeutically not useful (Stolorow, Atwood, and Brandchaft, 1994).

The intersubjectivists are radical. They do not even give the therapist the prerogative of knowledge of the "objective" reality of the therapeutic situation. They replace the term *transference distortion,* which implies a nonveridical perception of the therapist, by the understanding of transference as the patient's organization of experience (Stolorow, Brandchaft, and Atwood, 1987). This organization is to be elucidated rather than criticized. Intersubjectivism tries to move away as far as possible from the stereotype of the analyst who points out the patient's errors in understanding an objective reality the analyst knows. They try to show that many of the clinical phenomena described by authors like Kernberg, who subscribe to developmental moralism, are actually an iatrogenic artifact of their therapeutic technique. The intersubjectivists' alternative is their model of therapeutic work as a dialogical exploration of modes of experiential organization.

It seems to me that the most interesting developments in psychoanalysis are those which are moving away from developmental moralism and toward the other pole of Freud's thinking, radical narrativization. The promises of psychoanalytic theory in the strong sense have turned out not to be realistic, but it seems that we can become better clinicians and more interesting thinkers if we renounce a claim to knowledge which is illegitimate.

My use of the art world as a model for psychotherapy is intended as an ethical and therapeutic device. Only therapists are capable of taking ironical distance from their own particular ideal of maturity, if they have a grasp of the contingency of their own position, and refrain from mistaking it for a reflection of the natural order, can we create true solidarity with our patients' attempt to achieve their own form of individuality. Pluralist self-consciousness is not a metatheoretical luxury for psychoanalysis, but a therapeutic necessity.

Once the claims to theory and the moral ordering of the human universe, which constituted one of the two strands in Freud's thinking, became less dominant, new creative energies were becoming available to psychoanalytic thinking. The tremendous impact of feminist thinking on psychoanalytic thought and practice shows how interesting new perspectives are being generated. These latter developments, which fuse sophisticated cultural criticism with psychoanalytic thought, bring us to a position where celebration of individuality rather than pathologization of differences come to characterize the emerging psychoanalytic avant garde.

REFERENCES

American Psychiatric Association (1980), *Diagnostic and Statistical Manual of Mental Disorders*, 3rd ed. (DSM-II). Washington, DC: American Psychiatric Press.

Aron, L. (1996), *A Meeting of Minds. Mutuality in Psychoanalysis.* New York: Analytic Press.

Atwood, G. E., & Stolorow, R. D. (1993), *Faces in a Cloud: Intersubjectivity in Personality Theory.* Northvale, NJ: Jason Aronson.

Auden, W. H. (1939), In memory of Sigmund Freud. In: *Selected Poems.* New York: Vintage, 1979, p. 91.

Balint, M. (1935), The final goal of psychoanalytic treatment. In: *Primary Love and Psychoanalytic Technique.* London: Tavistock, 1965.

Becker, E. (1973), *The Denial of Death.* New York: Free Press.

Beckett, S. (1952), *Waiting for Godot.* New York: Grove Press.

Bellah, R., Madson, R., Sullivan, W., Swidler, A., & Tipton, S. (1985), *Habits of the Heart. Individualism and Commitment in American Life.* Berkeley: University of California Press.

Benjamin, J. (1989), *Bonds of Love. Psychoanalysis, Feminism and the Problem of Dominations.* New York: Pantheon.

——— (1995), *Like Subjects, Love Objects.* New Haven, CT: Yale University Press.

——— (1998), *Shadow of the Other: Intersubjectivity and Gender in Psychoanalysis.* London: Routledge.

Berlin, I. (1951), The hedgehog and the fox. In: *Russian Thinkers.* Harmondsworth, U.K.: Penguin, 1978, pp. 22–81.

————— (1958), Two concepts of liberty. In: *Four Essays on Liberty*. Oxford: Oxford University Press, pp. 118–172.

Bion, W. (1961), A theory of thinking. In: *Second Thoughts*. London: Tavistock, 1967, pp. 110–119.

————— (1970), *Attention and Interpretation*. London: Tavistock.

————— (1987), *Clinical Seminars and Four Papers*. Abingdon, U.K.: Fleetwood Press.

Bloom, H. (1973), *The Anxiety of Influence*. Oxford: Oxford University Press.

————— (1994), *The Western Canon*. New York: Harcourt Brace

Bollas, C. (1987), *The Shadow of the Object*. London: Free Association Books.

————— (1989), *Forces of Destiny*. London: Free Association Books.

————— (1992), *Being a Character*. New York: Hill & Wang.

————— (1995), *Cracking Up*. New York: Hill & Wang.

Breuer, J., & Freud, S. (1893–1895), *Studies on Hysteria*. Standard, 2. London: Hogarth Press, 1955.

Browning, F. (1993), *The Culture of Desire. Paradox and Perversity in Gay Lives Today*. New York: Crown.

Buswell, Jr., R. E. (1992), *The Zen Monastic Experience*. Princeton, NJ: Princeton University Press.

Chasseguet-Smirgel, J. (1984), *Creativity and Perversion*. London: Free Association Books.

Chodorow, N. (1989), *Feminism and Psychoanalytic Theory*. New Haven, CT: Yale University Press.

————— (1994), *Femininities, Masculinities, Sexualities*. London: Free Association Books.

Cocks, G., Ed. (1994), *The Curve of Life: Correspondence of Heinz Kohut, 1923–1981*. Chicago: University of Chicago Press.

Coltart, N. (1992), *Slouching towards Bethlehem*. New York: Guilford Press.

————— (1996), *The Baby and the Bathwater*. London: Karnac.

Cooper, J. (1993), *Speak of Me as I Am: The Life and Work of Masud Khan*. London: Karnac.

Copleston, F. (1946), *A History of Philosophy*, Vol. 1. New York: Image.

Danto, A. (1978). The artworld. In: *Philosophy Looks at the Arts*, ed. J. Margolise. Philadelphia, Temple University Press, 1978.

Davanloo, H., Ed. (1980), *Short Term Dynamic Psychotherapy*. New York: Jason Aronson.

Deleuze, G., & Guattari, F. (1972), *Anti-Oedipus,* tr. R. Hurley, M. Seem, & H. Lane. New York: Viking, 1977.

Diamond, J. (1991), *The Rise and Fall of the Third Chimpanzee.* London: Vintage.

Drews, S., & Brecht, K. (1971), *Psychoanalytische Ich-Psychologie* (Psychoanalytic ego psychology). Frankfurt aM, Germany: Suhrkamp.

Eigen, M. (1986), *The Psychotic Core.* New York: Jason Aronson.

—— (1992), *Coming Through the Whirlwind.* New York: Chiron.

—— (1993), *The Electrified Tightrope,* ed. A. Phillips. Northvale, NJ: Jason Aronson.

—— (1996), *Psychic Deadness.* Northvale, NJ: Jason Aronson.

Eissler, K. (1953), The effect of the structure of the ego on psychoanalytic technique. *J. Amer. Psychoanal. Assn.,* 1:104–143.

Ellenberger, H. (1970), *The Discovery of the Unconscious.* New York: Basic Books.

Ellis, B. E. (1991), *American Psycho.* New York: Vintage.

—— (1994), *The Informers.* New York: Knopf.

Eribon, D. (1987), *Michel Foucault,* tr. B. Wing. Cambridge, MA: Harvard University Press, 1991.

Ferenczi, S. (1987), *The Clinical Diary of Sándor Ferenczi,* ed. J. Dupont; tr. M. Balint & N. Zarday Jackson. Cambridge, MA: Harvard University Press.

Foucault, M. (1961), *Histoire de la folie.* Paris: Plon.

—— (1964), *The Birth of the Clinic. An Archaeology of Medical Perception,* tr. A. Sheridan. New York: Random House, 1973.

—— (1966), Les mots et les choses. In: *The Order of Things,* tr. A. Sheridan. New York: Vintage, 1970.

—— (1975), *Discipline and Punish. The Birth of the Prison,* tr. A. Sheridan. New York: Random House, 1977.

—— (1976), *The History of Sexuality,* Vol. 1, tr. R. Hurley. New York: Random House, 1978.

—— (1983), *The Care of the Self,* tr. R. Hurley. New York: Random House.

—— (1987), *Michel Foucault, Politics, Philosophy, Culture,* ed. L. D. Kritzman. London: Routledge.

Freud, S. (1895), Project for a Scientific Psychology. *Standard Edition,* 1:281–391. London: Hogarth Press, 1966.

—— (1910), Leonardo da Vinci and a memory of his childhood. *Standard Edition,* 9:14–53. London: Hogarth Press, 1996.

———— (1911), Formulations on the two principles of mental functioning. *Standard Edition*, 12:213–226. London: Hogarth Press, 1958.

———— (1912), Recommendations to physicians practising psycho-analysis. *Standard Edition*, 12:109–120. London: Hogarth Press, 1958.

———— (1915), Observations on transference love. *Standard Edition*, 12:157–171. London: Hogarth Press, 1958.

———— (1927), The Future of an Illusion. *Standard Edition*, 21:1–56. London: Hogarth Press, 1961.

———— (1930), Civilization and its Discontents. *Standard Edition*, 21:57–145. London: Hogarth Press, 1961.

———— (1933), New Introductory Lectures on Psychoanalysis. *Standard Edition*, 22:1–182. London: Hogarth Press, 1964.

———— (1937), Analysis terminable and interminable. *Standard Edition*, 23:209–253. London: Hogarth Press, 1964.

———— (1940), An Outline of Psychoanalysis. *Standard Edition*, 23:139–207. London: Hogarth Press, 1964.

Friedan, B. (1965), *The Feminine Mystique.* Harmondsworth, U.K.: Pelican.

Gadamer, H. J. (1960), *Wahrheit und Methode.* Munich, Germany: Niemeyer.

Garfield, S., & Bergin, A. (1978), *Handbook of Psychotherapy and Behavior Change,* 2nd ed. New York: Wiley.

Gay, P. (1988), *Freud, A Life for Our Times.* New York: W. W. Norton.

Gellner, E. (1985), *The Psychoanalytic Movement.* London: Fontana.

Gergen, K. J. (1991), *The Saturated Self. Dilemmas of Identity in Contemporary Life.* New York: Basic Books.

Giddens, A. (1991), *Modernity and Self-Identity. Self and Society in the Late Modern Age.* Cambridge, U.K.: Polity.

———— (1992), *The Transformation of Intimacy: Sexuality, Love and Eroticism in Modern Societies.* Cambridge, U.K.: Polity.

Gilman, S. (1993), *The Case of Sigmund Freud: Medicine and Identity at the Fin de Siècle.* Baltimore: Johns Hopkins University Press.

Goldberg, A. (1995), *The Problem of Perversion.* New Haven, CT: Yale University Press.

Goodman, N. (1978), *Ways of Worldmaking.* Indianapolis, IN: Hackett.

Greenberg, J., & Mitchell, S. (1983), *Object Relations and Psycho-analytic Theory*. Cambridge, MA: Harvard University Press.

Greenson, R. R. (1967), *The Technique and Practice of Psychoanalysis*. New York: International Universities Press.

Grosskurth, P. (1986), *Melanie Klein*. London: Maresfield.

—— (1991), *The Secret Ring*. New York: Addison-Wesley.

Grünbaum, A. (1984), *The Foundations of Psychoanalysis*. Berkeley: University of California Press.

Habermas, J. (1968), *Knowledge and Human Interest*, tr. J. J. Shapiro. Boston: Beacon Press, 1971.

Hadot, P. (1995), *Philosophy as a Way of Life: Spiritual Exercises from Socrates to Foucault*, ed. A. Davidson, tr. M. Chase. Oxford: Blackwell.

Hale, N. G. (1995), *The Rise and Crisis of Psychoanalysis in the United States*. Oxford: Oxford University Press.

Haley, J. (1973), *Uncommon Therapy. The Psychiatric Techniques of Milton Erickson, M.D.* New York: W. W. Norton.

Heidegger, M. (1927), *Sein und Zeit*. Tübingen: Niemeyer.

Hillman, J. (1989), *A Blue Fire. Selected Writings of James Hillman*, ed. T. Moore. San Francisco: Harper.

Hulme, T. S. (1924), Classicism and romanticism. In: *Speculations*. London: Routledge.

Hume, D. (1762), *The History of England, From the Invasion of Julius Caesar to the Revolution in 1688*. Chicago: University of Chicago Press.

Isaacs, S. (1948), The nature and function of phantasy. *Internat. J. Psycho-Anal.*, 29:73–97.

Juno, A., & Vale, V. (1993), *Research,* Vol. 1, *Bob Flanagan, Super-masochist*. San Francisco: RE-search Publications.

Kagan, J. (1989), *Unstable Ideas. Temperament, Cognition and the Self*. Cambridge, MA: Harvard University Press.

Kant, I. (1787), *Critique of Pure Reason*, tr. M. Muller. Garden City, NY: Doubleday/Anchor, 1966.

Kernberg, O. (1975), *Borderline Conditions and Pathological Narcissism*. New York: Jason Aronson.

—— (1976), *Object Relations Theory and Clinical Psychoanalysis*. New York: Jason Aronson.

—— (1987), Institutional problems of psychoanalytic education. *J. Amer. Psychoanal. Assn.*, 34:799–833.

Kerr, J. (1993), *A Most Dangerous Method: The Story of Jung, Freud and Sabina Spielrein*. New York: Alfred Knopf.

Khan, M. (1979), *Alienation in Perversion*. London: Hogarth Press.

Klein, M. (1957), *Envy and Gratitude*. London: Hogarth Press.

Koehler, W. (1938), *The Place of Value in a World of Facts*. New York: W. W. Norton.

Kohut, H. (1971), *The Analysis of the Self*. New York: International Universities Press.

——— (1977), *The Restoration of the Self*. New York: International Universities Press.

——— (1979), The two analyses of Mr. Z. *Internat. J. Psycho-Anal.*, 60:3–27.

——— (1984), *How Does Analysis Cure?* Chicago: University of Chicago Press.

Kramer, P. D. (1993), *Listening to Prozac: A Psychiatrist Explores Antidepressant Drugs and the Remaking of the Self*. New York: Viking.

Kristeva, J. (1982), *Powers of Horror: An Essay on Abjection*. New York: Columbia University Press.

Kuhn, T. S. (1961), *The Structure of Scientific Revolutions*. Chicago: University of Chicago Press.

Kundera, M. (1984), *The Unbearable Lightness of Being*, tr. M. H. Heim. London: Faber.

Little, M. (1985), Winnicott working in areas where psychotic anxieties predominate. A personal record. *Free Associations*, 3:9–42.

Lacan, J. (1953), The function and field of speech and language in psychoanalysis. In: *Écrits, a Selection*, tr. A. Sheridan. London: Tavistock, 1977.

Lyotard, J.-F. (1979), *The Postmodern Condition: A Report on Knowledge*, tr. G. Bennington & B. Massumi. Minneapolis: University of Minnesota Press, 1984.

Marcuse, H. (1955), *Eros and Civilization*. Boston: Beacon.

McDougall, J. (1983), *Plea for a Measure of Abnormality*. New York: International Universities Press.

——— (1995), *The Many Faces of Eros*. London: Free Association.

Messer, S., & Winokur, M. (1980), Some limits to the integration of psychoanalytic and behavior therapy. *Amer. Psychologist*, 35:818–827.

Mill, J. S. (1859), *On Liberty*, ed. G. Himmelfarb. Harmondsworth, U.K.: Pelican, 1974.

Miller, J. (1993), *The Passion of Michel Foucault*. New York: Simon & Schuster.

Mitchell, S. (1993), *Hope and Dread in Psychoanalysis*. New York: Basic Books.

——— (1997), Influence and Autonomy in Psychoanalysis. *Relational Book Series*, Vol. 9, Mahwah, NJ: Analytic Press.

Molino, A. (1997), *Freely Associated: Encounters in Psychoanalysis with Christopher Bollas, Joyce McDougall, Michael Eigen, Adam Phillips, Nina Coltart*. London: Free Association Books.

Murdoch, I. (1992), *Metaphysics as a Guide to Morals*. London: Chatto & Windus.

Nabokov, V. (1980), *Lectures on Literature*, ed. F. Bowers. New York: Harcourt.

Nagel, T. (1971), The absurd. In: *Mortal Questions*. Cambridge, MA: Cambridge University Press.

——— (1986), *The View from Nowhere*. Oxford: Oxford University Press.

Noll, R. (1994), *The Jung Cult*. Princeton, NJ: Princeton University Press.

Nussbaum, M. (1995), *The Therapy of Desire*. Princeton, NJ: Princeton University Press.

Ogden, T. (1986), *The Matrix of the Mind*. New York: Jason Aronson.

Phillips, A. (1993), *On Kissing, Tickling and Being Bored*. London: Faber.

——— (1994), *On Flirtation: Psychoanalytic Essays on the Uncommitted Life*. Cambridge, MA: Harvard University Press.

——— (1995), *Terrors and Experts*. London: Faber.

——— (1998), *The Beast in the Nursery*. London: Faber.

Proust, M. (1913–1927), *A la recherche du temps perdu*, Vols. 1–7. Paris: Pléiade, 1954.

Putnam, H. (1981), *Reason, Truth and History*. Cambridge, U.K.: Cambridge University Press.

Rapaport, D. (1960), The Structure of Psychoanalytic Theory: A Systematizing Attempt. *Psychological Issues*, Monogr. 6. New York: International Universities Press.

Ricoeur, P. (1970), *Freud and Philosophy: An Essay in Interpretation*. New Haven, CT: Yale University Press.

Rieff, P. (1959), *Freud: The Mind of the Moralist*. Chicago: University of Chicago Press.

Rorty, R. (1980), *Philosophy and the Mirror of Nature*. Princeton, NJ: Princeton University Press.

——— (1991), *Contingency, Irony and Solidarity*. Cambridge, MA: Cambridge University Press.

Rosen, S. (1982), *My Voice Will Go With You. The Teaching Tales of Milton H. Erikson.* New York: W. W. Norton.

Rousseau, J.-J. (1762), *The Social Contract,* tr. G. D. H. Cole. Harmondsworth, U.K.: Penguin, 1970.

Samuels, A. (1989), *The Plural Psyche, Personality, Morality and the Father.* London: Routledge.

———— (1993), *The Political Psyche.* London: Routledge.

Sartre, J.-P. (1963), *Being and Nothingness,* tr. H. Barnes. New York: Random House, 1956.

———— (1963), *Les Mots.* Paris: Gallimard.

Schafer, R. (1968), *Aspects of Internalization.* New York: International Universities Press.

———— (1970), The psychoanalytic vision of reality. In: *New Language for Psychoanalysis.* New Haven, CT: Yale University Press, 1976, pp. 22–56.

———— (1976), *A New Language for Psychoanalysis.* New Haven, CT: Yale University Press.

———— (1983), *The Analytic Attitude.* New York: Basic Books.

Segal, H. (1994), Interview: In: *Psychoanalysts Talk,* ed. V. Hunter. New York: Guilford Press, pp. 41–80.

Shorter, E. (1997), *A History of Psychiatry: From the Era of the Asylum to the Age of Prozac.* New York: Wiley.

Spence, D. (1981), *Narrative Truth and Historical Truth.* New York: W. W. Norton.

Spezzano, C., & Gargiulo, G. J., Eds. (1997), Soul on the Couch. Spirituality Religion and Morality in Contemporary Psychoanalysis. *Relational Books Series,* Vol. 7. Mahwah, NJ: Analytic Press.

Spinoza, B. (1677), *Ethics,* tr. R. H. M. Elwes. New York: Bell, 1883.

Stern, D. (1985), *The Interpersonal World of the Infant.* New York: Basic Books.

Stoller, R. (1985), *Observing the Erotic Imagination.* New Haven, CT: Yale University Press.

———— (1991), *Pain and Passion: A Psychoanalyst Explores the World of S&M.* New York: Plenum.

Stolorow, R., Atwood, G., & Brandchaft, B. (1994), *The Intersubjective Perspective.* Northvale, NJ: Jason Aronson.

———— Brandchaft, B., & Atwood, G. (1987), *Psychoanalytic Treatment, an Intersubjective Approach.* New York: Analytic Press.

Strenger, C. (1991), Between Hermeneutics and Science. An Essay on the Epistemology of Psychoanalysis. *Psychological*

Issues, Monogr. 59. Madison, CT: International Universities Press.

—— (1998), *Individuality, the Impossible Project: Psychoanalysis and Self-Creation.* Madison, CT: International Universities Press.

Taylor, C. (1975), *Hegel.* Cambridge, U.K.: Cambridge University Press.

Waelder, R. (1930), The principle of multiple function. In: *Psychoanalysis: Observation, Theory and Application.* Madison, CT: International Universities Press, 1998, pp. 68–83.

Wallerstein, R. S. (1988), One psychoanalysis or many? *Internat. J. Psycho-Anal.,* 69:5–20.

Wiesel, E. (1984), *Souls on Fire. Somewhere a Master.* Harmondsworth, U.K.: Penguin.

Williams, B. A. O. (1981), *Moral Luck.* Cambridge, U.K.: Cambridge University Press.

Winnicott, D. W. (1949), Mind and its relation to the psychesoma. In: *Through Paediatrics to Psycho-Analysis.* London: Hogarth Press, 1958.

—— (1960), Ego-distortion in terms of true and false. In: *The Maturational Processes and the Facilitating Environment.* London: Hogarth Press, 1965.

—— (1963), On communicating and not-communicating. In: *The Maturational Processes and the Facilitating Environment.* London: Hogarth Press, 1965.

—— (1965), *The Maturational Processes and the Facilitating Environment.* London: Hogarth Press.

—— (1971), *Playing and Reality.* London: Tavistock.

—— (1972), *Holding and Interpretation. Fragment of an Analysis.* New York: Grove.

Wittgenstein, L. (1953), *Philosophical Investigations,* tr. E. Anscombe. Oxford: Blackwell.

Yalom, I. (1975), *Theory and Practice of Group Psychotherapy.* New York: Basic Books.

—— (1980), *Existential Psychotherapy.* New York: Basic Books.

—— (1989), *Love's Executioner.* New York: Basic Books.

NAME INDEX

SUBJECT INDEX

263